APPLYING MARKET RESEARCH IN COLLEGE ADMISSIONS

Larry H. Litten
Daniel Sullivan
David L. Brodigan

College Entrance Examination Board
New York 1983

Figure 1-2 is taken from Katharine H. Hanson and Larry H. Litten, "Mapping the Road to Academe: A Review of Research on Women, Men, and the College-Selection Process." In Pamela J. Perun, ed., *The Undergraduate Woman: Issues in Educational Equity*. Lexington, Massachusetts: Lexington Books, D. C. Heath and Company, 1981. Figure 1-3 appeared originally in Larry H. Litten, "Different Strokes in the Applicant Pool," *Journal of Higher Education*, 53, 4 (July/August 1982), 383-402. Figure 2-2 is reprinted from L. H. Litten, "Market Structure and Institutional Position in Geographic Market Segments," Research in Higher Education, 11:1, 1979.

Copies of this book may be ordered from:
  College Board Publication Orders
  Box 886
  New York, New York 10101
The price is $15.95.

Editorial inquiries concerning this book should be directed to:
  Editorial Office
  The College Board
  888 Seventh Avenue
  New York, New York 10106

Library of Congress Catalog Card Number: 83-71937

Printed in the United States of America

9 8 7 6 5 4 3 2 1

Contents

Tables

Figures

Foreword

Most non-Americans would be perplexed by a book dealing with academic institutions as enterprises that must market themselves and persuade students—who are at once consumers and, when graduated, "products,"—that the benefits of their institution outweigh the costs of attending. In most centralized, state-controlled systems of higher education, grants to universities are not tied directly to enrollments. This pattern tends to protect the traditional high culture and saves esoteric subjects from elimination when there is limited student clientele for them. But in such systems, the entrepreneurial spirit of faculties and of institutions is not encouraged, and, response to the interests of students being limited, inventiveness in what is delivered to students may also be limited.[1]

In contrast, in the United States virtually all enterprises are subject in some degree to the constraints of the market, even our churches. When Alexis de Tocqueville was journeying through the America of 1831, he did not bring with him the characteristic French Catholic's judgment on American Catholicism: he did not criticize the United States because parishes are not given in the landscape, so to speak. Instead, he saw that it was an asset for the maintenance of Catholic religion that priests could not take parishioners for granted, but had to enter the marketplace along with the proponents of other religions; in contemporary parlance, they had to market their wares. Although the Church is strengthened by its voluntary character, some Americans today are jarred by the recognition that churches are enterprises or going concerns that are competing in a larger ecological environment: competing not only with other churches and sects, but with all supposedly secular activities that try to claim the time and resources of individuals.

Correspondingly, the three authors of this volume recognize that many academicians in the most selective colleges and research universities, typified by the big and little Ivy Leagues, will view with

---

1. What cannot be achieved through the market may eventually be attempted by political means, as in the drastic political reforms in Western Europe in the late 1960s.

distaste a book that discusses how private colleges that aim for high selectivity and claim some intellectual distinction can market themselves effectively in order to maintain both selectivity and distinction. The concept of a student market is linked in the minds of these academicians to their distaste for commerce, and their identification of marketing with the shoodier sorts of zealous salesmanship, as in the image of the used car salesman.[2]

In business and in academia, reflexive marketing is a two-way affair. Marketing has made it possible for millions of Americans to express their preference for Japanese and European cars, which have been more fuel-efficient, less in need of recalls, examples of providing front-wheel drive, and so on. Consumer preferences had to be educated to some of these advantages. In the case of academic marketing, it is of course possible to swindle some students by deceptive claims, for example, of the postbaccalaureate success of recent graduates or of the presence of facilities that turn out to be absent or defective. However, the authors of this volume insist that scrupulous marketing requires an institution to consider students' needs as well as wants, and also the other "products" of an academic institution, including its contributions to high culture and scholarship. Furthermore, they insist that a better understanding of why students choose an institution can help the institution both in efforts to educate potential applicants as to long-run benefits and to examine itself to assure that benefits explicitly or implicitly promised are in fact promoted by the educational and cocurricular programs. In other words, the marketing agencies of a college, including its public relations department, should not exist in isolation from the faculty and its committees, the academic side of administration, or from the dean of students and the director of admissions.

In the business world, monopolies seek to avoid the constraints of the market, and can do so until substitutes begin to impair their strategic grip. With colleges, as with churches, there are no monopolies. State-supported higher education depends primarily on support linked to full-time-equivalent students as the base for operating revenues. Tuition is kept at a low level and is not necessarily something that a particular institution can consider as an independent source of funds. Indeed, major state universities have

---

2. In "Avoiding and Stemming Abuses in Academic Marketing," Larry H. Litten presents a cogent discussion of specific abuses, such as telephoning prospective students rather than the less intrusive use of the U.S. mails, discounting tuition to meet a competitive college, and other more complex abuses, suggesting mechanisms of research and regulation, and serious journalistic scrutiny, as forms of control (see *College and University*, Vol. 56, No. 2, Winter 1981, pp. 105-122).

in recent decades built up their private foundations as sources of support which provide marginal freedom from the market, allowing, for example, for novel research enterprises or providing a cushion for salaries or sabbaticals, etc. State institutions, of course, compete with one another. They also compete both with local private institutions in the same geographic catch basin, and with the relatively small number of nationally recognized private colleges and universities.

None of the latter possesses a monopoly. To be sure, the highly overapplied institutions do not require marketing strategies to publicize their names. But this does not mean that they are passive vis-à-vis prospective students. For example, they actively cultivate potential black and other minority applicants. Their coaches are eager to have scholar-athletes apply, though they do not bribe them. Some, like my own institution, may be brand names pretty much throughout the United States, but it does not follow that Harvard will be salient to a bright potential scientist in Galveston, for whom Rice University or the University of Texas at Austin can offer distinguished faculty and ample facilities. Indeed, the authors have a chapter on the Dallas/Ft. Worth market for selective private institutions in the East, the Middle West, and the Far West, and they present data supporting the widespread recognition that indigenous Texans possess notable home-state loyalty, while the state harbors sufficiently fine and diverse educational institutions so that there is no want of options. High-ability students in Texas are aware of Princeton and Stanford and rank them among the best, but only a small fraction of these students will actually venture out of state.

The best market research differs from much social science theorizing in its closeness to data. The former seeks to disaggregate what would be overgeneralizations about, for example, the American consumer. For instance, some market researchers understand the insecurities that lead many blacks to prefer brand-name products, even if these are more costly, not so much, as is commonly thought, out of a desire for status, but out of a fear of being cheated by discounted products. Similarly, the authors of *Applying Market Research in College Admissions* have not only analyzed the preferences of high-ability high school seniors in the Dallas/Ft. Worth area in terms of the usual variables of gender, socioeconomic status, the education of both parents, religious preferences, and so on, but they have also applied similar analysis to the Denver/ Boulder area and to the Twin Cities.

In all these cases, the focus is on actual and potential interest in Carleton College, and secondarily in the colleges and universities that compete with Carleton for high-ability students. In the case of the Twin Cities, Carleton is a salient presence, dividing the selective college market with its Northfield neighbor, St. Olaf College. Some Twin Cities students apply to both, something most unlikely in the East or Far West. Both colleges are overshadowed, even for students of high ability, by the University of Minnesota, which along with Ohio State is the only combined flagship and land grant university in the capital and metropolis of a state. Moreover, in the Middle West, Far West, and South, the public universities have the cachet of being seen as democratic and diverse, whereas selective private colleges, even though most make great efforts to recruit nonwhite and low-income students, are more likely to be seen as snobbish and exclusive.

Carleton College, the authors note, can position itself to take advantage of what in the East is the handicap of its Midwestern location by acquainting prospective students with its relative informality, its considerable geographic and ethnic diversity, its lack of a "preppy" image. However, there is not much it can do to counter the perception in other parts of the country that Minnesota is snowy and cold, although it can play up its cross-country ski team, which competes nationally, and help prospects realize that Northfield, which is south of the Twin Cities, is several hundred miles away from the northern, truly frozen tip of Minnesota.

Carleton's market research evolved slowly over a period of a decade, one idea leading to another. The researchers interviewed admitted students concerning reasons for their choice of Carleton and why, since most had made multiple applications, other possible alternatives were rejected.[3] Student tour guides were also inter-

---

3. The more selective the institution, the more likely it is that an applicant will have made multiple applications, if only to be sure of finding a place somewhere. Suppose he or she is admitted to all or most of them? Each institution, no matter how venerable or overapplied, seeks to turn those it admits into what admissions officers call their yield, that is, those who accept admission. To this end, they mobilize their alumni and alumnae amateur recruiters and their inhouse admissions staffs, and they may flood the accepted applicant with literature and personal letters. For of course the highly selective institutions are all in competition with each other, as well as increasingly in competition with state-supported universities of high quality and far lower tuition.

An article in *The Chronicle of Higher Education* reports the greatly increased costs of recruiting, both absolutely and per recruited student, over the past three years; understandably, the greatest expense per student is among the selective liberal arts colleges (closely followed by other private colleges) which must spread the costs of increased mailings and telephoning over a diminishing pool of a traditional constituency of high school seniors. See Beverly T. Watkins, "The Cost of Recruiting a Student Is on the Rise, Survey Finds," *The Chronicle of Higher Education*, Vol. XXVI, May 4, 1983, p. 7.

viewed, uncovering the interesting fact that more of these volunteer guides were evangelical Christians than their relatively small proportion in the Carleton College student body. The guides reported what I think is the reassuring finding that parents and students were impressed by the Carleton Observatory, a landmark one does not find on a high school campus, but they related that people on tour remarked negatively about the apparently small library which, built on a hillside, erroneously appears to be only one story high from most campus perspectives. Indeed, the other side of market research, the impact on the institution, is reflected in the college's decision greatly to expand its library, a decision long in the making and long in the financing, whose priority as a capital expenditure was aided by the market research findings, although not dominated by these.

As the market research expanded into the type of area studies already referred to, the realization came to Carleton's admissions staff that different geographic market segments responded to different facets of Carleton; the same standard messages were not equally efficacious everywhere. In Minnesota, where high-ability students see Carleton as tough and demanding, even harsh, it is important for recruiters to emphasize that Carleton students not only work hard but play hard, and that they are serious but not solemn. Moreover, as it is the most expensive college in Minnesota, Carleton must show that it provides an education far more valuable for many students than the mammoth university can, and that it is less costly than colleges of equal or somewhat greater selectivity in the East. In contrast, in the East Carleton's lower cost is an ambivalent asset. In the areas where private higher education still has hegemony, and very high tuitions — in terms of national norms — are taken for granted, Carleton's somewhat lower cost can be seen as signifying lower value: a Buick rather than a Cadillac education. On the other hand, the point can be made in Eastern recruitment that the lower cost reflects lower rents and other costs of living in Northfield and not any lesser quality in terms of faculty and facilities.

Indeed, the market research documents in detail the widely recognized reluctance even of many relatively high-income families to spend for their children's education. My own random interviews with twelfth-graders and with admitted students from such families has led me to conclude that the "me generation" includes the parents as well as the college-bound children: families are living hedonistically, up to and beyond the limit of their credit cards, and where their income forbids their bargaining for a hefty financial aid package, students may be encouraged to attend a far less costly, distinguished, but local public institution. Or the difference of a few hundred dollars in net costs, taking account of financial aid, may tilt the student toward a somewhat less selective college, overlooking the fact that the difference in costs, amortized over a lifetime, will appear negligible.[4] To illustrate, there are students at Auburndale Community College, in a plush suburb of the Twin Cities, who have high academic ability and who come from professional and managerial families of more than average middle-class incomes. (Status degradation is associated with attending a community college in the East, but not in the rest of the country; in California, many bright, well-to-do students attend the commuter community college for two years and then transfer to one of the campuses of the University of California system.) Sometimes, the parents will offer a daughter or son a trip to Europe and a car if they will attend a community college or state college for two years and then transfer for the upper-division years to a costlier private institution.[5] Such pursuit of short-term comforts is almost unimaginable in Japan, where parents and children engage in frenzied cooperation to secure the children's admission to the most selective government universities and their elite private counterparts.

The marketing surveys in the Dallas/Ft. Worth and Denver/Boulder areas were undertaken in cooperation with the College Board. The Colorado study indicated, by zip code areas, the geographic areas where marketing efforts might be fruitful on the basis of attitudes of students and their parents that were sympathetic toward small, private colleges and toward leaving home to attend college; these are areas where both parents are well educated, and at least one parent has an advanced postbaccalaureate degree. Boulder, of course, is a prime example. In the Washington/Baltimore area, a similar pattern emerged. Particularly in Washington, D.C., there is an interesting difference in the knowledge and attitudes of parents and children: many more parents than chil-

---

4. An increasing number of colleges, desperate for able students who do not quite qualify for financial aid, are providing scholarships based on merit rather than need; there is also a growing practice of dubious bargaining for students by meeting and surpassing the financial aid offers of a competitor. Academicians may be happy that scholars are now being treated like athletes, but skeptical about the lessons learned by matriculants who have played the college admissions game in an auction-like way.

5. This observation ignores the many young people, perhaps especially young women, who are reluctant to impose their college-going costs on their parents. They are considerate not only of the parents' achieved standard of living but also of the needs of younger siblings. Rather than being hedonistic, young people who choose to limit what they ask of their parents are often self-sacrificing and generous.

dren are likely to have heard of Carleton College and to have a negative attitude toward California institutions, which appeal to the younger generation. (In the Minnesota survey also, the parents are reported to care more about the qualities of teaching at a liberal arts college than do the prospective applicants, for whom good teaching may be equated with "excessive" amounts of work and an anemic social life.) In the Dallas/Ft. Worth area, the authors conclude that the selective private colleges and universities belonging to the Consortium on Financing Higher Education should engage in cooperative recruiting efforts, which would not be economically practicable for any single institution (except perhaps for its desire to recruit Hispanic and black students), but which might wean some bright Texans away from their loyalties to home base.

The professional marketers who have moved in on a number of liberal arts colleges, taking over their admissions and sometimes their public relations and development offices, have no doubt learned a good deal about the student as a consumer, and what promotional techniques will sell the college.[6] But market researchers do not generally operate under the canon of publishing their findings, which are thus subject neither to criticism nor to use by others. *Applying Market Research in College Admissions* is an attempt to present the market research done by Carleton College in cooperation with the College Board in a form that has already been shared with Carleton's competitors and with the group of selective universities and colleges that constitutes the Consortium on Financing Higher Education (COFHE), of which Larry Litten, former director of institutional research at Carleton, is associate director. The college, in other words, is prepared to share what others would regard as "trade secrets." Thus the college is insisting that its market research be subject to academic rather than commercial norms. (Its scrupulousness may not aid it in the short run.)

Academic market research also differs from commercial market research in its attitude toward the student as consumer. Commercial marketers study consumer behavior with an eye to the con-

---

6. Cf. "Auditing College Catalogues," in David Riesman, *On Higher Education: The Academic Enterprise in an Era of Rising Student Consumerism*, San Francisco: Jossey-Bass, 1980, pp. 240-243, 267-268. The Litten-Sullivan-Brodigan book is concerned with interinstitutional competition, but those in academic life will recognize that marketing occurs in intrainstitutional competition, both among departments and among faculty members within departments. In many state universities a course in certain fields cannot be offered if there are fewer than ten students signed up for it.

sumer's desires, as these can be developed by exposure to the product or to advertisements for it.[7] The admissions office at a selective college that aims at more than survival, when guided by academic market research, can learn where it is feasible to try to persuade students to consider what they will need in four years rather than what they want on graduating from high school, and to show them that the college is responsive to their needs but not slavishly obedient to their wants.

In general, in a number of Ivy-type overapplied colleges, the admissions officers are dedicated alumni or alumnae. They are intelligent, fair-minded, and work impossible hours; but they are amateurs in that they have not studied institutional or market research. Some are given to anecdotage about students they have admitted who seemed to be high-risk candidates on the basis of their records and who then have done phenomenally well in college. Such success stories can distort the actual profile, which would show that other students of similar risk, though they generally succeed in graduating, are poorly matched with the institution and end up alienated and mistrustful of self and others. Admissions officers in the relatively small number of colleges in the United States which are truly selective — I would make a rough guess that there may be a hundred such institutions — are one of the several intended audiences for this book. The authors hope that the detailed analysis of what students know about a college of which they have only a vague idea, and the various segments of the student market, will help admissions staff do a better job of matching an ever-changing student population with a by-no-means-static institution.

The authors of *Applying Market Research in College Admissions* insist that no adequate market research can be undertaken without the support and cooperation of the academic sides of the institution, including faculty, academic dean or provost, and president. For example, some faculty leaders in selective and costly liberal arts colleges have regarded it as a dilution of the institution to pay any attention to postbaccalaureate careers other than graduate and professional school. They have no objection to an office of placement and career guidance. But they would strongly object, as antithetical to the liberal arts, to a minicourse on computer program-

---

7. As advertising is often attacked for its manipulative intent, it is important to note that certain goods sell themselves by their presence without advertising; indeed, the allure of Western or once-Western consumer products is worldwide, and chic wristwatches, designer jeans, and many other portables are in demand in the Soviet Union without advertising.

ming or one in applied mathematics, or a course in fine arts aimed at aiding students who wish to work in advertising; they would see these courses as compromising the liberal arts ideal. My own view is different. I would like to see undergraduates given the comfort and discipline of a craft that will make it possible for many of them, if they do not go on immediately to further postbaccalaureate study, to stay off the supermarket stockroom floor or avoid waiting on table at Howard Johnson's while planning their next move toward a career in which at the moment there may be few openings. Obviously, it is a question of degree. A certain amount of career security can encourage undergraduates to become more involved in their own pursuit of learning, investing in that learning in terms of a lifetime's interests rather than in terms of an immediate job. This is a matter of campus climate as well as of curriculum. The climate is, of course, only partially within the institution's control. Certainly, one can get to a point where such direct career offerings as accounting, health technologies, and so on can tip the institutional neighborhood toward immediate vocational pursuits without inculcating the professionalism of the craftsman.

Academic market research may here again play a part by revealing that there is a place, although a narrow niche, for liberal arts colleges that do not waive all requirements, nor inflate grades, nor promise immediate postbaccalaureate employment to virtually all graduates.[8]

Many professional and managerial families in the Northeast quadrant of the United States take for granted that everyone makes multiple applications, is rehearsing for the SATs, and is planning a high school record that will show that one is out of the ordinary as well as bright and, therefore, worthy of admission to the most selective Ivy institutions. An article in the *Washington Post* refers to

> ... a time of obsession with the mail carrier's punctuality and whether envelopes from colleges [which thousands of high school seniors across the country] have applied to are thick—implying acceptance—or thin. At [Walt Whitman High School in Bethesda], ranked among the top 10 academic high schools in the country, students are particularly obsessed

---

8. See, for example, the account of the marketing strategy of the University of Bridgeport, which took a full-page advertisement in the *New York Times* to declare "... the liberal arts graduate who doesn't know how to make a living in the real world is not a happy person.... the University of Bridgeport is nothing less than a dress rehearsal for reality." (Muriel Cohen, "Universities Looking Out for No. 1," *Boston Globe*, February 2, 1983, pp. 1, 13.)

with whether they were admitted to Ivy League schools and other prestigious colleges.[9]

A less parochial perspective would lead to the recognition that at least 80 percent of the students in the United States do not make multiple applications and may not even make a single one; they show up at the nearest "available college," be it a community college, a four-year state college, or an open-admissions private college (the great majority of which have today virtually no selectivity); they do not make a conscious college choice. Many of the local state-supported institutions do not engage in active marketing, let alone market research in search of the shrinking cohort graduating from high school. However, they may actively market their outreach programs for older students, mostly enrolling part time, who hope to complete or continue their educations and who may be lured by a huge diversity of programs appealing not only to vocational concerns but to hobbies and other leisure interests. Many of the community colleges have been notable for their flexibility in adapting themselves to the shape of consumer behavior.

If it were published, which it rarely is, the market research conducted to explore consumer behavior along educational dimensions would tell us, as other market research can potentially do, a lot about the variegated spectrum of American attitudes: perspectives on the future, on the status of degrees and credentials, on the sometimes ambivalent status of being a learned person, and on the degrees of curiosity, verbal and visual acuity, and musical intelligence in at least that majority of the population that has completed high school.

I have in the course of this Foreword referred to a few of the items of Americana turned up in *Applying Market Research in College Admissions*. However, the main aim of the authors is not to explore American values and aspirations but to understand the interaction between what a college actually offers to students from diverse backgrounds and what the perceptions of it are, if any, among those students of sufficient ability to be capable of attending and of sufficient venturesomeness to consider not only leaving home but moving outside of what I have sometimes referred to as

---

9. See also a book by a Yale psychiatrist and others which assumes that all high school seniors are anxious about which colleges will admit them: Herbert Sacks and associates, *Hurdles: The Admission Dilemma in Higher Education*, New York: Atheneum, 1978.

"laundry range," that is, too far from home for easy weekend so-journs. Only a minority of students even of high ability are pre-pared to make that move. The Ivies have deliberately sought to find and cultivate such potential students. They have done so out of a belief that there is value in geographic diversity per se. The authors of this volume support that belief by showing how different are the attitudes of students and their parents in the various mar-kets they have examined. Thus, the authors show that in terms of scale—that is, in terms of the massiveness of the student body— high-ability Texans prefer universities to colleges (recognizing, of course, that many colleges are called universities, and some called colleges—such as Dartmouth—are in fact universities). They note in passing that students from the Bay Area are different from the students they have sampled in other markets. Denver differs from Boulder, Baltimore from Washington. The belief in domestic con-vergence, that is, that every part of the country is becoming uni-form in the way that its airports and their surrounding motels are fairly uniform, is not the case—despite national media, constant interstate mobility, and all the other homogenizing features of our epoch.

However, nationalizing tendencies are strong enough so that no selective academic enterprise can count on a perpetually secure market share. Harvard and Stanford compete on a nationwide basis. So, to a somewhat lesser degree, do Carleton and Pomona. To a degree, this competition encourages institutions to be of ser-vice to their undergraduates rather than to count merely on cre-dentialing them with a "name diploma." Institutional market re-search can break down the generalizations drawn from the work of Alexander Astin and others who have studied college-going popu-lations and only broken them down in terms, for example, of liberal arts colleges, women's colleges, and residential four-year liberal arts colleges. Market research can say what is specific about a par-ticular student mix. If there are believed to be adverse conse-quences of the mix, for example, utterly ruthless and aggressive competitiveness, marginal efforts may be made to alter the mix to introduce more cooperative students, although all such efforts must proceed with the recognition that if an institution announces that it wants cooperative students, the mark-hounds will find ways of posing as the most generous cooperators. Market research can lead to more sophisticated judgments of the types of students an institution seeks to attract, but it can never substitute for the con-crete judgments of admissions officers and their relevant faculty committees concerning both the performance and the promise of a particular student. Of course, the authors do not overstate what market research can do. They see their book as a modest prolegomenon to future, more differentiated research on students and on institutions and on optimal matches between them.

David Riesman
Professor Emeritus
Department of Sociology
Harvard University

Introduction

This book is about higher education and the student markets in which colleges and universities operate. More specifically, it demonstrates and discusses techniques for studying these markets and responsible means of administering colleges in light of the knowledge obtained from such study. We hope to instruct, and perhaps even to provoke, both marketers and academicians. Those academicians who still bristle at the increasingly common assertion that marketing is an inescapable aspect of all manner of enterprises, including higher education, will dislike our agreement with this position. Many marketers will take exception to our insistence that higher education has some particular attributes and responsibilities that require appropriate marketing of colleges and universities to run counter to some of the most hallowed principles of the marketing profession. We hope, however, that a useful discussion of these various positions will be advanced by this publication.

In addition to promoting discussion of the relationships between marketing and higher education, we trust that something of practical value will result. This book is in part a case study of a specific college's market research program and its findings; we discuss a series of modest market research projects that were conducted over a six-year period and then devote a large part of the book to a major study of students and parents in six metropolitan areas (the Six-Market Study). We use the concrete institutional example, however, as a vehicle for a general exploration of basic marketing principles and techniques and market research for colleges and universities (hereinafter referred to as *academic marketing* and *academic market research*). By approaching these matters through *the particular*, we seek to move beyond the vague generalities that have characterized the previous writings of both the advocates and the critics of higher education marketing and market research — for example, the presumed but undemonstrated benefits of market research, of distinctive institutional specialization (or positioning), and of student-oriented institutional behavior in a traditional marketing sense. One of the principal messages of this book is that a homegrown, evolutionary, and incremental market research program is a powerful tool for generally heightening the insights and sensibilities with which an academic institution's marketing planning is conducted and related decisions are made. These diffuse effects are difficult to demonstrate, but we can show their "causes" — the market research activities and findings that provoke thought and refined observations of the world.

Formidable economic and demographic circumstances face colleges and universities today, and the severity of many of these challenges is only likely to increase during the coming decade. As a result of these pressures, increasing competition for students and resources and the possible demise of a substantial number of institutions have been predicted by various analysts (Crossland 1980; Stewart and Dickason 1979; Glenny 1980). One reaction by colleges to these phenomena has been to hunker down and continue to do business more or less as usual, perhaps with a little more intensity and maybe with a bit of deeply hidden anxiety. Another reaction has been to embrace the idea that colleges and universities can meet their challenges more aggressively.

Among those who subscribe to the latter approach are many who believe that higher education can exploit effectively the marketing practices that have contributed significantly to growth in the business sector of the economy. Marketers are advising colleges to be more responsive to consumers, to engage in more intensive market analysis and strategic planning, to develop new programs, and to improve their promotional, pricing, and delivery systems (see Johnson 1972; Barton 1978; Berry and Allen 1977). Many academic administrators, and even some faculty, have adopted marketing terminology and are trying to conduct their affairs in accordance with "the marketing concept" (see Chapter 1).

Marketing has a great deal to offer colleges and universities. One of the most significant contributions is the advancement of academic market research. Higher education can benefit substantially from a thorough and rational approach to its concerns, from greater attention to the relationships between colleges and their environments, and from the thoughtful and purposeful administration of academic affairs. Understanding an institution's market through market research has been stressed as an essential activity by the several authors who have advocated applying marketing concepts and principles to higher education. The detail they have provided, however, on how to conduct market research, what can be learned from it, how to apply the results, which research is worth the costs, and when it is worth the costs has been sketchy at best. It is particularly unfortunate that this void exists in the application of marketing principles to higher education, an enterprise that professes a strong commitment to understanding phenomena prior to taking action—that is, a commitment to informed action.[1]

This is not to say that market research is not being done in or for colleges and universities. Indeed, institutions and academic consortia are engaging in a variety of such activities. Entrepreneurial firms are aggressively promoting their research services to academe. With the development of this market research, however, a serious normative problem has emerged. An antiacademic disposition has cropped up regarding the dissemination of results from such efforts. The sharing of results for both the criticism by competent peers and the edification of others is a fundamental norm for the conduct of inquiry in academic institutions. Nevertheless, a proprietary attitude toward the findings has accompanied much of the market research being performed in higher education, both in studies for individual institutions and in studies sponsored by several institutions (such as the subscription effort promoted by the survey research firm Yankelovich, Skelly, and White about the time the principal research reported here was conducted). Such a stance is consistent with practices in the business world, but it flouts essential academic principles. We reject such attitudes and offer this book as partial evidence of our convictions. Previously we have made the results of Carleton's market research available through presentations to a wide variety of professional groups, including major groups of competitors in Minnesota and the nation at large. The data have also been made available for use by the staff of a national consortium of which Carleton is a member—the Consortium on Financing Higher Education (COFHE).

Although we do not maintain that research in and of itself will solve the problems of colleges and universities, we do believe that it makes an important contribution to their effective management.[2] Research promotes an examination of assumptions, a testing of both experience and intuition. Furthermore, sharing research results promotes further research (with its attendant benefits). We commend this practice to others and refer the reader to an article

---

1. A few notable examples of market research and its findings have been published, with the work of Maguire and Lay at Boston College and Leister and his colleagues at Pacific Lutheran University standing as exemplary instances. Larkin (1979) and Gaither (1979) contributed the first basic, introductory expositions of academic market research techniques.

2. We would not dismiss the positive effects of inspired genius or the need for wise and dedicated administrations; colleges cannot bank on the former, however, and the latter will benefit from sound information.

by Litten (1981a) for further discussion of the degree to which academic market research might enter the public domain, how soon, and through what mechanisms.

This volume is intended to help fill the voids created by the advocates of academic market research who have failed to demonstrate either its techniques or benefits, and by the practitioners of academic market research who have kept their work under wraps. We seek to provide a practical model for the conduct of academic market research, as well as to contribute new information about academic markets for those who manage the affairs of colleges. The Carleton College–College Board project that provides most of the data reported in this volume (the Six-Market Study) was conducted with a painful awareness of the paucity of models for executing such research. The Six-Market Study was originally intended — from the College Board's perspective — as an experiment to determine whether a college could obtain valuable market information from this kind of inquiry and — from Carleton's perspective — as an attempt to obtain information that would help a specific college make decisions about how to say what to whom about the college, how to price the college's offerings, and where demand for its services might be strongest or might be cultivated. We were also looking for evidence of when we might be barking up an empty tree (or cactus). We sought answers to questions about how people view colleges and their characteristics, what they believe they need to know about colleges they or their children might attend, and how they want to learn these things; who Carleton's competition is; how visible Carleton is (compared with the competition); and how these phenomena differ among various groups in our society. We suspected, from the beginning, that the answers to these questions might be of interest to other institutions, to higher education analysts, and even to other students of American society. When the College Board agreed to contribute resources to the Six-Market Study and to permit the use of names from its PSAT/NMSQT files for a sample (the Board continues its standing policy, which prohibits the use of these lists for institutional or consortial research purposes), Carleton in turn agreed to produce this volume, which would permit other members of the College Board to benefit from this experiment.

The project results certainly proved of value to Carleton; the information also appeared too rich to keep under wraps. The data provided basic insights into higher education and the public's views of it, and into the college-selection process and the influences on it. We believe also that the project involved methodological advances in the application of general market research techniques to higher education.

INTENDED AUDIENCES

College administrators are our primary audience, especially admissions officers, academic planners and institutional researchers, finance and financial aid officers, and the principal directors of all academic marketing—deans and presidents. The volume should also be of use to members of various campus committees and committees of trustees who are concerned with understanding a college's market and making institutional decisions that will affect the college's relationship to that market.

Marketers—business professors, consultants, and personnel in the firms that provide marketing services to the business community—have shown an increasing interest in higher education and its problems. All too often, however, they have shown a poor understanding of higher education—its institutions, its processes, and its purposes. We hope that this volume will help these professionals better understand academic marketing and promote a more effective application of their craft and imagination to the enterprise of higher education. We expect that it will also aid academic personnel in dealing knowledgeably with these external marketers.

Finally, this book may provide some substantive material to other students of higher education—sociologists, economists, historians—and perhaps even to those who seek broader insights into our national culture, or aspects of it, through examination of American attitudes toward higher education.

SPECIFIC OBJECTIVES

At one level this book provides an example of how one might try to understand a market, or markets, for higher education—that is, how to obtain and analyze market research data. In this effort we do not seek to be exhaustive of market research techniques or even comprehensive; this is not a market research text. Rather, it is an account of a highly targeted applied market research project designed to provide practical information for a specific college. We hope that this practical focus of our efforts will increase instead of detract from their exemplary utility, even though the reader will have to make the translation to a particular institutional situation. (We believe that market research techniques are more readily transferable between business and higher education, and across institutional types, than marketing practices are.)

At another level information is provided about the current market for higher education. Specific attention is directed to the traditional undergraduate market—recent high school graduates in their late teens. The focus is on the upper-ability segment of that market, as measured by standardized academic tests (we repeat—our data are from an applied marketing project for a selective, national college). Thus, the direct substantive interest of the material will be greatest for those who seek to serve this particular market; we expect, however, that our methods and materials can serve as a methodological and analytic model for others, even though their specific questions or research subjects may differ.

Another objective is to explore the *marketing implications* of the information obtained through our market research. Research that does not translate into marketing policies or programs is of limited use to college and university administrators. Although we are unable to report on the actual realization of many of the marketing activities these data suggest (much of this effort is still in progress at Carleton and some of the strategies derived from the research require considerable further research), we carry them beyond a simple report of interesting facts about the market or a college; too much market research stays fixed at that abortive level. We have also attempted to keep from losing sight of another critical set of questions, although the answers are extremely elusive: When is research information worth the cost of obtaining it? When are the marketing applications suggested by the research likely to be worth the cost of implementing them? We have no firm answers to these questions but attempt to indicate when and where they should be asked and how the answers might be sought.

We confront two intriguing conflicts in conducting the kind of research reported here and in addressing the audiences we are seeking to reach. One conflict pits the researcher against the marketer—the researcher's dream can be the marketer's nightmare. Neither wants to indulge in illusions about reality. Nevertheless, the researcher hopes to find variance in the world—different groups behaving in different ways or having different attitudes. The social positions, past experiences, and so forth, of these groups can then be used via appropriate theory to explain their different attitudes and behavior. On the other hand, the practitioner, while recognizing that people have distinctive interests and that these form the basis for effectively matching specific students with specific colleges, also hopes to keep differentiation to a minimum. To the degree that operations can be standardized, the less work there is to do. For example, a discovery that men and women use different sources for information about colleges is fascinating to the researcher; the absence of such differences is a relief to the practitioner, since he or she can use the same media for both sexes. For the researcher, the temptation is to look too hard for minor differences; for the college admissions director, the temptation is to look the other way.

Another conflict arises between the social researcher and the market researcher. (The authors were primarily trained as social researchers, as are many faculty members or institutional researchers who undertake market research on behalf of colleges and universities.) The social researcher, by training and professional inclination, seeks to explain observed phenomena through theory or general models; these models generally take account of a number of variables in explaining certain attitudes or behavior, but they blur or obscure the constellations of attributes that distinguish one group from another. The market researcher, in order to be of service to the marketer, tends to be relatively less interested than the social scientist in explanation, general theory, or general models; the market researcher is more interested in distinctive groups, the differences among them, and the way these phenomena affect the relationships of various types of individuals to the marketer's product or service.

We have indulged in some explanatory analysis by seeking to determine when socioeconomic phenomena might account for the relationships between attitudes and behavior (see Chapter 4). We have tried, however, to keep our social scientific egos under rein. In many instances we have simply documented differences among groups and moved on to considerations of how a given institution might take account of these differences in developing its marketing strategy and tactics (Chapters 6 to 9). We still believe strongly that the more theoretical understanding we have about things, the greater the probability that our attempts to deal with them will be effective. We also believe that efforts to achieve explanation are expensive and time-consuming and can distract from action-oriented agenda. Prudent conduct of marketing research calls for an effective (and unprescribable) balance between understanding and action, between generalized models and differentiation strategies.

Two traps await market researchers who pursue the segmentation snark—that is, researchers who look for differences among groups of people so that specific marketing strategies can be developed for specific groups (see Chapter 1). One is the temptation to make too much of differences that are relatively small; we have encountered much market research that focuses on statistically significant differences (differences that are unlikely to have happened by chance) that are less than 10 percentage points. The costs of implementing differentiated strategies for groups that show such small differences are not likely to be justified. The other trap is to give the wrong kind of attention to some sizable differences among groups when, even with these differences, only a minority of a given group exhibit a particular trait.[3]

We are researchers and not admissions officers, but we have tried hard to keep our fascination with group differences under control. When we do stray into the realm of small differences, however, it is at least partially a conscious effort to alert other researchers to directions for more detailed study and to provoke practitioners to test our findings against their own experiences.

In several instances, especially in the later chapters, our analysis also focuses on very small groups that can render even large percentage differences among groups subject to error or chance. We have persisted with our analysis in these cases, however, in order to demonstrate ways of conceptualizing problems and analytic approaches. We have tried to remind the reader when we are entering these realms of tentativeness and urge careful reference to the tables where the relevant numbers are clearly reported.

AN INTRODUCTION TO CARLETON

Since this is a case study of a market research program that was conducted by a specific college, a brief introduction to the institu-

---

3. We have seen researchers make the following kind of mistake (fictitious example for illustrative purposes only): Suppose that 30 percent of the students from urban high schools indicate that they would like Christmas break to start at Thanksgiving, and only 7 percent of the students from rural high schools exhibit this preference. Many researchers are inclined to focus on the fact that urban students are 22 percentage points (or over four times) more likely than rural students to favor this calendar feature and to suggest that colleges that seek to attract urban students should seriously consider such a development. They fail to give attention to the fact that students with such preferences still constitute fewer than a third of the urban student population. A college may seek specifically to attract this "early dismissal" subsegment of the urban population. The college, however, should not be misled into thinking that it will have an advantage with the majority of urban students if it adopts such a calendar, even though urban students show a strikingly greater incidence of preference for such a calendar than do their rural peers.

tion will help the reader understand both the problems addressed and the analysis performed; further detail on Carleton College can be found in the direct-mail brochure reproduced in Appendix B.

Carleton is a four-year, liberal arts, coeducational college, located in a town of 12,500 (including the students from Carleton and St. Olaf College), approximately 40 miles south of Minneapolis/St. Paul. It was founded in 1866 and, though of Congregational origins, is a nondenominational college. In the 1950s it emerged as a national institution and now recruits 57 percent of its students from 14 Midwestern states, 21 percent from the East, 10 percent from the South, 9 percent from the West, and 3 percent from other sources. It has an on-campus enrollment of approximately 1,700 and currently accepts 50 percent of its applicants; matriculating freshmen have average SAT-verbal scores of 607 and SAT-mathematical scores of 633; 48 percent were in the top 5 percent of their high school class. The college has 18 academic departments. It is located on a 900-acre campus (50 acres are occupied by academic buildings) and has an endowment of $62 million. The college is widely recognized as being in the set of highest-quality liberal arts institutions in the nation (see various college guidebooks and Solmon and Astin 1981).

ACKNOWLEDGMENTS

Many individuals and organizations have contributed to the realization of the Carleton College market research program and the production of this book. To name them all would result in a minor volume in itself. We must acknowledge the special contributions of some of them, however.

We wish to thank the officers and the staff of the College Board for their moral, organizational, and financial support of the Six-Market Study and of the production of this book. The financial support of the Northwest Area Foundation and of the Robert Sterling Clark Foundation is also gratefully acknowledged.

To our many colleagues on the faculty and the staff at Carleton we owe an inestimable debt. Not only are they a substantial part of the college that serves as focus and impetus for these endeavors, they contributed in countless ways to the realization of the research we are reporting—from serving on related committees to providing individual sources of counsel and criticism. Above all we would recognize and commend their supreme academic spirit in rising above the proprietary temptations that research such as ours so often provokes and in supporting the publication of our findings and analysis. We would also pay tribute to the officers of St. Olaf College, who have exhibited this same spirit in permitting us to draw upon St. Olaf as an example in Chapter 6.[4]

Among the Carleton staff who deserve special recognition are President Robert Edwards, who gave us his full support for all our projects, including this volume; Dean of Admissions Richard Steele, upon whose area this work impinges most directly and who used the fruits of our research labors; George Dehne, formerly Director of College Relations and now with the C. W. Shaver Company, who gave us strong support and sound criticism and so effectively exploited the early results of our studies; Walter Reeves, formerly Vice-President for Development and also now with C. W. Shaver, who helped us secure funding for the Six-Market Study and then shape it; and Kathleen Foley, who aided us with a great deal of computer work.

The students at Carleton who contributed to our various efforts at various times are far too numerous to list by name. We thank them all—the questionnaire respondents, the sociology methods course members, the research assistants and interns in the Office of Institutional Research. Several of these individuals are acknowledged through citation of their reports in our References. In addition we should note several others who made extraordinary contributions: Kim Honetschlager, Joan Peterson, Pam Vettel, Mona Sadow, and Susan Quinlin.

Several Carleton alumni also made substantial contributions to our thinking about these matters. We thank them all. We must specifically acknowledge, however, the extraordinary assistance extended by Richard Cardozo, Larry Youngblood, and Art Schultze.

Members of the staff of the Consortium on Financing Higher Education provided invaluable assistance. Katharine Hanson, the Executive Director, extended essential and generous moral support and helped criticize this manuscript. Carol Finney performed major amounts of computer work on the Six-Market data, offered valuable criticism of this manuscript, and, along with Timothy Welsh, helped write the COFHE report, which forms the basis for Chapter 9. Christine DeBold did a heroic job of typing draft after draft of each chapter and then of the entire volume.

---

4. We shared a draft of Chapter 6 with St. Olaf because we used data from the questionnaire item that specifically named that institution; all other data on specific institutions that are reported in this volume came from information volunteered by our respondents regarding their perceptions, applications, and so forth.

The following sociologists, admissions officers, academic administrators, and marketers read our first complete draft and offered invaluable criticism: David Riesman (Harvard University), Donald Dickason (Pennsylvania State University), Joseph E. Gilmour, Jr. (University of Maryland), William Turner (Washington University), and Richard Cardozo (University of Minnesota). Kay Litten gave us major editorial assistance on that draft.

With the considerable assistance of so many individuals and organizations duly noted, we, the authors, must finally assume the sole responsibility for any errors or oversights. We discovered that we had humblingly finite capacities for absorbing and accommodating the rich array of perspectives and suggestions offered by our readers.

Finally, we must acknowledge and express our gratitude to our families for relinquishing many hours of family time and suffering considerable postponements of domestic projects to permit this book to be written. We dedicate this book to our children, who during the next two decades will enter the realms about which we write, and to their mothers, who will have helped guide them there.

Larry H. Litten
Associate Director
Consortium on Financing Higher Education
Cambridge, Massachusetts

Daniel Sullivan
Vice President for Planning and Development
Carleton College
Northfield, Minnesota

David L. Brodigan
Coordinator of Institutional Research and Registrar
Carleton College
Northfield, Minnesota

1.

An Introduction to Marketing Concepts and Principles and to the Particular Nature of Academic Marketing

Marketing consists of a powerful set of concepts, principles, and practices designed to increase the effectiveness with which organizations relate to their publics (or individuals achieve desired social responses).[1] Marketing has been most highly developed in those spheres of human activity where the entrepreneurial spirit reigns supreme and where the concept of a market has long been accepted — in business and commerce. For over a decade, however, marketing has been advocated as a useful aid for academic institutions when they are dealing with their several challenges and problems. It has also been promoted as a valuable tool for many other non-profit organizations in health care, politics, religion, government, arts and cultural affairs, and professional services (see readings by Lovelock and Weinberg 1978 and Bibliography by Rothschild 1981; see also texts by Kotler 1975 and by Rados 1981).

Beginning with seminal pieces by Fram and by Krachenberg in 1972, marketers began to promote their craft to higher education. These pioneers were followed by other marketers (Bassin 1975; Berry and George 1975; Berry and Allen 1977; Gorman 1974; Lovelock and Rothschild 1980; and other articles by Fram 1973, 1974/1975), by administrators from within higher education (Huddleston 1976; Ihlanfeldt 1980), by higher education associations (College Entrance Examination Board 1976, 1980; Council for the Advancement of Small Colleges 1979), and by entrepreneurs whose firms sought to provide marketing services to higher education (Barton

---

1. A precise definition of marketing has proved elusive. It has been defined as broadly as the "science of transactions" (Hunt 1976) or "any social unit seeking to exchange values with other social units" (Kotler 1972, 10), but Webster (1974) has pointed out that such definitions include all types of human activity, including a parent's asking children to go to bed or a man's kissing his wife (p. 91). We prefer a definition that restricts the term "marketing" to activities intended to advance the interests of an organization or an individual through management of relations with its (or his or her) social/economic environment. The actor can be a singular or a plural entity, but the object of the action has to be plural.

1978; Johnson 1972). One of the giants of general marketing theory, Philip Kotler, also commands a central position in the early application of marketing perspectives to higher education and in the subsequent development of academic marketing thought (Kotler 1975, 1976, 1979).

SOME MARKETING BASICS

The references cited in the preceding section can be consulted for details on the ways in which members of the marketing discipline and profession view and relate to the world. This section introduces some principal marketing concepts (after noting a general problem related to the use of technical terminology), lists some basic marketing strategies, and indicates the kinds of questions that market research can address. Following that discussion we consider higher education marketing as a particular kind with a particular set of problems (and opportunities).

Key Marketing Concepts

Any reasonably sophisticated activity develops its particular orientation to the world and requires a specialized vocabulary for the participants to communicate efficiently with one another. This vocabulary becomes technical terminology to the practitioner and jargon to the lay person. Much of it can be translated into the vernacular, but it often loses its full set of meanings and its precision in the process. Marketing and higher education each have their respective vocabularies. Appendix A sets forth key marketing and market research concepts and suggests translations for academic or lay audiences.[2] The reader who is unfamiliar with marketing terminology may wish to peruse this appendix before plunging into the following text.

Let us briefly consider five key concepts from marketing and relate them to higher education.

The Marketing Concept. The basic premise of marketing is that an institution or an individual will be able to advance its (or his or her) interests most effectively by taking into account the interests of others (e.g., consumers, clients, publics). This principle has been

---

2. Some of these marketing and market research terms, however, have particular meaning in the context of our work that may differ from general marketing usage. Therefore, we have used italics for concepts and terms that are elaborated in Appendix A when they first appear in the text.

dubbed "the marketing concept" and has been variously defined and elaborated. Kotler has formulated what is probably the most widely cited set of definitions. In one variation he defines the marketing concept as "a management orientation that holds that the key task of the organization is to determine the needs, wants, and values of a target market and to adapt the organization to delivering the desired satisfactions more effectively and efficiently than its competitors" (1976, 14).

Later in this chapter we discuss some of the problems that the marketing concept presents for higher education because of the discrepancies that can exist between individual *consumers'* or society's *needs* and *desires* (see Appendix A for a definition of the italicized words), and the relative inexperience and lack of maturity of traditional consumers of higher education when they make the complex decisions relating to college selection. In general, however, it is safe to say that the purposes of academic institutions will be achieved best if the development of policy and practice takes the perspectives of their various publics into account.

Marketing Mix. The phenomena that can be altered by a *marketer* in order to influence the relationships a product or an organization has with the market, or with specific *segments* of the market, constitute the marketing mix. The specific nature of a *product*, its *price*, its availability, and the efforts made to inform people about a product constitute the basic elements of the marketing mix. These are known as the Four *P*'s of marketing—product, price, place, and promotion. The components of the marketing mix can be varied separately or in combination. In academic marketing, the marketing mix consists of a host of phenomena—curricular and extracurricular programs and activities, along with their associated personnel (product); dollar costs, financing arrangements, psychological costs associated with student effort and stress, prerequisites for admission (price); location of programs, academic calendars (place); recruiting and public relations activities (promotion).

Segment, Segmentation. A market segment is a group of people who exhibit characteristics, behavior, desires, needs, perceptions, or other phenomena that are similar within the group but are distinct from the rest of the market or from other groups in the market. Segments may be defined on the basis of objective attributes (race, age, sex, occupation, education, religion) or subjective phenomena (values, perceptions).

Segmentation is the division of a market by a marketer into segments in order to deal with a particular segment in a particular way. For example, a marketer may try to develop products or services that meet the needs of a particular segment, or different promotional strategies may be used with different segments in a segmented approach to marketing. The objective of segmentation is to enhance the relationship between a given product or organization and the particular desires, perspectives, behavior, and so forth, of a given segment. Segmentation recognizes a differentiated market and seeks to capitalize on the advantage a product will have with a given segment if it conforms to the preferences of people in the segment better than its competitors do. Objectively defined segments make a segmented marketing approach easier to execute than do subjective segments; the latter may be more closely related to product differences, however. (Indeed, benefit segmentation — segments defined by the way people use products and what they want from them — is a powerful basis for segmented marketing and positioning a given product.)

Position, Positioning. Position has two principal marketing meanings. In the broadest usage, a product's position describes how it relates to other products in a variety of ways — its particular market share (e.g., is it a leader with the largest market share? a growth product with an increasing share?); its objective attributes (e.g., is it higher quality? lower priced? more sophisticated or complicated than its competitors?); its subjective perceptions and evaluations by people in a market (i.e., how do consumers perceive and evaluate its objective attributes relative to other products? does it carry or convey more or less prestige, have a more youthful image, than its competitors?). In a somewhat more limited meaning of the term, a particular brand is said to have achieved position when it is the primary brand associated by consumers with a particular product or type of product (e.g., IBM with large computers, Cadillac with high-quality American cars). This latter condition is really a *leadership* position (see Geltzer and Ries 1976).

Positioning is the establishment of a particular market niche for a product — a distinctive set of attributes, price, availability (or each of these); a primary association with a particular set of benefits; a set of perceived advantages over alternative products. Because of differences among market segments, a given product or organization may occupy different positions across various segments.

Market Research. Market research consists of all formal or informal activities intended to increase understanding of a *market* and *consumer behavior* in that market. The objective of market research is to improve the conduct of *marketing* activities. (Economics, sociology, and psychology also study many of the phenomena associated with markets and consumer behavior simply to increase knowledge about them; the theories and findings of these disciplines can contribute substantially to the objectives of market research.) Market research can, and should, range from careful observation during the conduct of marketing activities, and disciplined reflection on those observations, through formal surveys and controlled experimentation. We will use the term this broadly, although the Six-Market project, on which we concentrate, was a formal survey conducted via mailed, self-administered questionnaires.

Basic Marketing Strategies

The marketing objective in profit-making businesses is to increase profits for the firm; nonprofit marketing has different purposes. In most instances the objectives for the latter are to provide better services (and to attain the attendant increases in status), to promote organizational growth, or both. The idea of growth is not particularly attractive to most academicians, even those who are acutely aware of the financial pressures visited upon their institutions by an inflationary economy. Nevertheless, in a competitive market or in a declining market, the strategies that are appropriate to fostering growth are also often the strategies that contribute to the maintenance of the status quo for a given institution. Without such strategies, the demand for the institution usually will shrink, either as it shares in the general decline or as its market is siphoned off by competing institutions that market their services more successfully.

Four basic marketing strategies can be implemented to expand an institution's market; combinations of the several approaches are also possible.[3]

---

3. We will focus on approaches one, two, and four in our work. Approach four is the highest-risk approach of the three from a marketer's perspective (it may also be the most responsible approach, however, from the educator's perspective). Most liberal arts colleges do not tend to have the flexibility to change institutional offerings in response to new or short-term demand in the market. The future may change that.

1. Find people who seek your institution's benefits but who now aren't getting them or don't know where to get them; make these people aware of your institution and facilitate their access to it.

2. Find people who seek your benefits and are now going to the competition to obtain them; then

    a. provide a better set of benefits than the competition;

    b. provide the same benefits at lower costs;

    c. provide better benefits and lower costs;

and then make people aware of your institution and facilitate their access to it.

3. Identify benefits that people want, which are not now being provided in the market and which are different from the benefits now provided by your institution; provide them.

4. Convert people who now do not prefer your institution's present benefits into people who do.

What the Marketer Needs to Learn from Market Research

Kotler (1975) has proposed an elaborate model for conducting a comprehensive market audit; such an exercise can provide useful information, but at considerable cost. We take a more modest approach to the questions that academic marketers would like to answer through appropriate market research. These questions include the following:

1. What are people seeking from, or in, a college, and why?

2. How do people conduct the college-search-and-decision process? What influences the way in which it is conducted and its outcomes?

3. How do people perceive and evaluate the *type* of institution the marketer represents? How do they perceive and evaluate that particular institution?

4. What is the nature and the structure of competition for the marketer's institution (in people's minds and as evidenced by their behavior)?

In each of these areas the marketer is interested in knowing specifically if groups of people differ in these respects, particularly segments within his or her own markets. When searching for relevant market segments, the marketer seeks correlates of these differences (objective attributes, behavioral phenomena, etc.) that will permit successful differentiation of marketing activities; it does little good to know that people have different needs, desires, or concerns, if different promotional materials or programs cannot be directed specifically and effectively to the intended type of person.

THE PARTICULAR NATURE OF ACADEMIC MARKETING

Marketing thought and practice have much to contribute to higher education. The advocates of greater use of these tools by colleges and universities have done a good job of presenting these benefits. They have not so consistently attended to the several risks that the development of marketing approaches to academic affairs might involve. Much of what is promoted and much of what is even carried out in the name of marketing is probably inappropriate for higher education. The differences between academic organizations and other institutions are often overstated by academicians. On the other side, they are all too often unrecognized or ignored by marketers. A few *marketers* have dealt with the limitations on the transfer of marketing theory and practices to higher education (Hugstad 1975; Lovelock and Rothschild 1980; Surface 1971); in general, the advocates of academic marketing within academe have not been so balanced in their enthusiasm.

Marketing thought was introduced into higher education during a period in which the marketing profession was in an expansive phase; the academic extension was part of the larger move toward marketing for nonprofit organizations (Kotler and Dubois launched these developments in 1969). It became apparent several years ago, however, that while there were commonalities across types of organizations that made marketing concepts and principles widely applicable, different types of organizations also faced distinctive marketing problems. From the academic end, the suggestion was made that other types of marketing might be more appropriate for higher education than the most prominent kind—consumer goods marketing (Litten 1980a). Gelb (1976) suggested that "industrial marketing" had a particular relevance for colleges and universities (see the section on Absentee Consumers later in this chapter). As general marketing theory matured, differentiation within the field developed at a rapid pace. The most important development for academic marketing occurred within the past few years with the emergence of a strain of marketing theory specifically focused on service organizations; this branch of marketing thought effectively blossomed with the first conference on the subject, which was sponsored by the American Marketing Association in 1981 (see

Donnelly and George 1981, for the proceedings from this meeting).[4] The emergence of "services marketing theory" promises to be at least as important for higher education as the initial embracing of general marketing thought (since the latter had some serious potential for corrupting as well as aiding colleges).[5]

This section first briefly considers higher education from the perspective of services marketing. Then we examine some of the particularities of higher education that set it apart further. Finally a diagrammatic picture of the college-selection process is sketched to establish the context in which the market research reported in this volume is embedded.

Services Marketing Theory and Higher Education

An ongoing and heated debate has developed within marketing over the differences between the marketing of goods and the marketing of services. One camp stresses the similarities (Enis and Roering 1981; Levitt 1976) and the other emphasizes the differences (Lovelock 1980; Shostak 1977, 1978, 1981). The specified differences are compelling considerations for higher education. Services are generally characterized by relatively high degrees of the following characteristics:

- Intangibility
- Inseparability (simultaneity) of production and consumption (consumer involved directly in production)
- Heterogeneity in quality
- High perishability (uninventoriability)
- Fluctuating demand (seasonability)
- Labor intensiveness

Because of these properties, consumers face particular problems in evaluating purchases of services, and marketers have particular problems in scheduling production, ensuring quality control, and informing consumers about their offerings and the benefits of their offerings. Indeed, each element of the marketing mix is affected by these properties of services.

Guseman (1981) has observed that some services present rela-

---

4. The first professional meeting on services marketing was a workshop in France sponsored by the University of Aix and the European Institute of Management Studies in 1977. The American Marketing Association sponsored its Second Conference on Services Marketing in 1982 (see Berry, Shostak, and Upah forthcoming).

5. Lovelock (forthcoming) has written the first text devoted to services marketing.

tively higher risks for the consumer than do others. He character-
izes the high-risk purchase as having the following properties:[6]

- Infrequently purchased
- (At least) somewhat expensive
- (High) degree of (personal) importance
- (Relatively) small number of alternatives

Many services are also high-risk because they are "credence goods"
(Litten 1981b; Zeithaml 1981). A credence good is one that cannot
be evaluated through simple search or experience; it often involves
professional judgment to ascertain its quality, both before and
after "purchase."[7]

Zeithaml and Guseman have each suggested that consumers will
use several devices for dealing with the problems that result from
the particular properties of services, and that marketers will have
to take account of these phenomena as they devise their own
strategies. Price, physical plant, publications, and personnel will
all be used as evidence of quality in the face of intangibility. Personal sources of information, especially other customers (present
and former, both through testimonial and example), will be used
more than impersonal sources for information. Considerable brand
loyalty and relatively limited searches will be evidenced (the legacy
student and local attendance phenomena in higher education).
Service purchasers will be conservative when confronted with innovations and will seek guarantees of one sort or another. Even
after delivery, service consumers may seek confirmation of quality
in what they have purchased.

The properties of services and high-risk products described by
Zeithaml and by Guseman certainly apply, in varying degrees, to
higher education.[8] The academic marketer faces severe production
challenges — scheduling; efficiency; establishing an appropriate division of production responsibility between students and faculty;
maintaining quality control among faculty, students, and other

---

6. Parenthetical insertions added by the authors to highlight the relevance of
each property to higher education.

7. Professional training, socialization, and certification or licensing are often the
principal sources of consumer protection in the purchase of these services.

8. In a panel presentation at the AMA's Second Conference on Services Marketing, Lovelock presented a scheme for distinguishing among different types of services and their various marketing implications along several dimensions (for
example, whether the service is directed to the consumer's mind, body, or property;
whether it involves a continuing or a discrete relationship between provider and
consumer).

parts of the institution. Pricing becomes a difficult exercise in balancing quality and financial burden on the consumer and the production of short- and long-term benefits. Decisions need to be made about where and how to deliver educational services in order to minimize costs to the individual while maximizing benefits (many of which come via group experiences). Accounting for the many nonfinancial costs (psychological, social, etc.) is a major challenge. Promotional efforts face a plethora of service-related difficulties: demonstrating the generic, intangible benefits offered by the college and the particular benefits associated with a given college; promoting an appropriate self-selection and then exercising necessary admissions selection to enhance the match between the student and the production processes of the college and to gain the production benefits that various types of students can contribute to the college (the benefits of diversity); extending effective information and counsel through the "noncontrollable" information and influence channels that students use; using current students and alumni as effective carriers of information about the college — both through what they say and what they do.

Some Idiosyncracies of Higher Education

Although higher education is essentially a service activity, it has some characteristics that further differentiate its marketing problems from those of most services. (Not the least of these are some quasi-products such as knowledge, which can exist over extended periods of time, and students, who as alumni visibly live out the effects of the services received. The "consumption" of educational benefits can occur over an extended period after graduation, and certain resources can be inventoried via videotapes, books, etc.) We believe that it is important in a book on academic marketing to pause over some of the particular properties and responsibilities of higher education and to consider their implications for academic marketing.[9] We deal with five issues: (1) the multiple functions of higher education, (2) students as educational consumers, (3) absentee consumers with an interest in higher education, (4) the nature of intellectual life, and (5) the value of diversity within a college. In addition to the brief observations we make here, the reader is encouraged to consult David Riesman's extensive historical and sociological treatment of many of these issues, and more, in his recently published work, *On Higher Education: The Academic Enterprise in an Era of Rising Student Consumerism* (1980).

---

9. These observations are derived in part from Litten (1980a, 1980b, 1981b).

Multiple Functions of Higher Education. Instruction (the imparting of knowledge, training in skills, etc.) is only one of several services colleges offer students. Among the other services are certification of knowledge and skills possessed; socialization to the norms and standards of intellectual activity; an environment for psychological maturation; a setting and means for socialization to adult economic and social roles; and opportunities for physical development, for socializing and entertainment, and, in some colleges, for daily sustenance and for religious development. A college experience is both a long-term investment purchase and an immediate consumption expenditure for students. Institutions have to take cognizance of both these elements in their marketing and help to keep *both* in perspective for students, with both the benefits and their related costs – including student effort – kept in view.

The socialization functions of colleges present a particularly difficult set of problems to the marketer, especially to those marketers who would follow the traditional formulation of the marketing concept, which stresses responsiveness to the consumers' perceptions. Although often limited in the degree to which it is realized, the existence of a community of scholars and their apprentices who adhere to a particular ethos is still an important aspect of the academic ideal; to surrender allegiance to the ideal would be to forfeit even hope of such communities and their occasional invaluable realization. It is difficult to envision a "responsive institution" that exemplifies the ideals that socialize young people to the highest norms of intellectual life; responsive organizations, as typically discussed by marketers, are more likely to conform to the norms and expressed desires of consumers. Higher education also has the obligation to criticize the established order in order to improve it. The student market cannot set these agenda.

Students as Educational Consumers. Students vary in their sophistication, maturity, and desires. The most problematic set of consumers for the marketer (especially for the "responsive" type) is the traditional prospective student – the high school senior. Often these students are not reliable sources of information about important aspects of the academic marketing mix, especially what is important in the curriculum (the instructional "product" or service). A young person graduating from high school frequently knows only vaguely what educational benefits he or she wants and only a little about what he or she needs. Much of the capacity for judging and criticizing higher education can come only as a result of the knowledge and skills that are developed through participation in the very programs of higher education. Higher education is indeed high in credence qualities. Furthermore, a quality collegiate education ought to be a powerful source of personal change and development; unimagined perspectives on one's self, one's circumstances, and one's society ought to emerge from such experiences. In addition, the traditional student is enmeshed in a major period of maturing—another source of instability and change. Even the college senior, with capabilities considerably more developed than those of the prospective freshman, often lacks much of the necessary perspective on life after college that needs to be brought into many institutional marketing decisions.

It is also important to an understanding of the responsibilities of, and the constraints on, academic marketing to recognize that it involves a singular, intergenerational decision-making process. Parental authority and responsibility are involved (particularly since parents are expected to be major financial contributors) at the same time that college selection and attendance is a major step toward achieving psychological, economic, and social independence for the students. Students and their families can be at different levels of psychological development (both within and across families). Parents may variously be attending to their own needs and benefits, their children's interests, or both in this process. Parents can provide some of the perspective that students lack when making these decisions, but they can also contaminate the decisions with dated information and concerns that do not serve the best interests of students or society. Academic marketers need to be aware of these complications and to structure and conduct their marketing processes in ways that effectively advance their several educational purposes.[10]

Absentee Consumers. Higher education embraces a vast array of products and services, including some of the most complex and advanced "products" in our society. It is important to recognize that not only is instruction but one of the services rendered to students, service to students is only one of the several social, economic, and

---

10. Most of the research about how parents and students compare on their perceptions of colleges deals with students who are already enrolled and their parents; Seymour and Richardson (1972) review several of these studies. Bowers and Pugh (1973) focused on students' and parents' perceptions of colleges as they relate to the college selection process. Wright and Kriewall (1979) dealt with families as decision-making units. Recent theses also have focused on family decision-making processes and college selection, but they contain serious methodological shortcomings.

cultural functions of higher education. As Douglas Windham (1980) has observed, public subsidies for both institutions and students are justified on the basis of benefits to the public beyond the private benefits to student consumers.

Discussions of marketing and market research in higher education tend to focus on students, to the exclusion of other consumers. Students can answer market research questionnaires; the needs of the economy, the political system, and the society at large cannot be ascertained as easily. There are products and services of higher education that are not directly included in the instruction of students but which relate even to those processes in critical ways. Universities and colleges are expected to preserve knowledge and cultural and intellectual traditions and to discover and transmit the wisdom of the past. Likewise, the creation and the dissemination of new knowledge are fundamental functions of higher education. Important interdependencies exist between the several products and services of higher education. The nature and quality of scholarship affects the nature and quality of teaching, and vice versa.

We must look after the interests of a number of "absentee consumers" with real interests in the marketing decisions of higher education: the student who emerges from the educational process greatly changed from the high school senior who selects a type of college, a specific institution, and a course of study; the society and the economy that need the services of a highly educated citizenry; and the society that requires the pursuit of truth regardless of the popular fads or fashions of the times. These are all interests that must be protected and served even though they are not well accommodated in the current concepts and practices of marketing (it was the eventual-employment element of a college education that led Gelb [1976] to suggest the industrial marketing model for colleges, recognizing both employers and students as consumers). Colleges and universities have developed structures and practices to help attend to these more broadly conceived interests; we consider them briefly in the next section.

The Nature of Intellectual Life. Academic "firms" have three principal productive resources: personnel (faculty, support staff, and students—for in higher education the "consumer" is also a major resource for fellow consumers); a campus (principally buildings, but also equipment, books, and grounds); and a set of particular activities (and norms for the conduct of those activities) through which research and education occur. Sir Eric Ashby (1973) has observed that allocations of these resources are shaped by three forces for change and another force that resists change. The first three forces are manpower needs, the influence of patrons, and customer demand. The conservative force he calls "inner logic." It consists of "inertia" and participants' "belief in the purpose of the system." Ashby is correct in seeing these beliefs as a positive conservative force – a protection against the "capricious" nature of the other forces in the market that play upon colleges. He fails to do justice, however, to the *changes* that the inner logic can also produce; many innovations in education flow naturally from creative forces within colleges. Bennet and Cooper (1979) make similar arguments about production-based innovations in corporate marketing.

The belief system of academicians is a critical resource in colleges and universities. Shils (1978) has referred to it as the academic "ethos" (the spirit of the academic community, which is held and nurtured *by that community*, not by the market). In terms closer to those of economics than to marketing parlance, he has called it the "intellectual capital" of a college. This capital consists of

> ... much more than its physical plant or its library; it is also more than the stock of knowledge and skills that its academic staff members bring to their tasks. It includes the zeal for discovery, the moral integrity, the powers of discriminating judgment, the awareness of important problems, and the possibilities for their solution that their members possess. (Shils 1978, 196–197)

This intellectual capital is also a source of quality control in a service organization; it is protected and developed by a faculty member's long and expensive socialization into several intersecting professional cultures. Some basic institutions and norms have been developed within these cultures at great cost over the years in order for academic life to flourish. Among these are tenure, which provides a buffer against political and other external intrusions; academic freedom, which permits the pursuit of unfashionable or uncomfortable ideas; and professional norms such as rationality or the wide sharing of scholarship and research for criticism and use by others. These norms and institutions do not exist to maintain the status quo, but to permit changes to take place that conform to intellectual requirements and standards. In a real sense, these academic institutions are antimarketing. It will be a source of both provocation and challenge to work with the tensions created between academic norms and marketing principles and to bring a creative synthesis out of the two spheres.

Value of Diversity within a College. There is a tendency within marketing that pushes an organization toward specialization — finding and exploiting a particular ecological niche, developing a distinctive identity, serving a particular clientele. Much of the segmentation and positioning advice of marketers both assumes and furthers specialization and leads away from diffuseness and diversity. And yet, education thrives on diversity within the educational environment. Different types of people, different disciplines, different values bumping against each other, are precisely what education is often about. Chapter 4 reports evidence that students are aware of the value of diversity within an educational institution, although they may have limited perspectives on diversity and value it for its symbolic effects instead of for real, and risky, educational encounters with different people. Therefore, some of the advice of marketers, which is sound when one is trying simply to expand the pool of customers for a consumer goods product, is sadly wide of the mark when transferred to higher education. Expanding demand by seeking the specific types of individuals who are most readily attracted to an institution may in the short run sustain an income flow, but if it leads to homogenization, it may compromise the institution's long-term educational integrity. Our evidence suggests that it may also compromise the long-term student demand for the narrowed institution that would result. To a certain extent, an institution will seek to cultivate those segments of the market that are most readily attracted to its benefits and attributes. To be a true liberally educating institution, however, it will also have to manage its affairs in order to attract a variety of students and provide a variety of benefits (Litten forthcoming). This necessarily involves a degree of diffuseness of image, the antithesis of the condition that affords a unique position for an institution in the market and in the minds of consumers. To a certain extent, this problem can be overcome by separate marketing efforts for the various components of a complex institution, but the problem will always be there, especially when marketing to students who have not yet narrowed their own perspectives on what they want or should want from a college education and a college experience.

These considerations also require that an institution *not* jettison certain program areas if they are not contributing satisfactorily to overall institutional advancement at a given moment. If the modern languages or the physics departments are proving to be unattractive to students, they are not to be discontinued readily. In a liberally educating institution, efforts must be made to revitalize such areas — even with efforts that would be judged costly by business standards of direct financial returns. Current students or prospective students might not be greatly concerned about such departments, but they should be by the time they graduate – or several years later. Some of these problems may require institutional support for cooperative or collective efforts beyond academia.

Overview of College Selection and Recruitment

We are dealing with complex phenomena when discussing academic marketing and college selection. Both when designing the market research and when presenting the results, it is important to have a clear picture of the process and the actors in mind; the problems and the questions differ according to who is being studied, at which point in the process, and for which reasons.

A market has two sides to it – those who buy and those who sell, those who seek education and those who provide it. The process of coming together for the seeker–provider exchange to take place in higher education is really an interaction of two basic processes – the student's search for a college and the college's search for students. There are some parallels and some distinct differences between these two search processes. A basic appreciation of the components and sequencing of each process is essential for both the marketer and the market researcher.

From the institution's perspective, the marketing process has been described by a number of authors as a funnel (see Figure 1-1), with pools of decreasing size at successive stages of the process (Chapman and Van Horn 1974; Ihlanfeldt 1980; Turner 1978). It has been suggested also that specific recruiting activities or public policies may be differentially appropriate at various stages in the funnel (Jackson, in press). Models of institutional behavior in this process can also be developed that incorporate the different steps in promotion and recruitment – from creating awareness (or name recognition), to differentiating a given institution from its competitors, to counseling a given student regarding the match with a given college.

We are more directly concerned in this volume with the college-selection process from the student's perspective. In a sense, this process can also be likened to a funnel in which the student passes from having all postsecondary institutions as options in which to enroll to finally matriculating in a single institution. Such a conception of the process is an exceptionally unrealistic abstraction, however, since no student has all institutions as an option except when he or she sits down with a published college guide in hand; natural ignorance of most of these options exists, and given human

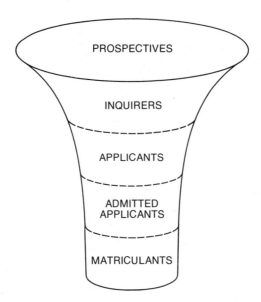

Figure 1-1. The College Admissions Funnel

information storage and processing capacities, that is not surprising.

The most detailed description of the steps in a college-selection process was developed by Lewis and Morrison (1975) when they studied college selection for the United States Navy as an example of "the complex, first-time decision." They interviewed students every other week during their senior years in high school and identified 13 discrete activities that were components of this process.[11]

Kotler (1976) proposed a simpler, six-step process in the pioneering volume on marketing for colleges and universities, which came from the first colloquium on the subject, sponsored by the College Board. Gilmour, Dolich, and Spiro (1978) reported that some intensive interviews with college freshmen empirically supported the essential aspects of Kotler's model. These steps have been consolidated by other authors into three basic stages, once the decision to go to college is made (see Figure 1-2; Hanson and Litten 1982;

---

11. Lewis and Morrison specified the following elements of the college-selection process: consult source; source provides name of new school; source provides information about school; source/information is evaluated; school is added; attribute is added to criteria; school evaluated for application; school is dropped; application to school; accepted at school; rejected at school; decision to attend; decision not to attend.

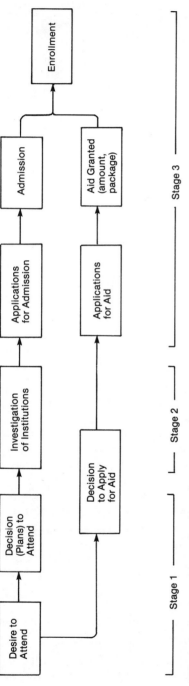

Figure 1-2. The College Attendance/Choice Process

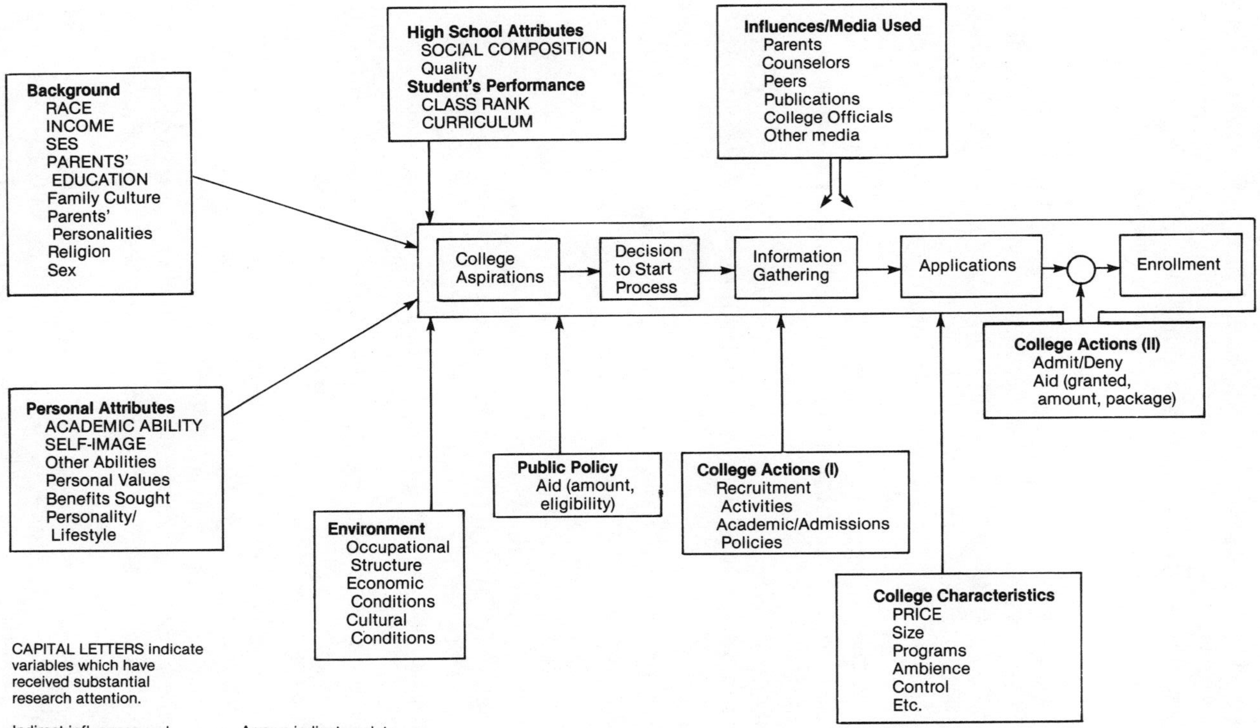
Background
RACE
INCOME
SES
PARENTS'
EDUCATION
Family Culture
Parents'
Personalities
Religion
Sex
High School Attributes
SOCIAL COMPOSITION
Quality
Student's Performance
CLASS RANK
CURRICULUM
Influences/Media Used
Parents
Counselors
Peers
Publications
College Officials
Other media
College Aspirations
Decision to Start Process
Information Gathering
Applications
Enrollment
College Actions (II)
Admit/Deny
Aid (granted, amount, package)
Personal Attributes
ACADEMIC ABILITY
SELF-IMAGE
Other Abilities
Personal Values
Benefits Sought
Personality/Lifestyle
Environment
Occupational Structure
Economic Conditions
Cultural Conditions
Public Policy
Aid (amount, eligibility)
College Actions (I)
Recruitment Activities
Academic/Admissions Policies
College Characteristics
PRICE
Size
Programs
Ambience
Control
Etc.

CAPITAL LETTERS indicate variables which have received substantial research attention.

Indirect influences and interactions between independent variables have not been drawn in in order to simplify diagram.

Arrows indicate points of principal influence, with influence generally continuing through remainder of process.

Figure 1-3. An Expanded Model of the College-Selection Process

Jackson, in press). It is important to keep this basic model in mind when conducting market research, when reading or interpreting market research results, or when designing a marketing program. Student perceptions and behavior may well differ at different stages in the process. Indeed, Gilmour and his colleagues suggest that different considerations are differentially important at different points and that influential persons exercise different types and amounts of influence at specific points.

The many personal and situational phenomena that influence the college-selection process, both in the way it is conducted and in its outcomes, have been studied by sociologists and economists. Most of the work in these research traditions has focused on the decision to participate in the process (i.e., the decision to go to college), with lesser attention to determinants of the kinds of colleges in which students enroll. Very little research has been done on the way students conduct the college-selection process. A good, and brief, review of these research traditions is given by Jackson. (Others have been produced by D. W. Chapman 1979; McPherson 1978; Gilmour, Dolich, and Spiro 1978 – each from slightly different perspectives.) Figure 1-3 schematically presents these influences.

CONCLUDING NOTES ON THE NATURE AND PLACE OF ACADEMIC MARKET RESEARCH

A solid philosophy of education has to be the starting point and the lodestar for the development of academic programs. It is the fundamental responsibility of professional educators to develop and to apply the standards of educational practice in colleges. The non-academic market cannot be permitted to drive the academic machine.

And yet it is naive to assume that the concerns, views, and misperceptions of the public can be ignored in a democratic, mass-education society. The kind of exquisite narcissism that has frequently characterized higher education in the past will be preserved only at the peril of both the institutions and the system. If for no other reason than to assure sufficient demand for the educational services offered, academicians will need to have information about the states of mind of people in the market to communicate effectively with them.

We hope that academic marketers who keep the essential nature of higher education obviously in mind as they conduct their affairs will be able to assuage the critics who fear that marketing will compromise the quality or the integrity of higher education (at least to the degree that such criticism doesn't simply mask an aversion to new perspectives on traditional ways). There have also been critics of academic marketing, however, who claim that it just won't work. Michael McPherson has observed:

> Everybody spending more on marketing is like everybody showing up two hours early to get a good seat at the big game. What happens in the aggregate is that everybody winds up sitting two extra hours in the same seat they [sic] would have had anyway. (1981, 20)

By equating colleges with athletic fans and students with stadium seats, however, McPherson's analogy fails to capture the nature of markets or of marketing. It's a rare world where everyone decides to do anything all at the same time (e.g., "showing up two hours early"), and if the stadium were shrinking as the traditional student market is, showing up early could indeed make a difference in whether one gets a seat. An individual can sit in only one seat at a time; organizations serve many individuals and can increase (or sustain) their shares of the market through effective marketing. Although seats may be passive receivers of posteriors, students *select* the institutions they will consider and they will attend. Marketing not only has to be "first," but, more important, it has to provide better benefits, a better price, easier access, better information, or some combination of these phenomena, than what is offered by the competition. When it does, the word gets around, and "the seats seek the sitters."

Furthermore, effective marketing by individual colleges shouldn't simply result in each institution's canceling out the effects of other institutions' activities. Certainly competitors will seek to counter any advantages achieved by a given institution through further marketing initiatives. Unless institutions choose, however, and are permitted, to exploit imperfections in the consumer's understanding of higher education, even "canceling efforts" should result in general improvements for students and the nation (improved programs, more effective pricing and financing arrangements, better delivery systems).

In addition to the antiacademic orientation toward the *use and dissemination* of research results, which we have observed in relation to academic market research (see Introduction), another antiacademic attitude often crops up regarding the *substance and foci* of such research. This is an insistence on "actionable" research and an eschewing of the "nonactionable." Although this is rather fuzzy jargon, it appears often to mean that research that does not lead directly to specific actions is not worth the cost. Nonacademicians are the principal carriers of such attitudes, although they are not alone. There are several flaws in such arguments. First, some things that are seemingly not actionable at first blush can indeed be the object of marketing actions. For example, although location often can't be changed for a college, off-campus programs can be developed to compensate for the limitations of some locations, or programs can be developed on campus that better exploit the advantages of a given location (e.g., the winter activities programs that began to emerge at Carleton). Second, knowledge of some liabilities that truly can't be changed can indicate how much effort may have to be applied to the development or promotion of other, compensating assets. Furthermore, colleges promote the ideal that self-understanding is good in itself, that basic insights into the nature of the world are of value even though their particular utility may not be foreseeable. This is especially true in a rapidly changing world, where changes in the financial or social infrastructure or the marketing initiatives of competitors can substantially and suddenly alter the order of things. The cumulative understanding that can be gained from ongoing or periodic actionable *and* nonactionable research is an important foundation for comprehending and dealing with a changing environment. The principal problems with the action-only orientation are that it often disguises a preoccupation with short-term problems and solutions instead of a concern for longer-term well-being, and that it focuses attention on easy solutions when the difficult issues may well be the more important. We believe that market research should have a strong practical aspect; we reject the notion, however, that nonactionable research is not worth its costs.

An interesting cleavage emerging among academic market researchers indicates two phenomena: (1) The field is maturing enough to begin to develop philosophical and stylistic divergences. (2) Academic market research is drawing on a number of other research traditions that are not always in full paradigmatic accord with each other. One camp seeks to develop formal models of market structure and consumer behavior. It is a deterministic approach to understanding the structure of the higher education market and a given college's market. Institutions are often counseled to respond to such data by adjusting their plans (future size, etc.) reactively to projections made on historical trends or current conditions. On the other side a more humanistic tradition is developing, which not only looks at slightly different data but also performs its analysis a little differently and comes to (or seeks) a different set of conclusions. This second approach attempts to understand the psychology of different types of "consumers" and to understand the cultures within which they make college-selection decisions. It looks not so much for deterministic forces but rather for opportunities for marketing initiatives, for openings in which an institution's situation can be developed in a more favorable manner or consumer behavior may be changed. We believe that both perspectives are important in a fully developed market research program (among ourselves we tend differentially to favor one or the other approaches). We have tried to attend to both perspectives in our own work.

Research cannot be permitted to lead to stereotyping. No research is definitive. Conditions change and particulars deviate from general patterns. We must always be alert to the singular event, the deviation from "the norm." This is especially true in educational matters, for they involve what is essentially *individual* growth, even though they require bringing larger-scale, institutionally organized resources to bear on these concerns.

An appropriate market research program can have powerful benefits for a college. Our conviction is grounded in the pragmatic effects of our own efforts at Carleton. Starting with the response of almost 20 percent to our Student Search brochure, which drew heavily on the results of the research (at the time the average response for single mailings through Student Search was 13 percent), the evidence has continued to mount. When the research began, Carleton had attracted an extremely able student body for over two decades. A self-selection by students, however, had some undesirable consequences for the college (or, more accurately, failed to deliver some desirable benefits).[12] As the research began to make its impact, Carleton's acceptance rate dropped from 82 percent in 1976 to 51 percent in 1981. This is not just selectivity for selectivity's sake. The increase in the applicant pool (up 44 percent over the same period) has permitted the selection of an educationally more exciting class, and the chance for a positive match between student and college has been increased. The latter is reflected in a decline in lower-division attrition from 17 percent for the class that

---

12. At a time when Carleton was twenty-seventh in selectivity (that is, it had the third-highest acceptance rate) among the 29 highly selective institutions in the Consortium on Financing Higher Education, it also had the eighteenth-highest average SAT-verbal scores for its entering freshmen.

entered in 1975 to 10 percent in the 1979 freshman class, measured at the start of the junior year.[13]

We should be clear, however, about the several mechanisms through which these results transpired and the place of the market research in the broader picture. The abilities of the particular persons who were managing the affairs of the college during these times should not be underestimated. At the same time the tools with which they were able to work were not inconsequential. Formal market research serves two functions — it provides answers to important questions; it also sharpens the questions themselves. The research findings contributed substantially to the decisions that were made about the marketing of Carleton. We believe, however, that even more important outcomes were that important questions were kept alive via the research and that sensibilities were formed and refined. Just as formal research should be used as a means of testing intuition and experience, it should lead to a sharpened sense of observation to validate and extend the results of the research. Market research is the institutional manifestation of the ideal we hold up to our students — the examined life. It is also a means by which private knowledge gained through experience can be flushed into public knowledge for use in institutional, collective decisions.

The mechanism through which market research is considered and exploited can be as important as the research itself. Carleton established several marketing task forces. The most recent group consisted of the dean of admissions, the dean for academic planning and development, the director of college relations, the director of third-world affairs, and the coordinator of institutional research. The research was an important springboard, but the extensive deliberations and careful decisions of this group were what really made the marketing difference for Carleton and the cost of doing the research worth it.

---

13. Research had shown that almost all the attrition at Carleton occurred by this point.

2.

Early Soundings in Carleton's Applicant and Inquiry Pools: The Evolution of a Market Research Program

This chapter reviews various early projects in Carleton's market research program, which began with a study of the college's current students and admitted applicants. Like charity, marketing insight begins at home. There are both philosophical and practical reasons for initiating a market research program in this way.[1] Current students represent successful institutional performances of social and economic functions — education and other services are being provided to at least some portion of the market. The marketing effort in place has indeed produced results. A college should not abandon lightly the performance of services to its current clients, even if it is not so successful at a given moment as may be desired.[2] Therefore, philosophically it makes sense for a college or university to try to understand why students are now coming to it, who they are, and how they get there. Pragmatically, current students constitute a kind of captive population that is inexpensive to study. When a study is begun with admitted students or applicants and with local research personnel, an opportunity is afforded to sharpen and refine, at minimal cost, the questions to be posed in subsequent, broader research. Such starting points also provide a foundation for testing the more generalized findings of the market research effort against the particular experiences and perspectives of persons within the institution. Although there are risks that research

---

1. A dramatic reduction in the number of applicants for an institution may require immediate focus on the market beyond the institution's applicant pool, even if the preliminary work with current students has not been effected. This constitutes a rational response to previous management that has not been optimally rational, however, and carries a number of attendant risks.

2. This is not to suggest naively that a given institution's resources may not be employed optimally to other ends, but simply to recognize that the risks of redeploying an institution's resources can be substantial.

conducted at this level will be infused with local prejudices and limited vision, at the beginning the risks are worth taking because of the benefits. Much more intelligent use of other "perspective-correcting" resources will then be possible when the time comes to use them.

Although many colleges have already executed some of the activities that will be described, this chapter serves several purposes. First, it sets the context for the later chapters and shows how some of the foci of the larger study, which is the main feature of this book, grew directly either from persistent concerns evident throughout the research program or from questions that emanated from these earlier research efforts. Second, this chapter provides perspectives on alternative ways of addressing some of the issues or dealing with some of the populations studied, even for institutions that have already entered these realms through their own devices. Finally, if market research does not contribute to the recurrent self-scrutiny of the institution that sponsors it, it is hardly worth undertaking. This chapter is our first effort to pull together in one place a review both of the findings contained in numerous reports and of the several methods used in our market research program at Carleton; as such, it affords a broader and deeper collective perspective on the research efforts, and others may find the exercise valuable as well.

The specific research activities and their sequence of execution at Carleton are not held up as a model; were we to do it over, we would make a number of changes in both activities and timing. And yet we firmly believe that the Carleton market research program was exemplary in important respects — it was an institutional effort, the research was evolutionary and incremental, and research became an institutionalized part of the college's life. Such a process enhances an institution's capacities for absorbing each set of data and for relating insights to further inquiry, which in turn leads to further insight; there is so much to be examined through market research that information overload is a serious threat. Indeed, this *internally generated and executed* research effort produced the outcomes of greatest value — not the specific research findings, but the heightened sensibilities referred to in Chapter 1. We hope that our historical approach to recounting this market research effort, with extensive citation from the primary research documents, will recover this developmental process and help the reader to participate vicariously in our discoveries and evolving market sense.

INITIATION OF THE RESEARCH PROGRAM

The admissions research effort at Carleton College was initiated in the early 1970s, following attendance by Paul Garman, director of admissions, and Richard Heydinger, associate director of data processing, at a College Board workshop on "Admissions and the Computer" at Indiana State University. A faculty member in the Department of Sociology, Daniel Sullivan, and the newly created Office of Institutional Research under its director, Larry Litten, were also involved at early points. The first reports, however, were primarily written by students, under professional supervision.[3]

Two principal kinds of market research studies were conducted at Carleton in the period from 1972 to 1978: (1) analyses of factors affecting Carleton's yield (percentage of acceptances who enrolled) and studies of prospects who had made some contact with Carleton (campus visit, written inquiry, etc.) but who subsequently did not apply for admission; and (2) studies of Carleton's market position relative to its competitors via further analyses of applications and acceptances. Both of these research foci are reviewed in this chapter.

The research began with analyses of data from records kept on recruiting contacts, data from the Carleton Admissions Application Form, and data from the annual freshman survey of the Cooperative Institutional Research Program (CIRP) of the American Council on Education. This first effort focused on the application-yield effects of three recruiting activities — contacts with prospectives by alumni, high school visits by admissions office staff, and campus visits by prospectives — and on the types of students that Carleton attracts.[4] It involved some very basic types of segmentation (type

---

3. The involvement of students has been a significant aspect of Carleton's market research all along. Internships have been important components in the Carleton institutional research scheme. Although student work has often been less "efficient" than a strictly professional job, students have contributed some valuable perspectives, and the activities have contributed invaluable educational experiences in social science research for students from a wide variety of backgrounds. The foci of the early reports were also shaped, more than were later efforts, by the interests of the particular student authors. Students were also instrumental in the creation of the essential computer resources that helped to accomplish the market research. Under the supervision of Graham Kimble and Carl Henry, student programmers created a statistical package that eventually developed into the Statistical Package for the Social Sciences (SPSS) now marketed by SPSS, Inc. for use on several of the Digital Equipment Corporation's minicomputers.

4. Metz and Evison, April 1973 and no date.

of secondary school, SAT scores, and location of home). In general it showed that referrals to alumni admissions representatives did not have a positive effect on students' propensities to enroll, except in the Midwest. It also noted, however, the possibility that other factors crucial to the recruitment process might be confounding that result because they were more often present in the Midwest (e.g., greater incidence of campus visits, general reputation of Carleton, and more media publicity). High school visits by Carleton admissions officers appeared to have no independent effect on matriculation probabilities. A visit to the campus was associated with a 50 percent increase in the probability that a student would be admitted and a 100 percent increase in the probability that a student would enroll; the effects were greater for students who lived near Carleton than for students from states that were farther away.

Analysis of data from the application form showed that Carleton was slightly more likely to admit students who exhibited past leadership activities than their less active peers, and slightly less likely to enroll such students; Carleton admitted students with lower levels of "social concern" at higher rates than their more "concerned" peers, and enrolled such students in relatively high proportions. In the CIRP data, Carleton's students did not appear very different from the students at similar colleges.[5] The first admissions research report concluded with the following questions for the Admissions and Financial Aid Committee:

> To what extent do we want to be distinctive with respect to any of the particular measures that we have here? To what extent do we want to recruit an entire student body that is turned on to art or politics or whatever? Do we want a mixture of student interests and objectives that generally reflect the society from which they come, in which they live and will continue to live following college? Or do we want a group of students that stands apart from the norms of the society, a group which more closely reflects unrealized ideals or which appears capable of helping to evolve new ideas? Is this a zero-sum situation in which these values are mutually exclusive or can we recruit a student body which is committed to art and to politics? What is the ideal and what is the realistic?
>
> Are we principally confirmers of ability, accomplishments, and values or are we principally educators? Should we be concerned principally about whether our entering classes are distinctive or should we be more concerned about assessing whether our graduates are distinctive, if indeed distinctiveness is what we seek? Should these data be the con-

---

5. We asked 24 colleges to share their data with us, and 5 did so.

cern of the Admissions Committee or should they be primarily of interest to [its] parent group—the Educational Policy Committee?

These first studies were, by later standards, oversimple and methodologically unsophisticated, but, as can be seen from the questions raised by the reports, they went to the heart of matters important for a college like Carleton to consider. They quickly stimulated thought and discussion; this was critical in creating a positive climate for market research and an emerging marketing sense at Carleton.

The second year's report was based on application-form data, a questionnaire to matriculating students, and a postcard to students who declined Carleton's offer of admission.[6] The report indicated that Asians were slightly less likely than other groups to accept our offer of admission, and that Minnesota applicants were somewhat more likely than residents of other regions both to be admitted and to enroll; the higher admission rates among Minnesota students were partially explained by their somewhat higher class rankings and SAT-mathematical scores. It was shown that Carleton's principal competition came from a geographically dispersed set of schools (among the top schools, seven were in the East, two in California, and five in the Midwest). Most of the admitted applicants that Carleton lost went to similar institutions; slightly over half of the losses went to institutions with somewhat higher "quality ratings" (on an index constructed at Carleton). The principal reasons that matriculating students chose Carleton were academic reputation, size, coeducation, and location. "Location" was the principal reason cited by nonmatriculants for declining Carleton's offer of admission, followed distantly by academic reputation. Nonmatriculating Asians were shown to cite location, almost to the person.

Geographic and ability segments did not exhibit more than minor differences in their reasons for nonmatriculation. People in the lowest income category and the second-highest income group were the most likely to indicate that financial aid was a cause for defection. This latter group encompassed middle-income families just above the financial aid cutoff. Students who went to the Ivy League institutions, the Seven Sisters, or the Little Three were the most likely to cite academic reputation as a reason. The "music program" was an especially strong attraction to Oberlin, "location" to Stanford, and "academic reputation" to Harvard and Princeton.

---

6. Young, August 1973.

The report of the second year's research was the first to make some specific marketing recommendations; it suggested that a list of other schools to which students were applying be obtained early, and specific characteristics of Carleton be emphasized to counter the appeal of these competitors. The report concluded: "None of the above should be interpreted as advocating a hard-sell admissions approach. It is only suggested that different kinds of questions will be the concerns of different kinds of people and that the admissions process can be improved by anticipating those concerns and alleviating them with the proper kinds of information."

In 1974 and 1975 the data for the analyses of determinants of Carleton's yield were obtained primarily from questionnaires that were an integral part of the Candidate's Reply Form, via which an admitted applicant notifies the institution of his or her intention to enroll (and which is accompanied by a deposit from matriculating students). These forms are printed in Appendix C.

The 1974 research also involved a survey of students who had inquired about Carleton but who had not followed through with an application. It was supported by a grant from the Hill Foundation (later renamed the Northwest Area Foundation) and was conducted by Daniel Sullivan. His report[7] was circulated to the entire Carleton faculty as well as to the admissions director and the Admissions and Financial Aid Committee. It was published with minor deletions and changes in the Northwest Area Foundation volume *Choice or Chance* (1976) and, with a 1975 update of the admitted applicants survey, it was published again in the College Board's *A Role for Marketing in College Admissions* (1976). Because of the prior publication, we present only a brief discussion of the methodological advances and major findings of this part of the research.[8]

The study of nonapplicants (inquirers who did not apply) showed them to be similar in ability and parental income to the applicant pool. To a large extent they went to institutions similar to Carleton, or to the institutions attended by Carleton's admitted applicants who did not come to Carleton. The nonapplicants tended to know less about Carleton than did the applicants. Most significant, however, was the discovery that Carleton has a marketing problem with Eastern students different from the one it faces with Midwestern students. Even though the tables have been published

---

7. Sullivan, August 1974.
8. Sullivan, 1976; Sullivan and Litten, 1976.

elsewhere,[9] we reproduce them here because of the importance of their message.

Whereas in the late 1960s Carleton's comprehensive fee was very close to those of its major Eastern competitors, by the mid-1970s, when the research reported here was conducted, Carleton was priced considerably below these institutions. At the same time Carleton had become more expensive than its Midwestern competition. Both trends have continued to the present. We asked nonapplicants if Carleton's cost was a negative factor in their decision not to apply; the results are reproduced in Table 2-1. Midwestern students were three-and-one-half times more likely to see Carleton's cost as a deterrent than were Eastern students. Carleton's cost advantage relative to Eastern schools was, and is, a positive factor in decisions by Eastern students to apply, and its cost disadvantage relative to Midwestern institutions is a negative factor in the calculations of Midwestern students.

These reactions by Eastern and Midwestern students to Carleton's cost, however, are offset by these students' perceptions of Carleton's academic reputation and its location. Table 2-2 shows that Carleton's academic reputation was much less often a "very positive" factor in the application decision of Eastern students than it was for Midwestern students.

Table 2-1. Nonapplicants (by Region of Residence) for Whom Carleton's Cost Was Negative Influence on Application Decisions

	Percentage	*N*
Midwest	47	273
South	36	70
West	36	59
East	13	87

Table 2-2. Nonapplicants (by Region of Residence) for Whom Carleton's Academic Reputation Was Very Positive Influence on Application Decisions

	Percentage	*N*
Midwest	67	278
South	61	71
West	55	60
East	43	87

9. Sullivan and Litten, 1976, 95.

Table 2-3. Nonapplicants (by Region of Residence) for Whom Carleton's Location Was Negative Influence on Application Decisions

	Percentage	N
East	74	88
West	59	59
South	48	71
Midwest	38	278

Table 2-3 shows that for about three-fourths of the Eastern students, Carleton's location was a negative factor; Westerners followed in the incidence of negative ratings of the location.

These data showed clearly and unambiguously the dimensions of a major marketing problem, and a set of opportunities that Carleton was not able to exploit fully until several years later, when these results were used to shape the publications prepared especially for use in the Student Search Service of the College Board. To attract more Eastern applicants, Carleton would have to deal effectively with its perceived lower academic reputation relative to its Eastern competitors and provide better information on its location, while exploiting the cost advantage. Midwestern students and parents would have to come to understand why Carleton is more expensive than other Midwestern schools — what value is purchased with the additional investment — and they would have to be told more clearly about financial aid. With Midwestern students and parents we would exploit the high esteem these people have for Minnesota and for Carleton.

Even more significantly, perhaps, in light of national demographic trends, Carleton's cost was less of a negative factor for Southern and Western students, and Carleton's reputation and location were more of a positive factor than for Eastern students. In the South and West, if Carleton could increase its visibility, we believed the response would be positive.

The preceding tables are exceedingly simple, but their messages were confirmed over and over in subsequent years' research, and the implications of these data have been profound for Carleton's student recruitment strategy.

The 1974 and 1975 yield studies involved a simple but major conceptual advance. We examined the effect of each variable on yield (e.g., reaction to a talk with an admissions representative and its effect on yield), taking into account whether or not Carleton was the prospective student's first choice at the time of application.

This was done because it was believed that the best test of a variable's impact on yield would be its effect within the group that had not started with Carleton as a first choice.

A further elaboration made the analysis even more interesting. We divided the group for whom Carleton was not first choice according to whether the students involved had been accepted by their first-choice schools. In other words, was the student's first-choice school an actual option at decision time? (Carleton was, of course, because the study population included only those accepted by Carleton.) Those students not accepted at their first-choice schools might, we hypothesized, be much more affected by aspects of the admissions process—for example, their reactions to an admissions officer. Because they were not allowed to make the choice they wanted, they might let their treatment in the admissions process have greater than normal effects. That is precisely what we tended to find, and these results led Carleton to pay much more attention to the impact of the recruiting and admissions process than we might have if we had used only our earlier analyses, which did not segregate the students who were denied their first choices.

Table 2-4, using data from our 1975 study, provides a good illustration of the result just described. We asked students who had had interviews with an admissions officer whether the interview increased or decreased their desires to attend Carleton. For each category of influence, we show the percentage of accepted students who enrolled at Carleton (the yield) separately (1) for those for whom Carleton was first choice, (2) for those *not* accepted at their first choices (not Carleton), and (3) for those who were accepted at their first choices (not Carleton). Yields for those who had not had an interview are also shown.

The impact of the interview on yield was much greater for the group not accepted at their first choices (these became known as "reluctant recruits" in Carleton admissions jargon). When the student said the interview was a highly positive experience, 74 percent enrolled; when, in the student's view, it had no influence or a negative influence, only 36 percent enrolled, for a difference of 38 percent. The effects of the interview experiences on yield for the other two groups were much smaller—13 percent and 7 percent, respectively. Those not accepted at their first choices were much more affected by their experiences with this aspect of the recruitment process than were the other groups. It was also evident that a positive interview (one which "greatly" or "slightly increased" the

Table 2-4. Matriculation at Carleton (Yield) by Influence of Admissions Interview on Desire to Attend Carleton for Three Categories of College Preference

	Carleton First Choice		Carleton Not First Choice			
			Not Accepted at First Choice		Accepted at First Choice	
Desire to Attend Carleton	%	N	%	N	%	N
Greatly Increased	85	100*	74	23	28	39
Slightly Increased	84	105	59	46	24	79
No Influence or Decreased	72	74	36	42	21	62
No Interview	86	92	51	74	17	98

Δ13% (Carleton First Choice) Δ38% (Not Accepted at First Choice) Δ7% (Accepted at First Choice)

Note: Δ = Difference.
* These figures indicate that 85 percent of the 100 students who had Carleton as first choice, and whose interviews greatly increased their desire to attend, actually enrolled at Carleton.

desire to attend) was associated with a higher yield than was no interview and that there appeared to be a higher probability of a positive interview than one that had a negative or no influence. This very important result was supported by other analyses not reviewed here. The Carleton Admissions Office now knows that it must pay careful attention to the nature of its contacts with prospective students, because the quality of the experience can greatly affect yield among students not accepted by their first-choice schools.

The 1974 and 1975 studies also highlighted the influence of parents on the final decision regarding Carleton and the positive impact of campus visits. In addition, those studies greatly increased our evidence on the roles cost and financial aid play in the college-selection process. With the huge increase in the inflation rate between 1974 and 1975, we saw a substantial decline in yield among those students who applied for financial aid but were determined by the college not to have need. The yield in that group declined from 37 percent in 1974 to 13 percent in 1975. Those applicants, children of middle-income parents who fell just above the financial aid cutoff, seemed to believe they needed help. When the economy worsened in 1975, they and their parents were much less likely to choose Carleton.[10] While not the only factor affecting the level of Carleton's fees in the several years just following that research, those results were influential in the college's decision not to increase its fees as fast as its national competitors did.

DEVELOPING A BROADER MARKET PERSPECTIVE

In 1976 there was a major development in the orientation of the Carleton market research program. The analysis moved beyond narrow admissions and recruiting research that focused simply on student characteristics, exposure to and ratings of Carleton's recruiting activities, and ratings of Carleton characteristics; we developed a sense of *the market* and began to examine market structure and ratings of both Carleton and competing institutions obtained via the admitted-applicant surveys. This reorientation came from reading general marketing literature and the application of the marketing and market research perspectives on college admissions that were being advanced through the efforts of the Northwest Area Foundation and the College Board.

---

10. Ibid., 101–102, presents the full analysis.

We started our examination of market structure by searching for patterns in application submissions by Carleton applicants, which might reveal *sets* of competitors that would help focus our marketing efforts. Beginning with the first admitted-applicant questionnaire in 1973, data on the other institutions to which Carleton's applicants had applied had been gathered (along with data on admission status and financial aid at each institution). Lists of principal competitors had been developed annually, but since Carleton applicants tend to submit several other applications, we began to search for overlap patterns. Unlike many marketing problems in other areas where only a few alternatives exist for the consumer, for many academic institutions the array of competitors is extensive, and some means of simplifying the picture can help move an institution toward the definition of specific marketing strategies. (There may also be individual competitors of such significance that strategies specifically directed toward those institutions will be warranted; the search for patterns can help identify these conditions.)

Some form of "mapping" the relationships among several products has been a major tool of marketers in their efforts to understand the structure of the supply side of a market. Graphs of "market space" produced through multidimensional scaling (MDS) of ratings of the similarities of pairs of colleges have been the principal means employed by higher education market researchers in analyzing market structure and the positions occupied by institutions within a given market. Such ratings present a rather cumbersome task for the rater. Our use of multidimensional scaling employed a simpler data collection procedure than did previous MDS applications; we derived market structure from students' market behavior—the submission of applications for admission.[11] We drew on a research tradition in the sociology of science—the analysis of the citation and cocitation of scientific articles (Sullivan, White, and Barboni 1977; Small 1973)—to produce MDS plots that show both the numbers of applications to given institutions and the structure of overlap among applications. Briefly, multidimensional scaling techniques involve the use of measures of "prox-

11. Multidimensional scaling has been used by a number of researchers to examine the structure of the market for institutions of higher education. Most uses of MDS to date have employed the more traditional—and more burdensome—technique in which respondents are asked to specifically rate pairs of institutions on the basis of their similarity. See, for example, the work of Leister and his colleagues; Sternberg and Davis 1978; Shaffer 1978.

imity" between objects to produce a geometric representation of their relationships, similar to a map. Each point in the geometric configuration produced by MDS represents an object (a college in our data), and the more similar two objects are (or are perceived to be), the closer their points will be on the map. Proximities can be any measure of similarity or dissimilarity between two objects, or measures of perceptions of similarities. Some data that are not directly proximities may also be converted to proximities for analysis through MDS. In our case we used overlap in applications as a measure of proximity, or substitutability—the greater the incidence of simultaneous applications to two colleges, the greater their proximity for MDS calculations.[12]

Since higher education institutions are tied to specific locations (as opposed to other, more portable products), we anticipated that the structure of competition would differ by geographic regions. Figure 2-1 presents multidimensional scaling plottings of the institutions to which Carleton applicants from four regions applied in 1976 and 1977.[13] These institutions were taken from the applicant's listing of the four top choices in his or her set of applications, including those to which the applicant was admitted and those that denied admission. By limiting the responses to four, we have possibly underrepresented "safety" colleges for applicants who submitted more than four high-risk applications.

A variety of information is contained in the figures. First, the sizes of the circles representing individual institutions are proportional to the number of applications submitted to that institution by students who also applied to Carleton. The proximity of the centers of two institutions' circles is a function of the incidence of applications to both of them by individual applicants (i.e., the more frequently students apply to two institutions, the closer they will tend to be on the plot). When Carleton lost the majority of the applicants who were admitted to both Carleton and the institution named, the name of the competitor is underlined.[14]

---

12. Two colleges' points can also be placed in close proximity on an MDS plot not because of their paired "similarity," but because they are both "similar" to a third college and both are placed close to the third institution's point.

13. We combined two years' data in order to increase the stability of the data and provide sufficient numbers of cases for disaggregated analysis.

14. These competitive advantage data are for 1976 and 1977; some of the advantages have been reversed since then. The data are also for total overlap, not disaggregated by region. The latter would provide much more analytic power, but the data from this era were not recoverable for such disaggregation.

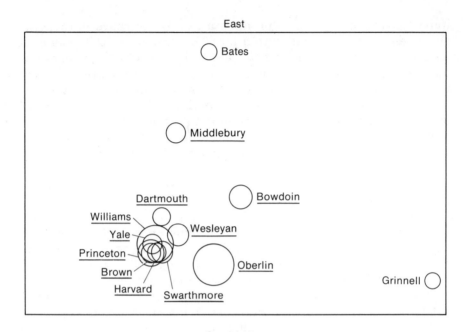

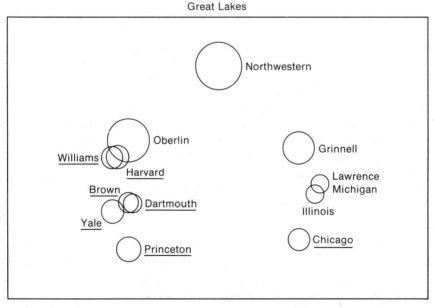

Figure 2-1. The Structure of Competition among Carleton Applicants in Four Regions

North Central

West

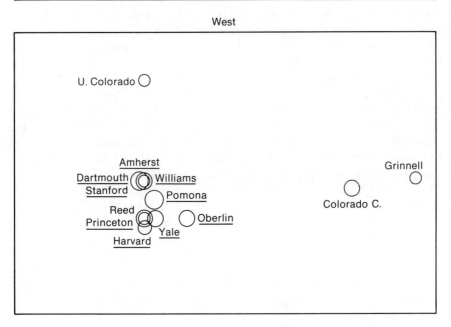

The data show how different the structures of competition for applicants were in the various regions, although in each region Carleton applicants also applied to a set of national private colleges and universities located in the East. Eastern private institutions dominated in both the East and the West, although Oberlin was a relatively more important competitor in the East. The two mid-continent markets each showed both a Midwestern and an Eastern component in the market; these two institutional sets were particularly well defined in the Great Lakes region, where Northwestern University loomed as a major competitor that straddled the two sectors—or vied for students who were oriented toward each sector. The nature of Carleton's pricing dilemma is also well illustrated here. Public sector competition for Carleton applicants was virtually nonexistent on the East and West coasts, whereas in the other two regions there were significant overlaps with public institutions. Furthermore, only one institution in the picture for the East had a comprehensive fee lower than Carleton's (Grinnell), but six institutions in the North Central region, representing over half of those appearing in Figure 2-1, were priced lower than Carleton. These results reinforced our sense that Carleton had to develop a regional marketing strategy that would take into account both the way in which Carleton is seen and the precise nature of the competition in each region, but that there were also some national competitors to be dealt with across the board.

Marketing stresses that decisions to purchase a product are not made in a vacuum; students have a variety of options, and we sought to determine how Carleton measured up—its relative strengths and weaknesses—in comparison with the competition. Students were asked to rate Carleton and other institutions on a number of dimensions (see the Candidate's Reply Form used in 1976 and 1977 in Appendix C). Students who were matriculating at Carleton were asked to rate the institution "you would most likely have attended had you not chosen Carleton"; nonmatriculating students were asked to rate the institutions they were planning to attend. The data in Figure 2-2 show how Carleton stacked up in relation to specific types of competitors, again within a specific region—the North Central market. (These "balance-sheet" graphs were developed for different types of institutions in different regions; see Litten 1979 for data on the Eastern region.)

The data show the relative ratings given to Carleton and a competing institution among students for whom the competition was an Ivy League institution or another member of a consortium called Associated Colleges of the Midwest (ACM), to which Carleton belongs. They show where Carleton was seen to be strong or weak relative to those two sets of institutions. For example, when compared with the Ivy League colleges, Carleton was accurately perceived to be less expensive and in general to have a superior admissions process, but no one thought Carleton's library superior. When compared with ACM schools, Carleton was seen by no one as inferior in academic quality, but Carleton's social atmosphere was more likely to be considered inferior than superior, as were its off-campus programs (many of which were run jointly with other ACM colleges—a true promotional failure!). Carleton's library was a neutral factor, and Carleton was uniformly perceived as more expensive. Carleton is just completing a major renovation of, and an addition to, its library, a project whose salience is at least partly a function of the negative perceptions of the current library that we saw in these data. The key point to be made here, however, is that these data indicated much more clearly what some of Carleton's marketing problems were with respect to specific sets of institutions in specific regions.

Too often in books like this, where results and influences on policy can be reinterpreted on hindsight, a sense of the groping for answers that went on at the time is not conveyed sufficiently. In such a report the researchers can be made to look much smarter than they were at the time. As the research process developed, we continued our efforts to refine our data collection and analysis in order to extend and clarify earlier research results, and began to test marketing ideas that had evolved in our discussions. A discipline we tried to enforce was always to try to answer the question "so what?" after we reported our analysis. To capture the spirit of this process and to provide concrete examples of the research-marketing linkages we considered, we reprint major excerpts from the concluding sections of the 1976 and 1977 reports.[15] These demonstrate how certain insights matured and new ones developed. Some of the suggestions, upon further consideration, had important effects on the marketing process; others were discarded. We begin with the 1976 report:

> Carleton's academic characteristics are rated high both by students who accept admission and by those who decline our offer. Ratings of geographic characteristics and of social atmosphere stand out as important correlates of the decision to enroll at Carleton. [Ratings of social atmosphere were *the most important* predictor of matriculation.]

---

15. Litten et al., September 1977; Litten, March 1978a.

C. Region: North Central
   School Type: Ivy League

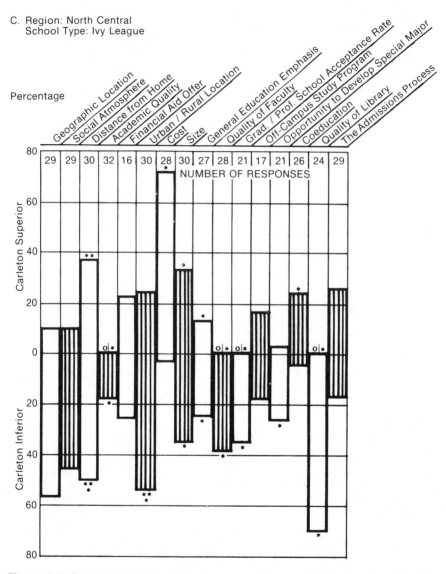

Figure 2-2. Relative Ratings of Carleton and Competing Types of Institutions in the North Central Region

D. Region: North Central
   School Type: Consortium

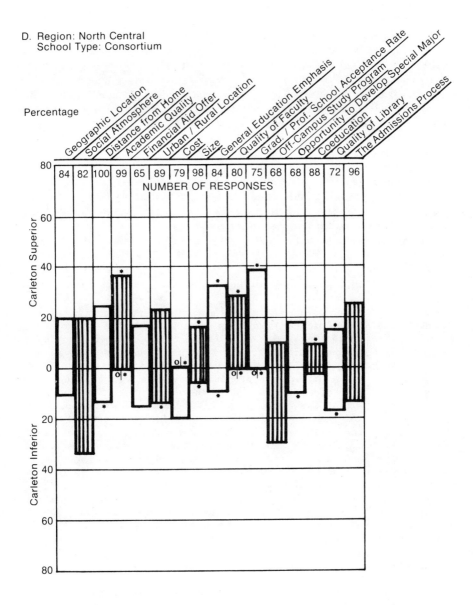

These associations are particularly strong when the ratings [of Carleton] *are relative* to [ratings of] competing schools (e.g., when our social atmosphere is perceived to be superior to our competitors', students are particularly likely to enroll).[16] The rating of graduate school acceptance rate is the academic quality characteristic which is most highly correlated with the decision to enroll. Particular departments (either presence or rated quality) are also reported by students to have been relatively important in this decision. Ratings of our price do not seem to be highly associated with the decision to enroll; *if anything, a positive rating of our price has a slight negative influence on attendance.*[17] When comparisons are made with other schools (as opposed to simple ratings of Carleton), however, the student's relative rating of the financial aid offers relates to the student's choice of college (attendance is more likely at the institution whose aid is rated better).

Men and women demonstrate slightly different patterns of influences on their decisions to enroll. Geographic considerations loom more important for women than for men. Cost and graduate school acceptance rate are relatively more important for men.

---

16. Our use of "difference measures" (one institution's ratings subtracted from another's) and multiple regression analysis to predict matriculation have been criticized by other academic researchers on the basis of methodological arguments in the social scientific literature (Maguire and Lay 1981). Two of the three citations given by the critics, however, are irrelevant both to the statistical nature of our difference measures and to our use of such measures; the third citation addresses only a minor limitation of this method. Indeed, the use of difference measures does obscure some aspects of the phenomena with which they deal; for example, the same difference scores between two institutions will be obtained for two raters when one rates institution A very high relative to the mean rating for all institutions and institution B near the mean, and when the second rater scores institution A near the mean and institution B very low. But there are tradeoffs, and we consider the benefits of difference scores over the use of individual institutional ratings in the prediction of choice behavior to outweigh their shortcomings. Principal among these benefits are preservation of the comparative framework that is implicit when a person is asked to rate two institutions side by side, and acknowledgment of the basic marketing principle that no decisions in the market are made through isolated evaluation of individual "products," but in a comparative framework in which other options are also evaluated. The use of individual institutional scores as suggested by these critics can produce results that are difficult to interpret. For example, ratings of the aid programs at the marketer's institution are *more important* than its specific academic programs in predicting enrollment at the marketer's institution, while the ratings of specific academic programs at the competition are more important than the competition's aid programs in predicting enrollment at the marketer's institution. (*op cit.*, 134)

17. Even though other results, as mentioned above, caused us to worry that Carleton might be too expensive, this finding led us to worry that students who were considering Carleton and more expensive schools saw price and quality as correlated with each other—the notion that if Carleton costs less, it may also be less good.

There are regional variations in the ratings of Carleton. Overall, New England, the Mid-Atlantic States and the Far West seem to have the most negative images of the college. Perceptions of our academic quality suffer most in New England. The South Central States, while smaller than some other regions in number of applicants, appear to have the most positive overall image of Carleton. Ratings of our location decline as distance from the college increases.

The relative ratings of Carleton and the competition by students who decline our offer of admission differ according to the types of institutions to which the students are going. The largest differences on the most numerous dimensions are reported between Carleton and public institutions. Irrespective of the types of institutions attended by students who decline our offer, our social atmosphere is [likely to be] seen as inferior by these nonmatriculants.

Several marketing implications of these 1976 findings were then discussed:

We have alluded to several strategies which flow from these findings. We will elaborate briefly on these at this point. Let us take as a case in point the ratings of social atmosphere, the characteristic which is most highly correlated with enrollment. One strategy for improving our yield might be to improve our social atmosphere through development of formal social activities, the development of social policies which improve social interaction or the social climate, or the provision of resources and facilities which facilitate a different social atmosphere. The hope would be that this improved social reality would result in improved ratings for Carleton and higher yield among admitted students (thereby permitting growth or greater selectivity or stability in the face of a declining college-age population).

A second strategy would be to alter the perceptions of our social reality. If students see Carleton's social life as nonexistent (and it would take further research to clarify the nature of the negative perceptions), it might be possible to stress the fact that social life is not absent, but rather that it is dispersed, less visible than at places with elaborate social centers, and closer to the places where students actually live. It might be possible to say, if it is demonstrably true, that there are periods of intense work and intense play—that people who form their impressions from one period or the other are distorting the realities of life at Carleton.

Of course, changes in the realities on which these perceptions and evaluations are based present some substantial risks (even beyond the difficulty of effecting such changes). Again, let us consider the problem of social atmosphere as an example. We saw [in one table] that approximately 87 percent of the students who accept our offer of admission rate [Carleton's social atmosphere] as equal or superior to the competition. By having such a high correlation with attendance, the ratings of social atmosphere indicate not only that a negative evaluation has a negative influence, but that a positive evaluation has a positive influence. And both evaluations are substantially represented in our pool of admitted students. If we change our social reality, we run the risk of turning the group with presently positive perceptions into the disaffected in our quest to woo the group who presently turn us down. And so, a third strategy would be to recruit more students of the kind who presently view our social atmosphere favorably (e.g., students in the Great Lakes and South Central regions). Another possibility, however, is to develop a more differentiated institutional reality, although we run the risk of trying to be all things to all people and then succeeding with none.[18]

Social atmosphere is an example which can be carried into other institutionally manipulable variables. Institutional engineering has to be done carefully, with due consideration given to both the costs (direct and indirect) and the presumed benefits, and with regard for the dispositions of both matriculants and decliners.

The case of social atmosphere also provides an example of the need for further research. What are the aspects of our social atmosphere about which students are informed; which are important to them; what, exactly, do they know about the things about which they feel informed, and how did they form these perceptions? To what extent is our problem an image problem instead of a reality problem? Who has more accurate information, those who come or those who decline?

The same problems can certainly be raised for the areas of academic quality and faculty quality. How do students form their impressions of faculty quality? What are the particular characteristics of faculty that cause the aspiring Ivy Leaguers to rate their chosen alma mater's faculty superior to ours? What kinds of contacts have they had with these faculty or how have they formed their impressions?

The 1977 replication of the previous year's survey produced highly consistent results. The occasion was used to expand the consideration of marketing implications:

Marketing our social atmosphere and our location seem to be the principal challenges which face us. Both of these tasks have two components to them. We can improve what we present about these aspects of Carleton or the way we present it. We can also change the institution in each of these areas.

To start with the seemingly impossible, let's examine location. We do not have detailed data on why our location is a problem, but we can make some analytic estimates. Location is primarily a problem for people on the two coasts. Distance from home is certainly a factor, particularly for women. Two approaches give promise in this regard. First we can try to locate and appeal to students with a sense of adventure, a

---

18. Evidence from an attrition study, however, also indicated that in the case of social reality, even students who continue at Carleton saw it as a problem area.

desire to break ties with home and discover a new culture. We can also develop and publicize a good personal support system which makes distance from home seem less formidable.

The Midwestern location appears to be a problem for two reasons. We are not the bastion of elite intellectualism that is New England or the avant-garde of American culture that is the West Coast. We are also given to intemperate winters. We don't have good suggestions to deal with the first problem—perhaps more stress on Midwestern progressivism and the crossroads concept. In the West and Southwest, where the population shift is, one might also emphasize the less formal, less closed nature of Midwestern culture (in relation to the East and the South).

The weather (in distinction to the cultural climate) is both a more severe problem and probably more amenable to effective marketing. A most promising development would be the creation of a more marketable institution—a college which effectively exploits the recreational and educational opportunities which our climate affords. An outings program, club and varsity sports which require our climate, courses which use our natural environment and climate, and arts and cultural events which focus on winter could all increase the attractiveness of Carleton. We could also seek students who have demonstrated a propensity to use instead of flee from or ignore the natural environment (e.g., Explorer Scouts).

The rural, exurban location can also be exploited in a variety of ways. There have been suggestions that more metropolitan campuses may be vulnerable in the face of heightened concern for security. We might be able subtly to work that theme into our recruiting. We could certainly make an effort to cultivate our proximity to the Twin Cities and to offer the best of both worlds, in reality and in publicity.

The social atmosphere question seems best addressed by seeking to provide more options for students (although we do not know how much of the response to this question refers to activities and opportunities and how much to an entirely different social concern—the social class of the student body). The new student center and a director or coordinator of campus activities seem to be promising on-campus developments. The challenge will be to exploit these resources effectively and to publicize them.

Differences in academic quality are perceived to a lesser degree than those which we have just mentioned, but they play an important role in these statistical "models" of the college-selection process. Innovative and exciting academic programs may alter these perceptions to some extent, but they will also have to be marketed effectively.

[These data] ignore many unpondered, if not imponderable, aspects of the marketing problem. We have not explicitly explored the role of better publicity regarding our alumni, more programs involving alumni, changes in facilities, student financing options, cooperative programming with other institutions—to name a few omissions. Much research remains to be done. The definitive research, however, never is accomplished, and the market marches on. The most important tasks are to recognize the existence of some reliable, if limited, data which suggest some problems and to mobilize both responsible offices and the entire community to respond creatively to the challenges.

In 1978 we attempted to obtain some more qualitative information on Carleton's strengths and weaknesses relative to the competition as they had been revealed by the ratings of Carleton and its competitors. We altered the Candidate's Reply Form questionnaire (see Appendix C) to allow for free responses to many of the same questions we had asked in earlier years under a structured format. This free-response format was designed to get us closer to the minds of the applicants by permitting them to phrase answers in their own words, and to help us get behind the ratings of attributes like "social atmosphere" to learn more precisely what students were rating. The following questions were asked:

- Where did you apply and what financial aid did you receive?
- What did you like best about the school you will be attending? (nonmatriculants) What did you like best about your runner-up school? (matriculants)
- Why did you choose the school you will be attending over Carleton? (nonmatriculants) Why did you choose Carleton over your runner-up? (matriculants)
- What aspects of Carleton might have made Carleton even more attractive if they had been different? (asked of both nonmatriculants and matriculants)

Students were also requested to rate Carleton on five dimensions (faculty, students, location, social atmosphere, image of the college held by the public) and to rate each dimension's importance to their decisions.

This type of open-ended questionnaire is cumbersome and expensive to analyze (complex coding operations are necessary to reduce the data to statistical form). The report is voluminous and difficult to summarize. Although we will not report them here, the qualitative data, for the most part, confirmed previous findings about the importance of various dimensions.[19] These data also afforded some refinements in our understanding of perceptions of phenomena such as location, and the qualitative data were useful in developing the contents of our admissions publications. Detailed profiles of Carleton's position vis-à-vis 10 principal competitors were also prepared. These profiles contained tabulations of the following information from the questionnaires of students who were attending each competitor: (1) what the student liked best

---

19. Litten, Layton, and Ross, November 1978.

about the institution chosen, (2) why that institution was chosen over Carleton, and (3) what might have made Carleton relatively more attractive. Samples of verbatim responses to these questions were reported for each institution.

EXPANDING THE ARRAY OF RESEARCH FOCI AND TECHNIQUES

In addition to studies of applicants and prospective students, we conducted a survey in 1977 of students who had left Carleton before graduation.[20] It confirmed suspicions that much of Carleton's relatively small attrition (24 percent over four years) was due to students' educational growth—they decided to enroll in a program of study not offered at Carleton. The report also sharpened our understanding of the problems some students encountered with Carleton's social atmosphere, its rural location, and the diffuseness of a liberal arts program (especially as it relates to specific careers). The report contained 13 specific recommendations of program developments that could address some of the issues raised; it also cautioned against changes that might make the institution more attractive to students who had left but might diminish its appeal to those who were persisting. Several of the recommendations reinforced or contributed to developments at Carleton, including the creation of a student center, the improvement of transportation to the Twin Cities, the expansion of the career-counseling and exploration program, and the establishment of some intensive curricular experiences through small courses.

Several other research efforts were also undertaken. The geographic locations of Carleton alumni and the sources of Carleton applicants were carefully mapped and compared. Various markets were examined for their economic and demographic projections. Such analyses provide perspectives that can contribute to the identification of promising markets; the data were used in selecting the markets to be studied in the major research project reported in this volume—the Six-Market Study. A careful historical analysis of Carleton's applicant, admission, and yield data was performed in the context of general demographic trends, and several projections were made using various assumptions regarding market share and yield (Sullivan and Zuckert 1979).

During the 1978–79 academic year, the director of college relations, George Dehne, and the coordinator of institutional research, Larry Litten, held a series of informal group interviews with

---

20. Litten et al., October 1977.

underclassman tour guides, who worked for the admissions office. The sessions were completely unstructured, although they focused on two areas: (1) We asked how these students had gone about the process of selecting a college; why they had investigated, or failed to consider, certain types of colleges; and why they had applied to, and eventually chosen among, their specific sets of colleges. We also asked questions about why their friends with similar characteristics and abilities had made other choices. (2) We asked the guides to report what kinds of questions students and their parents asked during a tour; what aspects of the campus seemed to be noticed (positively or negatively) by the people on tour; and what areas of the campus were the tour guides' favorite places to show, and why (this latter gave us some subtle indications of what aspects of the college appealed to current students).

The first set of questions yielded important insights. Escape-from-preppiedom was a major theme among students from the East (the avant-garde of the Save the Alligator movement); these students came to Carleton to find a kind of person different from their Ivy-League-bound peers with whom they had grown up. One very bright student also reported applying to a college that was more selective than Carleton as a "backup" college. Such behavior underscores how irrational and uninformed the selection process can be — a necessary and sobering reminder to the questionnaire-bound researcher. In another "interview" incident, one of the student research assistants in the Office of Institutional Research also provided some important perspective on the survey-generated data with which we were dealing and on students' naiveté. She was a senior when she confided, "When you asked me in the postadmission survey who had influenced my selection decision as a high school senior, I never realized how much my parents had influenced me by what they said — but even more by what they *didn't* say. Their failure to reinforce some of the ideas I came home with about possible colleges greatly directed my search in ways I never realized at the time."

Another finding of interest came from these tour-guide interviews, which might serve as an alert to both researchers and admissions directors. When we asked what other schools had been considered by these students, we were struck by the number of Bible colleges listed, sometimes as the only alternative to Carleton. It appeared that Evangelical Christians were attracted disproportionately to service as tour guides, and we inferred that perhaps religious enthusiasts tend to exhibit evangelical enthusiasms in other spheres of their lives.

The set of questions regarding the campus aspects that were noteworthy in the eyes of either the guides or those they guided also revealed some important perspectives. That students are looking for college experiences qualitatively different from their high school experiences (further evidence of this phenomenon emerges in our later work) was brought home by the guides' observations that Carleton's observatory, a registered historic landmark, was frequently noted by students on tour. This is the one building at Carleton that is clearly distinctive (both architecturally and functionally) from the structures on high school campuses. These interviews also threw into bold relief the problem that Carleton's library presented in a marketing effort. Students and their parents often remarked how small it was as they passed through the main part of campus and viewed the library from there. Carleton's library is built on the side of a hill that overlooks playing fields and the arboretum. From the main part of campus, what is really a four-story building appears to be only one story from a distance, and two stories from a closer vantage. Carleton publications began to feature prominent pictures of the observatory and a more revealing perspective on the library. The guides also reported that the underground tunnels, which connect many of the buildings, were favorite spots on their tours (from both the guides' and the tour takers' perspectives); these tunnels have decades' accumulations of graffiti—from the inane to the erudite. They also pointed with pride to an earthworks sculpture and the classic Great Hall, which is in one of the turn-of-the-century dorms. Again, these features were given more prominent play in the college publications. (Dehne held extensive interviews with freshmen in order to understand how they viewed and evaluated existing publications, and when new publications were designed, how the students reacted to those; these interviews were highly influential in the final design of these items.)

SUMMARY OF RESEARCH FINDINGS AND MARKETING APPLICATIONS THROUGH 1978

These various studies were part of a program we hoped would improve judgment and performance in our marketing of Carleton to prospective students and their parents. No striking revelations occurred; we did develop a gradual sense, however, that our understanding of Carleton's marketing problems and its opportunities was continually being refined.

Things Our Market Research Has Told Us

About the present and future market:

Although the U.S. is on the verge of a decline in 18 year olds, it will be relatively less severe in the western and southern states.

About Carleton's market:

Slightly over half of our applicants come from five states: 3 in the Midwest with moderate projected declines; 2 in the East with relatively high declines (76/77).

Slightly over half of our enrolling freshmen come from four states: 2 in the Midwest; 1 in the East; 1 in the West (76/77).

Approximately 125 high schools contributed three or more enrolling students in 1975/76; these schools account for two-fifths of our entering class.

Our yield from admitted applicants is lowest in the East.

Our attrition appears to be highest in the West and lowest in Illinois.

We have the highest acceptance/applicant ratio among the COFHE institutions, although our enrolling students have higher VSAT averages than 11 of them. If we continue to draw from our present major states, we are projected to admit over 90% of our applicants by 1985.

Our yield is exactly on the average for this set of schools [COFHE].

Nationally our greatest overlaps are with the following schools (listed in descending magnitude):

Oberlin	Colorado College*
St. Olaf*	Reed
Grinnell*	Yale
Northwestern*	Williams
University of Minnesota*	University of Chicago
Stanford	

Yield is in our favor for schools marked with an asterisk.

Overlap with a specific school varies, however, with the region. In the East we compete primarily with small, selective, private, eastern liberal arts colleges. In other regions our overlap tends also to be primarily from schools within the region, but it includes more large universities.

Figure 2-3. Summary of Early Market Research Findings Prepared for the CIA

About Carleton's admissions process:

Our admissions process is highly esteemed by both matriculants and those who decline our offer.

The campus visit is the "resource" which is most likely to influence positively a prospective student's desire to enroll, followed by present Carleton students, and alumni (for those who have contact with each resource).

On the other hand, our publications are our recruiting resource with the widest exposure.

Parents are second to our publications in the frequency with which they are reported as a source of information; they are the most frequently cited first source of information.

About Carleton's relative attractiveness:

Our social atmosphere is evaluated as a weak spot, regardless of the type of institution with which we are competing.

There are regional variations in both our absolute attractiveness and our relative attractiveness vis-a-vis competition.

East: our cost is attractive; location and academic quality are rated down; the best predictors of matriculation are ratings of our relative academic quality, social atmosphere, and geographic location (in order of predictive power).

Midwest: (excluding Minnesota): no outstanding plusses or minuses; relative ratings of our social atmosphere, academic quality, and geographic location are best predictors of matriculation.

Minnesota: ratings of library quality and location are unusually high; our cost is rated poorly; the best predictors of matriculation are the same as the rest of the Midwest, except that cost enters the picture only in Minnesota, just ahead of geographic location.

West: nothing consistently stands out for or against Carleton; relative ratings of academic quality, geographic location and social atmosphere are the best predictors of matriculation.

Women are slightly more likely than men to be influenced by geographical considerations.

In March 1978 a two-page document was circulated to the members of the CIA Research Program Task Force.[21] This document, shown in Figure 2-3, was produced on the eve of the research project that is the major focus of this book—the Carleton College–College Board Six-Market Study—and it summarized, in capsule form, much of what we thought we knew. It was circulated to the senior administrators and faculty members who constituted the governing body for the Carleton College–College Board project and who would be the implementers of the policies, practices, or structural changes suggested by the research findings.

In one way or another, the findings summarized in the 1978 document influenced or reinforced a variety of marketing decisions. Carleton's pricing policy ("to remain below, but not too far below, the price leaders") was influenced by the data on the different levels of concern about cost among the various geographic regions and the nature of regional competition. The data showing the very strong association between ratings of social atmosphere and yield, and leavers' comments about social atmosphere, reinforced a decision to renovate an old gymnasium and convert it into a student center. We concluded that such a center was both a functional and a symbolic necessity; part of the social problem seemed to be that social life was highly dispersed throughout the dorm and special-interest-house residential system—nothing spoke immediately and directly to the prospective student of the possibility of a social life or a place to turn for one. Concerns that students expressed about location contributed to the establishment of better transportation linkages with the Twin Cities. Negative attitudes toward the Minnesota climate led to discussions of an outings program and the expansion of a ski program, which eventually produced nationally ranked ski teams. Some of Carleton's perceived strengths—faculty quality, graduate school placement, and so forth—were also reinforced.

The most thorough exploitation of the research findings, up to the point at which the Six-Market Study began, was in the design and implementation of the college's recruitment publications program. The basic strategy was described in a document the director

---

21. The acronym CIA stood for "Carleton Institutional Awareness." The name was intended to nurture our sense of humor in the face of essentially very serious business. The referent of "institutional awareness" was purposely left ambiguous; the research was designed both to tell Carleton something about its visibility in the marketplace and to heighten institutional self-awareness.

of college relations produced to guide the design of this publications program; it drew heavily on all the research reported to date—both the formal surveys and the informal interviews. The document listed 19 "Facts or Near Facts" and for each one listed two to eight elements of a publications strategy to deal with the marketing problems or opportunities these facts presented. It was noted in this document that publications had appeared in the research as a major source of information about Carleton, and that Carleton's publications "had to represent Carleton, warts and all." The result was an extremely successful direct-mail brochure for use in Student Search, a copy of which is reproduced in Appendix B. By 1981 it was being mailed to over 80,000 high-ability high school PSAT/NMSQT-takers all over the nation and abroad in May of their junior year; a return of nearly 20 percent was realized.

The Search brochure was intended to answer questions that students would naturally have about a college, to help position Carleton advantageously in relation to competitors, to correct misperceptions and provide information that had been shown to be deficient, and to establish a desirable frame of reference for the college search process (i.e., to pose questions Carleton *wanted* students to be asking). Through a series of questions and answers (with the "questions" also providing information), the following issues were addressed:

Issue/marketing problem	*Question(s) in brochure*
Establish Carleton's membership in the most selective/elite set of colleges in the nation; establish appropriate criteria for making such comparisons (see also cost-related issues below).	"Carleton is reputed to be one of the best small colleges in the nation. How do you evaluate something like that?"
Establish Carleton's position among the small set of truly national institutions, one of the few in the Midwest.	"Is the fact that Carleton enrolls men and women from all parts of the country important to the students?"
Acknowledge Carleton's prevailing social image, but present a more inclusive and balanced perspective.	"Academic pressure is expected at Carleton, but how intense is it and what do students do to relax?"

Issue/marketing problem	*Questions(s) in brochure*
Deal with the locational problems revealed by students.	"What are the winters really like in Northfield?" "The Twin Cities of Minneapolis and St. Paul are known as culturally vibrant places. Can Carleton students take advantage of them?"
Establish graduate/professional acceptance rates while claiming an essential share of students who are bound for other postcollegiate pursuits.	"Carleton is known for its success in placing students in graduate and professional schools. But what about the men and women who wish to start a career immediately following college?"
Explain Carleton's price position and financial aid program; establish its "Eastern quality" at "Midwestern prices" by explaining cost differentials; present it as an educational bargain.	"Carleton has a significant endowment, but how does it benefit the students?" "Carleton's tuition is lower than that of many fine Eastern colleges. How does this affect educational quality?"
Establish faculty reputation for both teaching and scholarly quality.	"Carleton has a low student-to-faculty ratio, yet the faculty is well known for its scholarship. Does this mean Carleton's faculty stresses research rather than teaching?"

Through pictures the brochure also sought to convey Carleton's rural beauty and extensive campus; to show its faculty as both serious and jovial; to depict students engaged in a variety of academic pursuits, in casual interaction and relaxation, and in zany moments. The brochure was designed as a low-key, nonflashy document; it did not use full color, but employed subdued tones with sharp, clear photographs. Its informative questions and their answers and illustrations were responses to the problems the market research had revealed and were also efforts to exploit opportunities the research had suggested and to capture a desirable position for Carleton.

In addition to the brochure, regionally differentiated cover letters were developed, which stressed the points that were particularly salient in a given region — academic quality and reputation in the East, the benefits associated with Carleton's relatively high price and its financial aid program in the Midwest.

The market research had communications impact beyond the publications program. Because the results were shared, debated, and discussed widely throughout the Carleton community, they affected the college's communications with its constituencies in the broadest sense, and not just through its admissions literature. Administrators, faculty, current students, and alumni all came to understand Carleton's marketing problems in varying degrees and were thus able to respond more effectively to the questions and concerns of prospective students and parents. This effect is not as easily documented as a change in a publication, but we believe that it was a result of major consequence.

This summary of our earlier work demonstrates the market research process at Carleton College and its outcomes, and establishes the context in which the Carleton College–College Board Six-Market Study developed. We had learned much but had been limited to studies of students already familiar with Carleton College. To learn how to improve our success at recruiting qualified students not already aware of Carleton, we had to study representative samples of the nation's intellectually able students. That is what the Six-Market Study was designed to do, and we turn to it now.

3.

The Carleton College–College Board Six-Market Study: Its Origins and Execution

The market research program at Carleton College moved in ever-widening circles. It started with admitted applicants and then moved on to the much wider pool of prospective students who had come to the college's attention through inquiry or referral (admitted applicants continued to be studied annually as well; see Haselkorn 1980). Nevertheless, we realized that even the inquiry pool, which was five times as large as the applicant pool, constituted a very small percentage of the set of potential students who could both benefit from, and contribute to, an education at Carleton. Our understanding of Carleton's place in the market would be incomplete until we could put it in the context of the college choices of this considerably larger pool of desirable students. Furthermore, in the face of demographic declines, Carleton had to increase its share of the relevant market if it was to protect its applicant pool from erosion and to obtain the educational and financial benefits associated with selective admissions. This meant attracting noninquirers, some of whom might never have heard of Carleton. To do this, we had to discover how visible Carleton was (and where it wasn't visible); where noninquirers were going, and why; and what might be done to make Carleton better known or more attractive. We had to find a way to carry our research to potential students beyond the inquiry group, all of whom obviously knew about Carleton.

Our research had shown that parents were among the most important sources of information and influence on the decision to apply to and to attend Carleton; they were second only to our publications as a *source of information* about Carleton and were most frequently cited as the *first source* of such information. As an overall *influence*, parents were second only to the campus visit, ranking ahead of admissions officers and high school counselors. Other research had also shown that parents have a considerable influence on college choice (Gilmour, Dolich, and Spiro 1978; Lewis and Morrison 1975; D. W. Chapman 1979). Therefore, in addition to going beyond Carleton's inquiry group to study students, we needed to study parents and their perceptions of colleges and the college-selection process.

After deciding who is to be studied, the researcher has to determine when in the college-selection process (see Figure 1-2) to collect the relevant data. A number of studies, including the work described in Chapter 2, have used data obtained after the final choice of a college has been made; this is the principal perspective from which institutional market research (admitted applicant, nonapplicant) studies have been developed. (In addition to the Carleton work, see the studies cited in D. W. Chapman; Gilmour and his colleagues; Barton 1978; Lucas 1979). There are good reasons for locating research that is obviously an *institutional* effort at this point in the process. Institutional research at an earlier point can conflict with institutional recruiting efforts — studying and courting are not generally compatible approaches to the same "subject"; this post hoc approach also has the advantage of having the actual college chosen as the outcome measure. On the other hand, research at the conclusion of the process suffers the disadvantages of possible data contamination from postdecision rationalizations about the factors that influence college choices, and defective recall of relevant matters by the subjects. How serious such contamination is has not yet been determined by research; it is potentially a substantial source of error, however, particularly since the psychological effects of nonacceptance on applicants are often quite profound (Sacks and Associates 1981).[1]

We intentionally directed our attention to the earlier stages of application and selection, both to avoid these postprocess effects and to obtain data at the early points in the process when a college might have the most marketing options open to it. As noted previously, these early stages had not received much research attention. In the study conducted under the auspices of the College

---

1. A few research efforts have followed the selection process over a period of time (with periodic or at least before-and-after data collection), ending with the selection of the chosen college (Wright and Kriewall 1979; Lewis and Morrison 1975). This kind of research has the advantage of an actual choice of a college as the outcome, without the serious post hoc rationalization problem. At the same time, it has the considerable disadvantage of its extreme costs (and the necessarily very small samples that have been used) and the possibility of contaminating the student's selection process by the data-gathering efforts of the research (the Heisenberg Principle).

Board, the potential for research and recruiting conflicts was avoided. Our study of parents took place in the fall of their child's senior year, the time we believed parents' influences to be most important. Our working assumption, although the research evidence to support it is scanty, was that parents are an important influence at this early point in setting major boundaries for the college search.[2] Students were contacted later—winter of their senior years—at a point when most of them would have submitted their applications but few of them would have received their notices of admission or nonadmission (with the exception of early-decision applicants). This timing was intended to reduce postadmission rationalizations and give us a reasonably clear picture of the competition at this stage and the perceptions and values that lead to applications.

Originally, a massive, comprehensive research project was designed, which included studies of students, parents, Carleton alumni, and high school counselors. Funding was obtained from the Robert Sterling Clark Foundation for the first two studies; this work forms the principal basis for this book. Carleton and the College Board also contributed substantial resources to the execution of the project.

Carleton approached the College Board initially as a source of names of students who might meet the academic requirements of the college and who could be surveyed. Although it was not (and is not) the policy of the College Board to release names from its student files for research purposes, this project interested the Board for a variety of reasons. The nature and quality of Carleton market research was well known to the Board through previous work (Sullivan and Litten 1976). Carleton's proposal suggested that new methodological ground might be turned and that it would be useful to determine whether the proposed research could contribute significant information to a college's marketing program. It was agreed, therefore, that the College Board would become a partner in the research in order to pursue and evaluate this experiment. The Board hoped that the project would suggest services that could be rendered in the future to colleges and to students; at minimum, through publication of the results, the experience could

---

2. Gilmour and his colleagues reported in their 1978 study that "many respondents indicated that their parents made the decision that they were going to college for them. . . . In this stage parents also generally defined the cost, geographic and quality boundaries within which the respondents were to remain in making their college selection. Although parents were not cited as a strong influence in the succeeding phrases, this boundary setting had subtle but pervasive effects throughout the remainder of the college selection process."

be instructive to other member colleges about the risks and benefits of such inquiries.

The project benefited considerably from the guidance of two groups. Our efforts were kept on track by an internal advisory group at Carleton, which consisted of the dean of the college (Carleton's equivalent to an academic vice-president or provost), the dean of students, the director of third-world affairs, the director of development, the dean of admissions, the director of public relations, a faculty member, and a student. An external advisory group met twice during the development of the project; its counsel broadened our horizons and sharpened our thinking. This group was composed primarily of Carleton alumni who were selected for their professional expertise: the chairman of the marketing department in the business school of a Big 10 university, a vice-president of one of the nation's largest advertising agencies, the director of marketing for a division of a national food products corporation, a professor of sociology at a second Big 10 university, the director of marketing for a division of a major Eastern bank, a vice-president for public relations for a national paper products company, and a biology professor at another liberal arts college. In addition, a staff member of the College Board participated as a member of this group.

The names of students for our student sample, and those whose parents were sent the parents' form of the questionnaire, were drawn from the Admissions Testing Program (ATP) files of students who took the Preliminary Scholastic Aptitude Test/National Merit Scholarship Qualifying Test (PSAT/NMSQT) as juniors in 1977–78. The students were selected from among those persons in the file who had combined PSAT/NMSQT scores of 100 or greater (this is comparable, but not identical, with SAT scores on the verbal and mathematical sections that total 1,000). The students also had to have indicated an interest in one of several liberal arts majors, or have indicated that they were undecided about their majors. A complete list of the majors included in the sample is given in Table D-2 in Appendix D.

The students were selected from six metropolitan areas spread across the United States: San Francisco/Oakland; Denver/Boulder; Dallas/Ft. Worth; Chicago; Minneapolis/St. Paul; Baltimore/District of Columbia (the specific zip codes are given in Table D-1 in Appendix D). These cities represented places from which Carleton currently had a strong flow of applicants and areas that had been identified through the work described in Chapter 2 (Expanding the Array of Research Foci and Techniques) to have high potential for future cultivation.

Questionnaires were developed through extensive testing and refinement. The processes even included a test of phone interviews versus self-administered mailed questionnaires (with a sample of parents from the Chicago area drawn independently by the survey research firm that conducted the phone interviews). Details on the processes by which the instruments were developed are given in Appendix E. The surveys were sent from Educational Testing Service in Princeton, New Jersey, and returned to them. Both the questionnaires and the cover letters (reproduced in Appendix E) displayed the College Board logo. The cover letters stated that the research was being conducted by the College Board "in cooperation with one of its member colleges." Carleton College was not specifically identified as a cosponsor, although Carleton's project director, Larry Litten, and the College Board's project director, Darrell Morris, were listed on the questionnaire as study directors.

Five thousand students who met our sampling criteria were randomly selected from among the participants in the Admissions Testing Program; the sample was derived in equal parts from the six metropolitan areas (833 names per market). Five hundred randomly selected students in each market received questionnaires; 333 questionnaires were sent "to the parents of" the remaining names.

Questionnaires were mailed to the parents in October 1978. Three weeks later a reminder postcard was mailed; a final letter and another copy of the questionnaire were mailed in mid-December (successive mailings were to nonrespondents only). The children of these parents had just entered their senior years when the survey was mailed. (This was somewhat later than we had hoped to administer the survey — we were originally aiming for spring of the junior year — but we ran behind schedule and decided to wait until after the summer vacation.) We received 928 codable parents' questionnaires from a deliverable mailing of 1,970 for a 47 percent response. (Appendix D shows the response rate by metropolitan area and discusses response biases that may exist in the data.)

The student questionnaire was mailed in late February 1979. It was followed by a second mailing of the questionnaire one month later and a reminder postcard 10 days after that. This timing conformed exactly to the original design. We received a response of 1,456 codable student forms out of a deliverable mailing of 2,940; this represents a 50 percent response rate.

Questionnaire coding was carried out by Carleton students, under the close supervision of two of the authors. Keypunching was performed by a service bureau. Most of the data processing was conducted on the Carleton computing system (with some at

MIT because of the relocation of the Carleton project director). Carleton students performed enormous amounts of preliminary analysis of the data, both as research assistants and interns in the Carleton Office of Institutional Research and as members of a course on social research methods taught by Sullivan in the Carleton Department of Sociology.

We should note at this point that a number of market research projects were executed under the Robert Sterling Clark Foundation grant (or in conjunction with the Six-Market Study), which are not reported here. The Office of Third-World Affairs created a large map of the nation's high schools, showing National Merit Scholarship and National Achievement Scholarship qualifiers (colored pins identified schools by size of the groups). Both the Office of Third-World Affairs (under Charles Dickerson) and the Office of Institutional Research conducted extensive searches for promising markets, using the demographic and economic indicators provided by the Bureau of Economic Analysis and the summer issue of *Sales and Marketing Management*. Reports were written on the high school sources of Carleton applicants who had taken Advanced Placement Tests and on the institutional competition by field of study, SAT level, and minority status (using the ATP summary reports).

One of the most provocative documents was produced by an economist on the Carleton faculty, who analyzed high school students' college-search activities from the perspective of economic theory on search activities (Lamson 1978). He noted the marginal costs and diminishing returns of "extensive search" (adding institutions to the search list) and the value of "intensive search" (getting more information on a limited set of options). The use of personal sources of information about colleges (parents, etc.), the intergenerational "pooling" of information (college reputation), and the costs of obtaining information about geographically distant options were discussed. The different search problems (costs, benefits, etc.) experienced by students of various ability levels and the promotional needs (and benefits) of various types of institutions were examined. Lamson also cataloged an extensive array of search activities, beginning with the self-scrutiny achieved through preparatory work at the high school level. This document anticipated many of the observations that have recently been made in conjunction with services marketing theory (see Chapter 1).

All these activities sharpened our perspectives and kept important issues alive.

4.

A General Perspective on Preferences and Choices in College Selection

To understand the market for colleges and universities, it is necessary to know what students believe they want from, or in, a college; what they are getting from the colleges where they are enrolling; and how and why these two sets of phenomena might differ. Although much of the emphasis in this book is on the *differences* among geographic markets, this chapter uses the entire set of respondents to explore these issues within a general framework. This set is large enough to perform the necessary analysis and offers clues that can be explored in greater detail in the analysis of specific markets. It also provides a base for efficiently comparing and contrasting specific markets in the subsequent analysis. Finally, this chapter introduces the reader to the various measures used in the Six-Market Study.

Starting with a general discussion of how one can measure "what people want in a college," we then turn to what the data revealed about desires and preferences and the phenomena that influence them. We had not anticipated one of the most provocative findings of this research—*the pervasive influence of price sensitivity* (as opposed to income elasticity) on the choice patterns of college-bound students.[1] These results considerably increased our sensitivity to positioning via price, which had first been wakened by the research reported in Chapter 2. (These data are reported toward the end of this chapter.)

---

1. Price sensitivity (or elasticity) means a differential purchase response to different prices for a product (usually a lower price means greater purchases); income elasticity is a differential propensity to purchase a product across income groups. Research such as that reported by Spies (1978) has found little income elasticity in the demand for selective-admission higher education.

MEASUREMENT OF THE BENEFITS COLLEGES OFFER
AND THE BENEFITS PEOPLE SEEK

Students enroll in colleges to obtain certain benefits. Indeed, benefit seeking is fundamental to all spheres of human activity — people patronize firms and join organizations (and even cultivate friends and lovers) to obtain personal benefits that could not be achieved, or as easily or effectively achieved, otherwise. An equally basic fact is that different people seek different benefits from investments of their time, money, or efforts; these differences are demonstrated when people choose to allocate their resources to diverse activities. But it is also true that not everyone uses similar activities or organizations for identical purposes or benefits.

Organizations also vary. Not only do specific organizations have differing purposes, even those with similar generic purposes can be unlike in size, location, specific activities they conduct and the way in which these activities are conducted, governance, personnel, atmosphere, expectations of their publics. These differences affect the specific benefits (and combinations of benefits) an organization offers, the quality and quantity of these benefits, and the costs to the consumer of achieving them and to the organization of producing them. Thus, a specific organization cannot be all things to all people. It tends to do some things better than others, to provide some benefits and not others; it tends, therefore, to serve the specific needs or desires of some people better than it serves others. A basic marketing theorem states that people will tend to patronize or affiliate with organizations (or purchase products or services) that can best provide the particular benefits they seek at the particular costs (prices, time, effort, status) they are willing to incur.

In marketing, therefore, intentional efforts often are made to make an organization (or a product) different in desirable ways from others — to specialize, to do some things especially well, to offer a particular set of benefits, to provide benefits at an especially attractive price, and to inform people of these differentiating attributes. Marketers call this purposeful differentiation "positioning." Positioning is not only useful to make the provision of benefits efficient and effective; positioning is also necessary to gain the attention of the persons who are most likely to be attracted to an organization in a crowded organizational and information environment (Geltzer and Ries 1976; Ries and Trout 1980).

This chapter examines the various benefits people seek in colleges and the sizes of the groups that exhibit interest in different constellations of benefits. By addressing the particular needs (or desires) of a specific group, or groups, a college should be able to assume an advantage over less favorably positioned colleges in attracting students who desire the benefits it offers.[2]

It should be repeated here that what people want, particularly when it comes to a complex activity such as higher education, may not be everything from which they could benefit; at times it may even run counter to what they most need.[3] Nevertheless, what people say they want has to serve as a starting point in understanding the market and the attitudes and values people bring to college selection. If a college chooses to give people other than what they want (perhaps what they need, should it differ), it will have to find ways of convincing them that they want what the college offers, or that they should at least be willing to consider or try its particular benefits or means to given benefits. This will require relating the college's message to the existing beliefs or perceptions of people in the market. In a book unhappily titled *Positioning: The Battle for Your Mind*, Ries and Trout (1980) clearly identify the problem and the challenge from the perspective of marketing communications:

> To be successful today, you must touch base with reality. And the reality that really counts is what's already in the prospect's mind. . . .
>
> Today's marketplace is no longer responsive to the strategies that worked in the past. There are just too many products, too many companies, and too much competition. . . . we have become an overcommunicated society. . . .
>
> The mind, as a defense against the volume of today's communications, screens and rejects much of the information offered it. In general, the mind accepts only that which matches prior knowledge or experience.
>
> Millions of dollars have been wasted trying to change minds with advertising. Once a mind is made up, it's almost impossible to change it. Certainly not with a weak force like advertising. (5–7 passim)

Although higher education's marketers would have to reject Ries and Trout's ultimate remedy ("the best approach to take in our overcommunicated society is the oversimplified message"), we ig-

---

2. Specialization has its limits in higher education. In higher education, distinctiveness may well have to be achieved via quality, nature of the educational process (laboratories, fieldwork, seminars, lectures, video resources, and combinations thereof), and price instead of narrowing the fields of study offered. At the same time, quality discernment in higher education can also be difficult for the lay person. We refer the reader to our discussion of these issues in Chapter 1.

3. See Services Marketing Theory and Higher Education in Chapter 1.

nore their diagnosis of the problem and their basic solution at our own peril. What colleges have to say and, to a certain extent, what colleges have to offer will have to be related in some manner to the prejudices and preferences that exist in the minds of prospective students, parents, and others who influence their educational decisions. We may wish to reorient people, but we will have to start from the directions in which they are facing.

People think about, and talk about, organizations in several ways. One is to consider what personal or social benefits are offered by the organization, or might be obtained from it. Another is to think in terms of the characteristics that define the organization and make it similar to, or different from, other organizations. These characteristics produce or contribute to the benefits available to the individual customer or joiner. Although the personal and social benefits that organizations offer provide the ultimate rationale for their existence and the ultimate reason for an individual's interest in them, these ultimate benefits are often difficult, complex, and elusive phenomena to deal with – both for the lay person and for the researcher. Because the characteristics of organizations are much more tangible than the ultimate benefits they offer, people frequently use these characteristics when thinking and talking about organizations, and they become symbolic representations of the personal and social benefits with which the characteristics are associated.[4]

Three principal approaches have been developed for ascertaining what people want from colleges and what characteristics they seek in a college. We have tapped all three in this project in seeking to understand the market for Carleton, although our use of the three has been uneven.

The *first approach* has been to measure directly the benefits that people seek from a college; this often goes under the name of needs analysis, although desires and *rational* needs that relate to *rational*

---

4. Benefits segmentation – that is, finding out what different groups in the market seek from a product, and marketing specific products to specific groups – has an honored place in the marketing literature of business (Peterson 1979, Chap. 3 and Haley 1972).

There is disagreement in the theoretical literature on the marketing of services (education is closer to services than to goods when it comes to marketing), about the degree to which people use benefits or tangible attributes (personnel, facilities) in judging alternative purveyors. We believe the use of "benefits" per se is particularly difficult for the relatively unsophisticated student consumers who are making both consumption and investment decisions about a highly complex service when they search for a college.

ends are not well differentiated in this literature.[5] In this approach the researcher seeks to determine what specific benefits people — students or employers — desire from participation in an educational program (or what specific programs they desire). This approach is most useful, however, when several conditions are met. It is more applicable to the design of specific programs than it is to the marketing of the more diffuse educational offerings of most liberal arts colleges. It is also more appropriate for use with relatively mature adults than with traditional college-bound high school students. The former have a clearer idea than the latter about who they are, where they are going, and what they want from an educational experience. Even with relatively mature students, however, the possibility is strong that their perceptions of their options are undesirably constrained and that they may have a better understanding of what they *want* than they do of what they might *need* or could *benefit from* (Cross 1979, 11ff.).

The annual survey of college freshmen conducted by the American Council on Education and UCLA (Astin, King, and Richardson 1980) is probably the best-known effort to measure why students go to college (a proxy for benefits sought) by asking them directly. It exemplifies the problems associated with this approach: the reasons tend to be general and abstract, and the same reasons generally top the lists of students regardless of the type of institution in which they enrolled. Such undiscriminating indicators are of little use to the marketer who is trying to create a particular niche or position for a given institution, even though these measures do provide some clues about basic benefits that an institution might attempt to provide.

The *second approach* to understanding what people seek from a college is to determine which college attributes influence people's choices.[6] This approach has been the most widely used and can be done in a number of ways. Students have been asked directly what was important to them or what influenced them when they chose

---

5. See Lee and Gilmour (1977) or Coffing and Hutchinson (1974) for theoretical or prescriptive discussions of needs analysis; see Cross (1979) for a critique of its techniques, assumptions, and results; see Goodnow (1981) for a direct application of "benefits analysis" to the marketing of higher education for relatively mature adults and Saunders and Lancaster (1980) for an English application. See also Chapter 1 for observations on how desires may not equal needs.

6. We use the terms "attribute" to refer to generic or defining properties of an institution (e.g., size, location, control) and "characteristic" to refer to a given institution's specific quality or value on a particular attribute (e.g., "large" on the attribute size; "rural" on the attribute location; and "private" on the attribute control).

colleges (see Chapter 2; Astin, King, and Richardson 1980; Russick and Olsen 1976; Richards and Holland 1965; University of California 1980; Gilmour, Dolich, and Spiro 1978; Bowers and Pugh 1972). The approach is often flawed on several counts. The measures are taken mostly at the end of the decision-making process, with serious potential for post hoc rationalizations. These reports are often abstractions from complex judgments about specific institutions and may well reflect what the respondent believed was *supposed* to be important. The questions that elicit this type of information also often confound two distinct phenomena—attributes of institutions (e.g., size, location, program quality, costs) and influential individuals (e.g., parents, counselors).

Another type of assessment of important attributes, which avoids the problems of abstraction, asks students to rate specific institutions on a number of attributes and then correlates these ratings with their choices among the rated institutions (again see Chapter 2; see also Lay and Maguire 1982). This approach suffers frequently from the use of a single pair of institutions (often first- and second-choice institutions) and does not measure attributes that contribute to establishing a set of institutions to be investigated or applied to. Lewis and Morrison (1975) conducted a singular study of the college-selection process that avoided the problems both of abstraction associated with general questions about important attributes and of specificity limited to only a pair of institutions. They interviewed college-bound seniors every other week and coded the attributes the seniors mentioned ("factors") when they explained why specific colleges were added to or deleted from the set they were considering; the researchers carefully coded "generators" of information (influentials) separately.

The important-attributes approach provides some insight into which dimensions of higher education institutions affect the choice of colleges, but all such approaches fail to give the marketer essential information about the specific characteristics that will help or hinder in improving demand for a given institution. It tells us that cost, quality, location, and other attributes are important, but it does not reveal how specific characteristics (e.g., expensive, small, rural) might affect the attractiveness of a college. Another major limitation of much of this research stems from the researchers' primary focus on independent or net effects. Social scientists, and market researchers of such stripe, have developed sophisticated statistical techniques to sort out the independent effects of personal, social, and institutional phenomena on other phenomena of interest. They can tell you, *ceteris paribus*, just how much more important costs may be to college choice than location and other considerations. This is important information in understanding how people behave and why. But in the real world, the world to which the marketer must relate, all other things are not equal. People and institutions come in complex packages, and we have to be able to think in terms of bundles of attributes and complicated processes.

The *third approach* is to measure the appeal of specific institutional characteristics. This may be done by directly asking people about the characteristics they prefer; by directly measuring the characteristics of colleges esteemed by students, considered, applied to, or chosen (compared with colleges not chosen); or by a combination of these methods. Dealing with specific characteristics has both advantages and limitations. Characteristics are less abstract than the amorphous benefits often sought from higher education — especially by the traditional college-bound adolescent. Indeed, colleges and universities possess specific characteristics. They don't simply have sizes and locations; they are small, rural, and so forth. Institutions are defined by virtue of their characteristics; people often think about them, and differentiate among them, by focusing on their characteristics.

Focusing on specific characteristics also has an advantage over dealing with attributes. It permits the market researcher to investigate the appeal of *bundles* of benefits or defining attributes. Higher education institutions are particularly complex enterprises that are in the business of providing a complex set of services with a host of benefits. Much of the existing research on what people seek in colleges attempts to isolate the independent effects of a given institutional trait (e.g., public versus private). While the independent-effects approach is an important part of dealing with these issues, it also gives a peculiarly flat and lifeless picture of reality; it is therefore not sufficient unto itself for the market researcher who seeks to understand how demand for a given institution is formed, where it is located, and how large the demand is.

A liability of using reported preferences for institutional characteristics, as we shall see, is that people can limit the benefits or characteristics they say they *desire* on the basis of their perceptions of the possibilities of personally achieving them, particularly at a given price. This is a perennial problem in marketing, however. Consumers tend to think in terms of what they already know and can see. Using their terms of reference helps the marketer tap into the realities of perceptions and the decision-making processes; it can also tie the marketer down to the conventional. Higher education marketing will be greatly advanced when we develop a clear, comprehensive, and usable taxonomy of the benefits of college attendance—investment and consumption benefits—and ways of validly assessing consumers' perceptions of these benefits and responses to their availability.

Although some attribute measures permit derivation of the appeal of specific characteristics (e.g., when different institutions with specific characteristics are rated by students), it requires an additional, cumbersome, data-treatment step by the researcher, which is rarely taken and less frequently reported. That is, the specific characteristics of the institution rated more highly on a given attribute must be compared with the characteristics of those rated lower.

A few researchers have used the approach of correlating specific institutional characteristics with choice behavior. As noted earlier, this requires complicated codings of each institution's characteristics. To date such research has produced different findings, however, largely because different questions were asked at different points in the college-selection process (R. Chapman 1979; Tierney 1980; Anderson 1975, 1976).

DATA AND FINDINGS

Important Attributes and Preferred Characteristics

Important Attributes. Question 4 in our student survey (5 in the parent survey) asked the respondents to rate attributes of an institution according to their importance in the college-choice decision; each item was rated on a four-point scale ("not important" to "very important"). For the specific question wording and the responses listed on the form, the reader is referred to the questionnaires reprinted in Appendix E.

This was followed by a question that focused the attribute issue further by asking about *desired information.* This question (5 in the student form and 6 in the parent form) asked the respondent to state in his or her own words "the three most important things you wish to know about the college(s) or university(ies) to which you apply" (or "to which your child applies").

We found that the relative importance of various college attributes and information about colleges depends to some extent on who is asked and how their responses are measured. There are some striking consistencies, however, among parents and students and across measurement approaches.

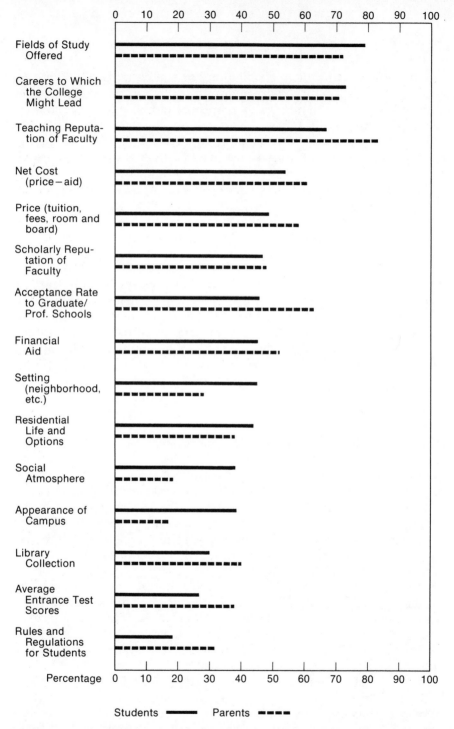

Figure 4-1. Attributes of Colleges Rated Very Important by Students and by Parents

What can be studied, what it will lead to, and how well it is taught are what high-ability students and their parents are most likely to consider very important attributes of colleges (Figure 4-1). These are the top three items for both students and parents—over two thirds rate them very important, and they have the highest average ratings. The order differs somewhat between the two groups, however, with students most likely to be interested in fields of study offered and parents most likely to report an interest in the teaching reputation of the faculty. Following this initial intergenerational consensus, patterns of attribute importance diverge for parents and students, and the measurement variations emerge.

Financial aspects follow closely the top three concerns for both students and parents—net cost is considered very important by over half the members of each group. (When measured by *average ratings*, however, its relative importance drops because of substantial numbers for whom it is of slight or no importance; this drop is less noticeable among the parents, who pay most of the bills.)

Although career outcomes are important to both groups, parents appear considerably more likely than students to see graduate or professional school as a step in this direction or to link admissions at this higher level to the nature of the undergraduate experience— at least as evidenced by parents' greater incidence of strong interest in such acceptance rates for a college's graduates.

Interest in residential life runs about the same in both groups. Students are considerably more likely than parents, however, to report the setting of the campus, its appearance, and the social atmosphere to be very important to them.

By restricting the question to the *three most important* types of information desired and then having the students and parents state them in their own words, some additional perspectives and insights were obtained. Admittedly, a college would never want to limit itself to providing only "the most important information"; students and their parents most likely use the larger array of information suggested in the preceding question in making the final selection of a college. Nevertheless, these critical aspects of colleges may well be the dimensions upon which the set of colleges that are seriously considered or investigated is based, and others are excluded.[7]

The variety of information that students and parents consider to

_____

7. In our survey this format also permitted subsequent linkage between specific types of information and preferred media, as reported below.

be among the most important is impressive – and a bit overwhelming. This variety demonstrates that the college-selection process is far from standardized, even though there are some major commonalities. As stated, many responses to this open-ended question were taken by the respondents from the list printed in the preceding question on the survey form. It was necessary to supplement this list of codes, however. Through an iterative process of coding and consultation among the coders and the project directors, 53 codes were finally developed to cover most of the responses (plus "uncodable" and "other" categories). This artificially constrained set of responses (with the respondent limited to only three items), which were coded by the project staff, provides a somewhat different picture of student and parent concerns than the one just presented. We will focus on items that appeared in any of the fields, from "most" to "third" in importance (Table 4-1).

With fewer options permitted, respondents spread them over a wider variety of information items than they do when they can rate as many attributes as they wish "very important." This reduces the general salience of any given attribute. Financial concerns stand out for both students and parents by this tabulation (we combined four separate codings – cost, aid, net cost, price – into

Table 4-1. Most Important Types of Information about Colleges*

	Students		Parents	
	Percentage	*Rank*	*Percentage*	*Rank*
Financial concerns	50 (735)†	1	55 (507)	1
Fields of study offered	40 (594)	2	29 (272)	2
General academic reputation	17 (242)	3	11 (102)	7
Location	15 (224)	4	12 (109)	5
Social atmosphere	13 (192)	5	11 (101)	7
Teaching reputation or ability of faculty	12 (180)	6	24 (219)	3
Academic standards or general quality	12 (175)	6	17 (161)	4
Campus activities	11 (159)	8	2 (22)	–
Careers to which college might lead	11 (158)	8	12 (109)	5
Total *N*	(1,456)		(928)	

* Types of information listed as one of three most important things to know by at least 10 percent of the students or parents; coded from free responses.
† Number who listed each item in one of the three spaces provided is given in parentheses.

one subsuming financial category). The category fields of study runs a close second for students and a distant second for parents. The relatively greater importance of the faculty's teaching reputation to parents is highlighted again by this method of posing the question.

These kinds of information provide some important data for the design of promotional programs; they also provide some clues regarding the concerns and values of individuals, which we will use below to help understand patterns of application behavior and esteem for colleges.

We should note, parenthetically, that the specific information media through which students and parents would prefer to obtain information vary substantially according to the specific information desired. Furthermore, students and parents tend to make different linkages between the desired information and the preferred medium. These relationships have been reported in detail elsewhere (Litten and Brodigan 1982).

Preferred Characteristics. The survey asked directly what specific characteristics students and their parents prefer in a higher education institution. Nineteen pairs (eighteen in the parent form) of characteristics were listed — for example, public or private, studious atmosphere or social atmosphere — and respondents were asked to indicate a preference for one member of each pair or to indicate no preference. The reader is referred to Appendix E for the format and the specific pairs of characteristics (Question 10 for students; Question 12 for parents).

We also draw on three other questions for evidence of the characteristics people want in a college. We asked them to list up to four characteristics that are *"most* important" in college selection and briefly state why (Question 11; Question 13 for parents). Students and parents were also asked in the first item on the questionnaire to give their emotional reactions to a variety of words and phrases associated with colleges or universities. Finally, after listing the institutions to which they were applying, in order of preference, students were asked to "briefly tell us why you prefer your first choice over your second choice" (Question 14). The corresponding item in the parent form is Question 15.

Certain institutional characteristics find almost universal acceptance in the populations we surveyed; others pretty evenly divide students and parents. Figure 4-2 shows the data on types of institutions preferred. Coeducational institutions are not only preferred

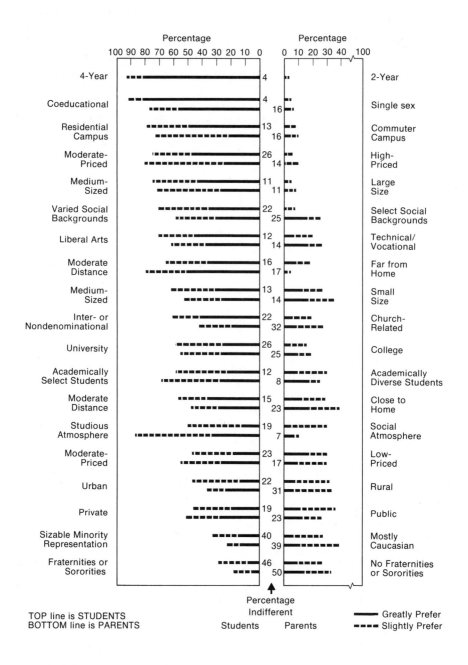

Figure 4-2. Characteristics Preferred in a College

by over 90 percent of the students, they are "greatly preferred" by over 80 percent. Parents also show a marked preference for coeducational institutions, although it is not as strong as students' preferences, and they are four times as likely as students to be indifferent to this dimension. A four-year institution (asked only of students), a university, a liberal arts program, a residential campus, academically select students, a studious atmosphere, a moderate distance from home, and a moderate price are other characteristics preferred by a majority of these high-ability students and their parents.

Respondents are rather evenly divided on their preferences for public versus private institutions (particularly students), rural versus urban locations, close to home versus moderate distance (particularly parents), the presence of fraternities or sororities, and the substantial presence of minorities; both students and parents exhibit considerable indifference in the last two areas.

Some of the characteristics preferred by large numbers of students evoke strong preferences; others are less enthusiastically endorsed. Both the total numbers exhibiting a particular preference and the strength of the preference are important for understanding a market. For the two most widely favored attributes—coeducation and a four-year college—almost 9 in 10 of the students who preferred each characteristic checked "greatly prefer." The third most popular attribute, residential campus, was "greatly preferred" by only 63 percent of those who desired it, and the sixth attribute in overall preference, students from varied social backgrounds, received "greatly prefer" ratings from only about half the students who preferred it over the listed alternative. Among the specific characteristics preferred between the paired attributes, a studious atmosphere had the most lukewarm endorsement among students—52 percent preferred it over a social atmosphere, but only 25 percent of these students "greatly preferred" it.

Some college attributes inspire sizable yawns. The dimensions that elicited the highest incidence of indifference ratings for students were the presence or absence of fraternities or sororities (46 percent), the racial composition of the student body (40 percent), and whether the institution is a college or a university (26 percent). Indifference looms large for parents on a greater number of issues: presence of fraternities or sororities (50 percent), racial composition (39 percent), religious orientation (32 percent), rural or urban location (31 percent), social backgrounds of students (25 percent), college versus university (25 percent).

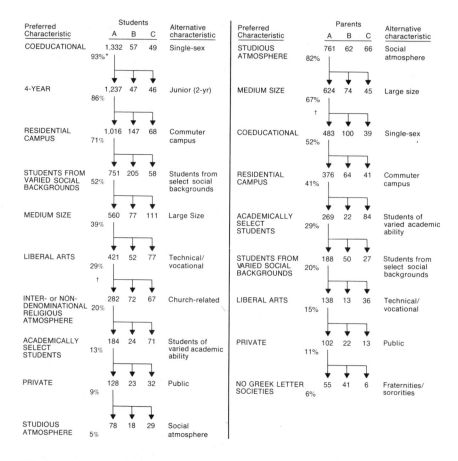

Preferred Characteristic	Students			Alternative characteristic	Preferred Characteristic	Parents			Alternative characteristic
	A	B	C			A	B	C	
COEDUCATIONAL	1,332 93%*	57	49	Single-sex	STUDIOUS ATMOSPHERE	761 82%	62	66	Social atmosphere
4-YEAR	1,237 86%	47	46	Junior (2-yr)	MEDIUM SIZE	624 67% †	74	45	Large size
RESIDENTIAL CAMPUS	1,016 71%	147	68	Commuter campus	COEDUCATIONAL	483 52%	100	39	Single-sex
STUDENTS FROM VARIED SOCIAL BACKGROUNDS	751 52%	205	58	Students from select social backgrounds	RESIDENTIAL CAMPUS	376 41%	64	41	Commuter campus
MEDIUM SIZE	560 39%	77	111	Large Size	ACADEMICALLY SELECT STUDENTS	269 29%	22	84	Students of varied academic ability
LIBERAL ARTS	421 29% †	52	77	Technical/ vocational	STUDENTS FROM VARIED SOCIAL BACKGROUNDS	188 20%	50	27	Students from select social backgrounds
INTER- or NON-DENOMINATIONAL RELIGIOUS ATMOSPHERE	282 20%	72	67	Church-related	LIBERAL ARTS	138 15%	13	36	Technical/ vocational
ACADEMICALLY SELECT STUDENTS	184 13%	24	71	Students of varied academic ability	PRIVATE	102 11%	22	13	Public
PRIVATE	128 9%	23	32	Public	NO GREEK LETTER SOCIETIES	55 6%	41	6	Fraternities/ sororities
STUDIOUS ATMOSPHERE	78 5%	18	29	Social atmosphere					

KEY: A — Number preferring characteristic in left column
    B — Number indifferent to characteristic in both columns
    C — Number preferring characteristic in right column
* Percentage below each line indicates the proportion of the original sample that remains after the addition of each successive attribute preferred. Each successive line consists of only those people who preferred the attribute on the left in the preceding line (e.g., for students, only those who preferred coed are included on the 4-yr/2-yr line; only those who prefer 4-yr are included on the residential/commuter line).

† If the distance variables had been included, a preference for moderate distance over close would have appeared here and the subsequent preferences would have been reordered slightly.

Figure 4-3. The Most Appealing Type of Institution

We have noted several times that institutions are combinations of many specific characteristics and that this constellation of characteristics defines an institution's market position and creates its appeal (or lack thereof). Figure 4-3 shows the combinations of characteristics that would appeal to the greatest number of students and parents — as described by the particular attributes listed on the questionnaires. It also demonstrates how much the potential market is narrowed as an institution is ever more precisely defined. Figure 4-3 starts with the characteristic preferred by the largest number of students (coeducation). Within that group we selected the characteristic preferred by the largest number (four-year college). By the time we had selected respondents who preferred a "coeducational, four-year, residential institution with students from varied social backgrounds," the group had been reduced to about half the original number. Adding medium size (versus large) and liberal arts reduced the number to less than a third its size at the first cut.

Both price and distance were excluded from the set of attributes included in this figure. The included characteristics all contribute to the definition of an institution in ways that affect the benefits it offers, regardless of its location vis-à-vis the student's home. As such they could be used in defining the general market opportunity for developing a new institution (something we are not thinking much about during the present decade, but the time may come again) or repositioning an existing institution. Of course, such an exercise would have to be carried out in the particular market for which a new or repositioned institution was being considered, and the existing institutions (the competition) that fit the particular description (or approximate it) would have to be analyzed. Distance from home is specific to each particular market and is not of the same "universal" order as the attributes we have included. Location is also an aspect of another component of the "marketing mix": the "delivery system." Price has also been excluded because it relates directly to the benefits perceived to be available from a particular institution — what people will pay depends to a considerable extent on what they think they will get for their money. It is difficult to deal with the price question in isolation, although each benefit listed above probably has a particular price (or value) to a given individual, as do their various combinations. We deal with the effects of price (or concern about price) on college choice at several other points.

Bringing this analysis home to our particular case, what do these data say about preferences for the kind of institution Carleton is —

independent of considerations of cost (or price) and location (in relation to the student's home)? We took five attributes that showed correlations with the ratings given to Carleton in the cities where it was known (the Twin Cities, Chicago, Baltimore/D.C., and Denver/Boulder) and selected the characteristics that describe Carleton (private, nondenominational or ecumenical religious atmosphere, studious, selective, no fraternities or sororities). We gave students a point each time they *preferred* the specific member of the pair of attributes that described Carleton, and by summing these points we created an index of preference for Carleton; those who scored high (5) we labeled Prefer a Carleton, or PAC. In all of our six markets combined, 4.3 percent of the students scored 5 on our PAC Index (see Chapter 5 for intermarket differences on this index).

For another perspective on potential demand, we expanded the number of attributes but loosened the "preference" requirement to include persons who were not opposed to Carleton's characteristics (i.e., we included all people who did not *prefer* characteristics that were *opposite* Carleton's). Selecting eight characteristics that describe Carleton, we created an index of openness to Carleton (college, private, academically selective, studious atmosphere, liberal arts, non- or interdenominational, rural, and small). We gave an individual a point each time he or she preferred, *or was indifferent to*, each Carleton characteristic. Those who scored high (8) we have labeled Open to Carleton, or OTC. In our six markets combined, 5.4 percent of the students received a score of 8; that is, they favored or were not opposed to all eight traits that describe Carleton. (Parents were slightly more likely than students to score at the highest level of this index. A score of 8 was achieved by 6.1 percent of the parents.)[8]

---

8. We removed the size variable from the OTC Index and recomputed the score for a basic-Carleton institution and for five other types of institutions to get our bearings on the scale of demand represented by these figures. The characteristics that were changed from the basic-Carleton type (Type I) are shown in uppercase letters. The results were as follows (these are "openness" indicators—"prefer" or "indifferent to"):

I. Private
Selective (academic)
Studious
Liberal arts
Nondenominational
Rural
College: Students–8.0%
Parents–9.3%

IV. Private
Selective
Studious
Liberal arts
CHURCH-RELATED
Rural
College: Students–5.8%
Parents–9.8%

Validity and Value of Stated Preferences. Later in the chapter we examine the usefulness of stated preferences for college characteristics in predicting application behavior. At this juncture, however, we briefly consider the validity of stated preferences cum preferences. As previously noted, approximately one-third of the students and one-quarter of the parents indicated a preference for public institutions over private colleges and universities. In a later question, after we asked about colleges to which applications had been made or would be made (Question 13), we asked whether there were colleges a student would like to consider, but which would not be considered because of tuition or living costs (Question 16). Among the students who indicated they preferred a public over a private institution in Question 10, 55 percent indicated there were colleges for which costs prevented their consideration. Of the specific colleges listed by this "propublic" group in response to the question, 79 percent were private. It appears that, to some extent, preferences reported in the abstract may be contaminated by what is perceived as possible or at least by an unwillingness to pay for certain "desired" benefits; thus, reported preferences should be tested against other behavioral and subjective indicators before great stock is placed in them.

Most Important Characteristics in a College. Following the question that asked for a choice between opposite types of institutions, we asked the students and the parents to list in their own words the

---

II. Private
Selective
Studious
Liberal arts
Nondenominational
URBAN
College: Students–6.3%
       Parents–8.3%

III. Private
Selective
Studious
Liberal arts
Nondenominational
URBAN
UNIVERSITY: Students–10.0%
       Parents–14.0%

V. Private
Selective
Studious
Liberal arts
CHURCH-RELATED
URBAN
College: Students–4.7%
       Parents–8.1%

VI. PUBLIC
Selective
Studious
Liberal Arts
Nondenominational
URBAN
UNIVERSITY: Students–11.7%
       Parents–10.9%

Note: Because the "indifferent" category was included in these "preferences," a given individual may be included in more than one of these groupings.

Table 4-2. Student Selection of Most Important Characteristics in Postsecondary Institution

Characteristic	*Percentage*
Coeducational	42*
Low to moderate costs	32
Close to moderate distance from home	28
4-year	25
Liberal arts	19
Residential	17
Variety, heterogeneity (especially social)	15
Medium size	14
Studious atmosphere	12
Small	12
University	10
	$N = 1,353$†

* Percentages do not add to 100 because each respondent could list up to four characteristics. Percentages indicate proportion of students who listed characteristic in answering Question 11.
† Number who listed at least one characteristic in response to Question 11.

four most important characteristics their colleges should have. The student responses are listed in Table 4-2.

A wide variety of characteristics were listed by students, many of which were taken from the list in the preceding question. Curricular references did not figure prominently in these answers, nor did items that could be coded in the categories of educational or academic quality, teaching quality, or other academic elements. Fewer than 1 percent of the students mentioned specifically that being a *college* is among the most important characteristics; the number who mentioned university status was over ten times as great. About an eighth of the students did mention small size; perhaps this is a more meaningful proxy for "college" in their minds.

In addition to asking what characteristics are most important, we also asked *why* they are important. This brings us back into the realm of inquiry regarding the benefits people seek. (We believe that the method of tying such questions to concrete characteristics probably reduced the incidence of conventional platitudes.) We can give only a sampling of these responses, but they do provide a taste of both the substance and the sentiments that high-ability students bring to the process of college selection.

Desire for a coeducational institution dominates the list of essential characteristics. (There is a *very small*, but important, market niche for the single-sex institution, witnessed to both by the fact that some institutions of this sort are flourishing and by our data.)

The reasons that students give for an interest in coeducation range from the sublime to the salacious.

- I have read Simone de Beauvoir and there are two sexes and both should have equal coeducational opportunities.
- Girls make learning more fun and create a more diverse set of values.
- I need to meet many types of people so that I can communicate with them (I'm to be a nurse).
- In class both views are often beneficial.
- I want to find a wife.
- I only human [*sic*].
- I like looking at guys.

Learning through exposure to a variety of people was an important theme, both for the respondents who mentioned social or other kinds of diversity and for those who said it was important that an institution be a university. Among those who cited social diversity was a student who wrote: "College needs to be a mixing of all people, ideas, and philosophies as part of an education." Another said: "Students of varied social backgrounds are necessary in order to learn to live and cope with the same people you will meet in everyday life." People who believed that university status was important noted both curricular and social diversity. Several simply indicated that universities provided better, or higher-quality, education, and several mentioned that they had better reputations. Students who thought that *public* status was an essential characteristic cited as reasons both lower costs and a broader variety of people ("opens up instead of closes your dealings with many people"; "everyone should have a chance at a good education"; "people of varied backgrounds").

Competition is not a dirty word among high-ability students. It was frequently cited as a benefit among the students who listed selectivity as an important characteristic and was implied by those who listed studious atmosphere as an essential characteristic. The latter group often acknowledged a need to be "kept in line so I don't stray from my purpose" or, as one student put it, "I'm not going to school to screw around."

A liberal arts orientation was seen primarily as a way to explore options and as the appropriate approach to education for students who have not yet settled on specific directions. The few persons who did mention "college" as an important characteristic noted that colleges are smaller, more personal and friendlier, and more focused on the undergraduate. "Private" was seen as offering more personal attention and sometimes as being of higher quality.

A concern for low or moderate costs was often expressed in terms of "that's all that I can afford" or "I don't want to overburden my parents." It was not often stated in terms of "there's no reason to pay more" or "higher cost isn't worth it." This suggests that if the differential benefits of higher-priced education can be demonstrated and promoted more forcefully, or if long-term financing can be sustained and promoted, demand for such education might be increased.

Interest in an experience that is qualitatively different from high school, particularly in the social exposure it affords, is a strong theme among these students. (Such a theme was also noted earlier in our interviews with tour guides about which buildings visitors notice at Carleton.) The college that can promote and deliver a qualitatively different and personally manageable set of varied academic and extracurricular experiences should be very appealing to the high-ability market.

The essential characteristics of an institution of higher education may not be the same as those characteristics that determine the relative attractiveness of specific institutions. Marketing theory indicates there may be minimal levels of a particular attribute that must be present for a given consumer, after which trade-offs may be made among other attributes. It also suggests that certain characteristics may have to be present before an institution can enter the set being considered, but then other characteristics come into the picture in order to differentiate among, and rank-order, those institutions being considered.

The formation of the set of colleges that are considered seriously, and the final choice of a college, are two separate phenomena; we are concerned primarily with the first. The criteria people use in making the final selection can also shed some light on basic benefits they seek to maximize, however. In most of the existing research, people have been asked what these specific criteria are or what attributes are important to them (in the abstract), or these dimensions have been derived from ratings assigned to a pair of institutions on a number of prespecified attributes. We took a slightly different tack by asking respondents to tell us in their own words why they ranked their first choices over their second. This established specific institutional referents for the response — perhaps reducing the probability of "socially acceptable" responses; it also had the advantage over most previous research of asking about this ranking before a sizable proportion of the students and the parents were rationalizing their choices after admissions actions had been communicated to them by the colleges under con-

Table 4-3. Reason for Selecting First-Choice College over Second Choice

	Students		Parents	
	%	Rank	%	Rank
Specific program better	18	1	13	4
Nearer home.	15	2	20	1
Less expensive.	12	3	14	3
Better academic quality	11	4	15	2
Better reputation	11	4	9	7
Prefer smaller school	9	6	12	5
Family connections			11	6
	N=1,306		823	

sideration. Table 4-3 shows the results of our coding of these open-ended responses (up to two reasons were coded for an individual). The results are a mixture of general attributes and specific characteristics. The differences between generations are slight but interesting. "Specific programs" are mentioned by the largest number of students and are mentioned more frequently by students than by parents. "Nearer home" is most frequently mentioned by parents (supporting the conclusions of Bowers and Pugh 1972), and mentioned by parents more often than by students. "Less expensive," "better academic quality," or "better reputation" contribute to these decisions for segments of both students and parents. The response "family connections" figures in the picture for parents but not for students.

Parents of men and parents of women exhibit several differences on a variety of the measures we have been discussing—important information, attributes of concern, and type of institution preferred. Furthermore, there are a few interaction effects between the sex of the parent and the sex of the student (e.g., fathers of sons are more likely to report a concern about the career outcomes of college than are fathers of daughters). These findings have been reported in detail in a previous paper delivered at a regional meeting of the College Board (Litten, Jahoda, and Morris 1980); it may be obtained from the principal author.

Student Perceptions of "Best" Institutions

The survey asked students (Question 7) and parents (Question 8) to list up to four colleges and universities they consider the "best" for students with "high academic potential." The question was asked principally because Carleton would like to have reasonably broad recognition as one of the best small colleges in the United States;

this is the position of preference for the institution. We were therefore interested in the degree to which this status has been achieved and where the incidence of such opinion was most likely to be found. We also sought to determine institutions with which Carleton would have to be associated (seen as similar to) and which it might have to displace in order to occupy this position in specific markets.

As we developed our analysis, we also began to use this question as a check on the stated preferences people reported for types of institutions. Stated preferences may well have an element of rationalized reporting of what people believe they *ought* to prefer. They are also abstractions that may not translate well into institutional realities. The listing of best institutions was one way of bringing the exercise down to concrete examples, to real institutions. By asking the question with an abstract person (students with high academic potential) as the referent, these data may also circumvent the practical considerations that may have intruded on the direct statements of preferred characteristics noted earlier.

There are also limitations, however, when one seeks to equate esteem for an institution with its desirability, especially for a specific individual. A student who reports a list of "best institutions" may truly not desire such an institution (and a parent may not wish such an institution for a child) for a variety of reasons. The "best" institutions may be viewed as too costly in one or more ways: too expensive, too exclusive, too much effort required for success, too far away. Instead of the "best," people may be seeking "best buys"—the best that can be obtained at a particular cost. A variant of this particular source of discrepancy between esteem and preference is the possible failure of an individual to identify personally with the abstract student with high academic potential who was the referent of our question. The concept of best institutions is also limited as a proxy for preferences by two kinds of ignorance: (1) The institutions listed may be little more than mythical beasts— names that have been heard but about which little more is known. (2) The list may not include many or any of the kinds of institutions which would most appeal to an individual simply because such institutions are not known; for example, a student might prefer a small, single-sex institution a moderate distance from home, but not know of any, even if one exists. Finally, there is the limitation we built in simply by constraining the list to four names (although one can argue that the most salient institutions and characteristics are captured by this method).

Table 4-4. Student Listings of Best Types of Institutions, Summer Intentions, and Actual Applications

	Best	Summer Intentions	Actual Applications
None private	5%	26%	37%
25–50% private	24	33	23
66–75% private	25	17	12
100% private	45	24	29
	99%	100%	101%
	N = 1,372	1,330	1,317
None very selective	16%	48%	59%
25–50% very selective	32	29	19
66–75% very selective	22	11	8
100% very selective	30	12	13
	100%	100%	99%
	N = 1,372	1,277	1,316

The types of institutions students list as the best colleges or universities are shown in the first column of Table 4-4. We have coded institutions for two attributes: public or private and selectivity. Other attributes would be of interest to Carleton and to other institutions—for example, in-state or out-of-state; college or university; secular or religious; urban or rural; and size—but there were practical limits on the amount of coding that we could attempt in this project.[9] Only 5 percent of the students listed public institutions exclusively, with 70 percent reporting a list that was over half private. These "best" institutions tend to be very selective, as defined by Cass and Birnbaum in their 1977 guide to colleges (we have combined their categories of "most selective" and "highly selective" into our classification of "very selective"). Slightly over half the students had lists that consisted predominantly of "very selective" institutions.

Institutional Types Students Consider and Choose

It can be argued that the kinds of institutions to which students apply and in which they eventually enroll provide the best evidence

9. The actual numbers of these two types of institutions that exist should be kept in mind. Of the 210 private institutions coded in our study, only 34 percent were "very selective by our criterion.

of college preferences. All things considered — benefits *and* costs — these are the most desirable institutions to the persons who choose them. There is a great deal of truth in this interpretation — and there are some serious limitations, particularly from the marketer's perspective. Institutions that are not known, or are poorly understood, will not be included among those considered and eventually chosen. The marketer seeks to overcome the effects of such ignorance through promotion. Choices represent preferences in the face of constraints, and constraints can be removed or reduced by appropriate marketing. Choices represent preferences based on existing levels of understanding of a particular institution's benefits; people can be helped to become better informed. Alterations in the level of benefits or in the level of costs associated with an institution, or in both, can alter its relative desirability. Marketing changes in these various phenomena can redistribute choices by changing the relative attractiveness of institutions; a major goal of the marketer is to alter the status quo (or to maintain it in the face of alterations in the competitive environment).

We asked two questions about choices and applications. Question 12 asked students about the set of institutions they carried into their high school senior years as candidates for applications; we call these institutions "summer intentions." This item was intended to explore who added, or dropped, institutions similar to Carleton after first considering them, and why such shifts might have occurred. Question 13 asked about actual or probable applications as of midwinter in the senior year; we refer to these institutions as "actual applications," or "choices."

For both questions, only the first four institutions were coded for analysis. The four institutions coded in Question 13 were the most preferred institutions because the questionnaire gave instructions to rank-order the applications by preference; the assumption of preference in the "summer intentions" question was imposed by the coders, who took the first four listed. It is possible that the institutions still under consideration at the application stage were most likely to be listed first in the summer intentions question, thereby underestimating the elimination of alternatives between summer and midwinter.

The second column of Table 4-4 shows that summer intentions lists contain fewer private institutions and fewer "very selective" institutions than do the lists of "best" institutions. Actual applications (column 3 of Table 4-4) show even further erosion on these counts. The greatest discrepancies between best and summer intentions lists occur on the selectivity dimension—over half (52 percent) of the students had lists of best institutions on which a majority of the institutions were very selective; almost half (48 percent) of the students did not list any very selective institutions among the four summer intentions institutions that were coded, and only about a quarter (23 percent) of the students reported intentions lists that consisted of a majority of very selective institutions. During the first half of the senior year (summer intentions to applications), the percentage of students who reported lists on which a majority of the institutions were private or very selective stayed just about constant (approximately two-fifths and one-fifth, respectively); there was an increase of 11 percentage points, however, for the number who listed no private or very selective institutions.

On the assumption that applications to the most preferred institutions are the most likely to be followed by matriculation (if admission is granted), we also examined the nature of first-choice applications and first- and second-choice sets (to see how deeply these preferences ran). Private institutions were named as first choice by 50 percent of the students; they constituted first- *and* second-choice institutions for 51 percent of the students who listed two or more applications. Thirty percent of the first-choice institutions listed by students were "very selective." Among students who listed two or more applications, about a quarter had both a first *and* a second choice that were "very selective."

Discrepancies among Student Lists of Best Institutions, Summer Intentions, and Actual Applications

These simple frequency counts obscure some discrepancy patterns across a student's three lists, which can be highly important to marketers. Of interest are the *extent* of such discrepancies: *who* exhibits them and *why*. The purpose of such information is to find ways of encouraging desirable movements (from a given institution's perspective) and arresting undesirable shifts. Table 4-5 shows both kinds of alterations in the composition of student lists of colleges and universities, with Carleton's characteristics (private, very selective) taken as the points of reference. Shifts away from private or very selective institutions we have called "erosion"; shifts toward private or very selective institutions we have labeled "augmentation." Because it is generally easier to sustain prior preferences through marketing activities than it is to create new

Table 4-5. Erosion and Augmentation of Private and Selective Institutions in Student Lists of Best Institutions, Summer Intentions, and Actual Applications (Choices)

A. Erosion

1. Private	% with Choice List Less Private than Best Set*	% with Choice List Less Private than Summer Intentions*	% with 1st Choice Public	% with 1st or 2d Choice Public
Best list 100% private.	49	–	–	–
Best 25–75% private .	71	–	–	–
Prefer private (Q. 10) .	39	22	17	36
Summer intentions list 100% private . .	–	12	9	13
Summer intentions 25–75% private . . .	–	48	51	75

2. Very Selective†	% with Choice List Less Selective than Best Set‡	% with Choice List Less Selective than Summer Intentions‡	% with 1st Choice Not Very Selective	% with 1st or 2d Choice Not Very Selective
Best 100% very selective	63	–	–	–
Best 25–75% very selective	84	–	–	–
Prefer academically select students . . .	64	26	62	70
Summer intentions 100% very selective .	–	27	6	11
Summer intentions 25–75% very selective	–	52	58	77

preferences, we concentrate primarily on erosion, and its causes, in the next two sections.

Incidence of Private Institutions. Students are much more likely to name private institutions as the "best" institutions for students of high ability than they are to apply to private institutions. Table 4-5.A.1 shows that among students who listed only private institutions as the best, almost half (49 percent) had application lists that were not 100 percent private. Erosion on the private dimen-

Table 4-5 (continued)

B. Augmentation

1. Private	% with Choice List More Private than Summer Intentions	1st Choice Private
No summer intentions private	19	11
Summer intentions 25–75% private . . .	34	–

2. Very Selective	% with Choice List More Selective than Summer Intentions	1st Choice Very Selective
No summer intentions very selective. . . .	8	4
Summer intentions 25–75% very selective	27	–

* Percentage of private applications is less than percentage of private institutions on best or summer intentions lists.
† "Most selective" and "highly selective" categories of Cass and Birnbaum (1977).
‡ Percentage of very selective applications is less than percentage of very selective institutions on best or summer intentions lists.

sion was even more pronounced among students who listed less than 100 percent private institutions on their best lists. Erosion of an orientation toward private institutions is also evident among students who declared preferences for private over public institutions in Question 10 of the survey; 39 percent had application sets with proportionately fewer private institutions than did their lists of best institutions.

Summer intentions are better predictors of application sets than are lists of best schools, but even here there is substantial erosion among students who are not exclusively oriented toward private institutions at the start of the senior year (i.e., students with 25 to 75 percent private intentions). Almost one-half (48 percent) of these students have application lists that are less heavily private than are the lists of institutions they were seriously considering at the start of the senior year; about one-half (51 percent) of these students list first-choice institutions that are not private, and three-quarters have public choices that appear in at least their runner-up positions.

Students who are solidly oriented toward the private sector at the beginning of the process tend to hold steadfast in this orientation; students without such strong preferences tend to drift into the public sector. Nevertheless, a few students move toward private institutions in the course of the senior year. Part B of Table 4-5 shows that almost 1 in 5 students who were not coded as having private institutions among the colleges they were considering seriously (before the senior year) added private institutions to their actual lists of applications; about 1 in 10 put the private institution in first place. Thirty-four percent of the students who had lists of summer intentions that contained private institutions (but were not exclusively private) reported applications lists that were even more heavily private.

Incidence of Selective Institutions. An even greater erosion of commitment occurs when selectivity is examined, as Table 4-5.A.2 clearly shows. Sixty-three percent of students whose sets of best institutions were 100 percent very selective had less selective application sets, and 84 percent had less selective application sets when their sets of best schools were 25 to 75 percent very selective. Erosion from a commitment to selective institutions was also pronounced when the summer intentions lists are compared with actual applications. Finally, as Table 4-5.B.2 indicates, students were somewhat less likely to add very selective institutions to their application sets than they were to add private institutions.[10]

Toward an Understanding of Students' Preferences and Behavior Patterns

We have seen in preceding sections that students exhibit various patterns of esteem for colleges and universities and a variety of application patterns. Frequently the institutions an individual regards highly are not the institutions to which he or she submits applications. We have also seen that students report varying preferences for specific institutional characteristics and that a variety of concerns about colleges are reported by members of the body

---

10. Recall our caveat in note 9 about the relative incidence of private and very selective institutions in the country.

scholastic. For both social scientists and marketers, these observations lead to a set of corollary questions — what kinds of students exhibit specific preference patterns, and why? Subjective perceptions, attitudes, or desires are of most use to the marketer if they can be associated with demographic or behavioral phenomena that let the marketer design a promotional strategy and the delivery of services so that they will reach the intended audiences or markets efficiently and effectively. If certain subjective phenomena (e.g., benefits or institutional attributes desired) are more likely to be found among one group than among other groups, then the "irrelevant" groups can be excluded from promotional efforts at corresponding savings in costs for the marketer (and a reduction in the noise level endured by people in the market who are spared inappropriate promotional assaults).[11] Similarly, the discovery that a marketer can supply the needs of one group or of several groups better than those of other groups leads to additional questions that facilitate the design, delivery, and pricing of the services being offered:

▪ Does the target group have economic circumstances that require particular pricing or financing arrangements?

▪ Do the life-style and culture of the group suggest particular considerations regarding the way the service is delivered, its quality, its associated benefits and images?

▪ Does the group get its information about potential services through certain sources?

▪ Is the group particularly influenced by certain types of persons, agencies, or circumstances?

To deal effectively with a specific group in the market, one must know not only what they want but who they are, how they behave, what they believe, and what influences them in these areas. This information can also be used as part of the basis for determining what would have to be changed in a college to permit it to appeal to groups that are not currently in its market, or — somewhat more risky — what it would take to change the desires of other groups to correspond to the present benefits offered by the college.

In this section we pay particular attention to why stated or re-

---

11. Of course, since these relationships are almost never perfect, there are always risks that useful information will not be delivered whenever people are excluded as targets for certain information or when programs or services are designed intentionally to serve one group as opposed to others. Nevertheless, it is necessary in the face of limited resources, on both sides of the market, to pursue some efficiencies by directing efforts where they are most likely to be valued.

vealed preferences for specific characteristics in colleges might not be realized in actual choice behavior. In keeping with the use of Carleton as a specific case through which to demonstrate the practical applications of such information, we focus on a preference for Carleton's type of institution and on the prediction of such preferences and correlates of failures to realize the same.

There are two principal approaches to determining whether there are particular groups in the market that are especially appropriate for a specific college to cultivate, and who they are. The first is to determine whether people have specific sets of desires, preferences, or needs and then to discover who the people are who want or need the specific things the given college offers. A variant on this approach is to learn whether there are particular types of people who are attracted, at present, to the college at rates greater than the attraction rate in the general population. The second approach is to identify specific groups the college seeks to serve and then to ascertain what it is they need or desire, and how to get what they need to them or how to get them to the college. Combinations of these two approaches are also possible, and indeed the informal marketing practices of higher education throughout history have exhibited various mixtures of these approaches — with a bias toward the second. Many instances exist where a college was established to serve a particular religious denomination, or a specific locale, and then the programs were developed that these people wanted (or that professional or educated judgment determined they needed). On the other hand, a number of secular institutions in the private sector have defined the benefits they intend to provide and then searched for students through testing devices, articulation arrangements with secondary schools, and other recruiting and referral devices.

A combination of these approaches has been used in this project. The market was initially defined as students with relatively high standardized test scores. We then searched for preference patterns within this group and will now search for social, economic, educational, and attitudinal correlates of these preference patterns.

We should pause briefly to note that we have not been able to use one of the most powerful analytic tools available to marketers for investigating these questions — the Automatic Interaction Detection (AID) program. This statistical device (it's from the University of Michigan, not the Starship Enterprise) has been used extensively by market researchers for segmenting a market — that is, finding people who are especially disposed toward a certain product and determining the size of this group. Unfortunately, the AID package was not available on either Carleton's or MIT's computers.[12] Some pioneering work with this package in admissions marketing has been conducted, however, at Boston College (see Lay, Maguire and Litten 1982); the reader is encouraged to consult this work as a companion to the approaches presented here.

We start with the identification of persons who exhibited an openness to Carleton, the OTC student described above in the section on Preferred Characteristics.[13] We have employed multiple discriminant analysis (MDA) in an effort to identify the student characteristics that might predict an openness to Carleton; MDA is a statistical technique found on most computerized statistical packages. It searches a data set for the best combination of variables that predict whether an individual will be found in a given group as defined by a "dependent variable." In the case that we are examining, the group (dependent variable) is defined as students who prefer (or are indifferent to) a Carleton type of institution. When MDA has specified the prediction model or functions (the combination or combinations of variables), it can then be used to classify individuals into the groups of interest; the percentage of correct assignments is a measure of the validity of the statistically derived prediction model.[14]

---

12. Financial resources were not available for remote computing. Furthermore, AID works best when the group that interests the researcher does not constitute an extremely small portion of the market; the market-share data we are using involve a very small percentage of a very small sample.

13. The OTC Index was selected over the PAC (positive preferences) because it resulted in a larger group and was less restrictive from a marketing standpoint; its principal limitation is that it is theoretically more difficult to predict or distinguish the "indistinguishable" or indifferent group than those with specific preferences, thus weakening the predictive model. For the MDA runs an individual was considered open to Carleton if he or she scored at the highest level (8) on the OTC Index.

14. The MDA examines the relationships between specified predictor ("independent") variables and the researcher's groups (i.e., the nominal, or discrete categories, dependent variable) and reports the relative contribution that each variable makes to predicting an individual's membership in the group(s). The MDA creates a prediction equation with specific predictor variables on the basis of statistical criteria, and excludes other variables that do not meet these criteria. The prediction equation also weights the relative importance of the included variables in making the prediction. A test of the success of the prediction function(s), or model, comes when MDA attempts to use the prediction function(s) to classify individuals in the data file (or, ideally, another file) into the specified groups. In other words, the computer assigns individuals to groups on the basis of the predictor variables alone. It then compares these assignments with the groups in which each individual actually belongs. The percentage of successful assignments, compared with some random or proportional assignment of individual to groups, is an indicator of the power of the MDA-derived prediction equation.

We have used two sets of predictive variables in our MDA models. The first set had only demographic or objective attributes; these would be the phenomena that would most readily permit the marketer to identify the targets. The second set added subjective reports of important attributes (Question 4) and emotional ratings of various college-related phrases (Question 1) to the first set of variables. The two sets of predictor variables are listed in Table 4-6.

Table 4-6. Predictor Variables Used in MDA Analysis

Objective Attributes	Subjective Variables
Own religion*	Ratings of:
City*	Character building
Race*	Concern for the whole person
Parents' educations	International programs
Mother's college type†	Traditional
Mother's college control‡	Independent study
Mother's college size	Computer-assisted instruction
Father's college type†	Information desired:
Father's college control‡	Admission rates
Father's college size	Social atmosphere
Father's occupation*	Campus activities
Verbal PSAT/NMSQT score	Rules and regulations
Mathematical PSAT/NMSQT score	Appearance of campus
	Net cost
	Faculty scholarly reputation
	Careers to which college might lead

* Dummy variables (each category is a separate variable).
† Liberal arts, etc.
‡ Private, etc.

Ten demographic variables (out of twenty-four)[15] were selected as part of the prediction function for OTC students by the MDA algorithm. The educational level of the parents was the most powerful predictor, followed by residence in the Colorado market, having a father with academic employment, residence in Minnesota, and having a father who was an alumnus of a denominational college (as opposed to public or secular-private). The higher the parents' educational levels, the more likely the student was to be open to Carleton's characteristics. Children of academically employed

15. These variables were mostly "dummy variables," which represented 12 attributes.

fathers were more likely than their peers to be in the OTC group. Students from the Denver/Boulder and the Twin Cities markets were also most likely to score high on this index. If the student's father graduated from a denominational college, the student was especially unlikely to be in the OTC group (probably because of its nondenominational component). By using the 10 variables included in the prediction function, 70 percent of all the cases in the sample were correctly assigned to the OTC/non-OTC groups, with 65 percent of the OTC group classified correctly (50 percent of the cases would have been assigned correctly by chance).[16]

Inclusion of some of the attitudinal measures improved the predictive power of the MDA model but required more variables. Eighteen variables permitted a successful, two-group classification of 74 percent of all individuals, with the correct assignment of students in the OTC group increased to 77 percent. The most powerful predictor was the importance of career outcomes (as an attribute of the colleges to which a student was applying), followed by the importance of net costs, parental educational levels, being from Colorado, the importance of computer facilities, having a father who was associated with an academic institution (faculty or staff),

---

16. The discriminant weights for these variables were as follows:

	10-Variable Model	18-Variable Model
Residence in Denver/Boulder	.40	.29
Residence in Twin Cities	.33	.26
Father denominational college alumnus	−.33	−.24
Mother nonsectarian college alumna	.29	.16
Black	−.15	−.13
Other race (not black, Hispanic, Asian, or white)	.27	.21
Parental educational level	.43	.29
Father in academic work	.38	.27
Father a doctor		−.14
Father an engineer	−.22	−.17
Rating: character building		.14
Rating: independent studies		.15
Rating: computer-assisted instruction		−.28
Importance: social atmosphere		−.16
Importance: campus activities		−.16
Importance: net cost		−.31
Importance: career outcomes		−.34
Importance: faculty teaching reputation		.27
Verbal PSAT/NMSQT	.18	

being from Minnesota, and having a father who was not a denominational college alumnus. The less important career outcomes, net costs, or computer facilities are, the higher the educational level of the family, being the child of an academician, and being from Colorado or Minnesota all increase a student's probability of being open to Carleton. Again, children whose fathers went to a denominational college are particularly unlikely to be in the OTC group.

We had some measures for the parents that were different from those for students. With the set we used, the MDA classification model was able to predict membership in the OTC/non-OTC groups for 69 percent of the cases with 10 objective variables, and for 73 percent of the parents with a combination of 14 objective and subjective measures (52 percent and 74 percent of the OTC group were classified correctly by each of these models, respectively). The probability of being an OTC parent is increased by residence in the Washington-area market, when the respondent has high educational attainment, when he or she gave a positive rating to the concept of racial diversity, or when the father filled out the questionnaire; openness to Carleton's characteristics is reduced when the father is a lawyer, computer-assisted instruction was rated positively, or when the respondent is the alumnus of a university.

These MDA models provide some clues regarding the kinds of people who are relatively well disposed toward the generic type of college that includes Carleton. They suggest that a "natural market" exists among high-ability students who come from more highly educated families and who are not particularly career-oriented; one might look for such prospective students particularly among children of college faculty and administrators. Children of alumni of denominational colleges, particularly when the father is an alumnus of such an institution, present rather unfertile soil for the type of harvest Carleton seeks. Among parents, a humanistic strain appears among those who are open to Carleton.

Pervasive Effects of Price Sensitivity on College-Choice Patterns. We now consider some of the causes of several basic shifts in orientations toward colleges that occur during the college-selection process; we do this through an examination of the movements away from private institutions and away from very selective institutions, which were noted above. We started with the pool of 627 students who declared preferences for private over public institutions in Question 10 (indifferent students were not included). Their first- and second-choice institutions, by type of control, were correlated with 27 variables, which included selected concerns about colleges (Question 4), preferences (Question 10), and background variables.[17]

Our direct question about whether costs were keeping students from submitting desired applications (Question 16) showed the highest correlation with the appearance of a public first-choice institution ($r = .30$), and with a public institution appearing as first or second choice (.33), among these students who preferred a private institution. A concern about price (tuition, fees, room and board) was the variable that showed the second-highest correlations with both these measures of failure to realize a stated preference for a private institution ($r = .25$ for both erosion measures). A concern about net cost (a more sophisticated financial measure) was also associated with the appearance of a public institution among the top-ranked applications, but the effects were less pronounced than the relationship between concerns about price and these measures of erosion (.16 for a public first choice). The weak hold that private institutions have on students who prefer them, but who have high levels of concern about the published price of a college, is shown in Figure 4-4.A. Financial concerns make an impact especially in the nature of the runner-up institutions; people with such concerns frequently seem willing to take a first-choice shot at private institutions, but are quickly ready to retreat to what are perceived to be less expensive public options.

Parts B through E of Figure 4-4 show how students move away from private institutions, even though they prefer them, when

---

17. The specific items were

Concerns: Admissions rates Net cost
Social atmosphere Teaching reputation
Religious atmosphere Career outcomes
Varsity athletics Graduate/Professional school
Price acceptance rate
Faculty doctorates

Preferences: Church/nondenominational
Studious/social atmosphere

Background: Mother's education Verbal PSAT/NMSQT score
Father's education Mathematical PSAT/NMSQT score
Combined parental education Combined scores
Professional father Jewish (dummy variable)
(excluding academic) Catholic (dummy variable)
Academic father City of residence
(dummy variables)

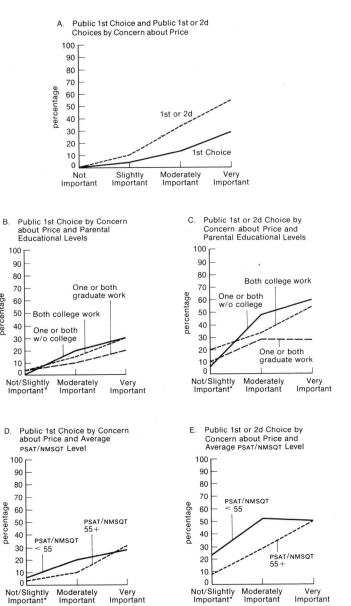

A. Public 1st Choice and Public 1st or 2d Choices by Concern about Price

B. Public 1st Choice by Concern about Price and Parental Educational Levels

C. Public 1st or 2d Choice by Concern about Price and Parental Educational Levels

D. Public 1st Choice by Concern about Price and Average PSAT/NMSQT Level

E. Public 1st or 2d Choice by Concern about Price and Average PSAT/NMSQT Level

*Combined due to small numbers

Figure 4-4. Erosion of High-Ranked Applications to Private Institutions among Students Who Prefer Private Institutions by Concern about Price

financial concerns intrude, and that these effects appear regardless of parental educational levels or students' tested abilities. (There is one exception — concern about price has a relatively weak effect in pushing people to second-choice public institutions in *highly educated families*, if the first choice is private.) In general, higher levels of parental education lead to stronger inclinations toward private institutions. The depressing effects of financial concerns, however, are present at each level of parental education, albeit slightly moderated among families where at least one parent has had graduate work.

Figure 4-4.D shows that the negative effects of a concern about price on private first-choice applications are found among students in both the lower half and the upper half of our ability spectrum; among the upper group, however, it takes a greater level of concern ("very important") for the negative effects to be evident to a high degree. When first and second choices are examined, we discover that concern about price has greater effects among the higher-ability students than among the lower-ability group. Among students with high levels of concern about price, the high- and low-ability groups are equally likely to have public first or second choices; among students with low levels of concern about price, students in the upper-ability group are much more likely to submit two highly ranked private applications than are students in the lower group.

Private applications also suffer with higher levels of expressed concern about the career outcomes of a college education, although the effects are not as marked as those observed for concern about price. This finding suggests that financial concerns may include a complex set of phenomena: affordability (income, current obligations, assets), cost/benefit relationships, financial sophistication, willingness to sacrifice for education, or other considerations.

The abandonment of academically selective institutions among students who say they prefer them is a more complex phenomenon than straying from the private institution fold. For this analysis we examined the behavior of the 834 students who indicated preferences in Question 10 for colleges with academically select students. As in the public or private situation, measures of concern about price are the variables most highly correlated with reporting less than very selective first choices (.31 for both Question 16 and the price measure in Question 4) and with having neither first nor second choices that are very selective (.38). Again, concern about net costs was less correlated with these measures of preference

erosion than was the gross price item.[18] The next most highly correlated variables with lower selectivity first choices were preferences for church-related institutions (.27) and levels of parental
education (−.26 with our measure of parental education). Figure 4-5
shows these relationships.

In the private versus public institution choices, flight to public
second choices increased noticeably as the importance of price
increased. Although somewhat fewer students have both first and
second choices that are very selective than the number who have
very selective first choices, movement away from such institutions
via the second choices is not as dramatic as with public and private
institutions. Students who tend to have very selective first-choice
institutions tend also to have very selective second-choice institutions, regardless of levels of concern about price, parental education, or desires for church-related institutions.

In general, the effects of concerns about price are more damaging
to desires for very selective institutions than to desires for private
institutions. Among the selective-oriented students who express no
concern about price, only 20 percent indicate they are applying to
less-than-very-selective first-choice institutions; this figure rises to
almost three-quarters among students with very strong concerns
about price. More than three-quarters of the children of relatively
less educated families who desire selective institutions list less-
than-very-selective institutions as first choice; this figure drops to
less than half among students who have two parents who have had
graduate work. Among students who strongly prefer church-
related schools and who prefer selective institutions, it appears
that the church considerations frequently win out; fewer than 10
percent list very selective institutions as first choice.

_____

18. We do not have a measure of how students perceive selectivity. Some may well
consider institutions that fall below our cutoff to be selective institutions. Indeed,
among students who prefer a selective institution and whose lists of best schools is
at least half "very selective" by our standards, 49 percent had a very selective first
choice ($N = 498$). Among students who were indifferent to the selectivity dimension
or who preferred an institution with academically diverse students, 21 percent listed
very selective first choices ($N = 199$). Among students who indicated preferences for
selective institutions, but whose lists of best institutions were less than half very
selective, only 6 percent listed very selective first choices ($N = 568$).

However, the correlations between our concern and preference variables and the
nonfulfillment of desire for selective institutions (by our criterion of "very selective") are very similar for the group that prefers selective *and* lists very selective
institutions (by our definition) as best, and for the entire group that simply prefers
selective institutions.

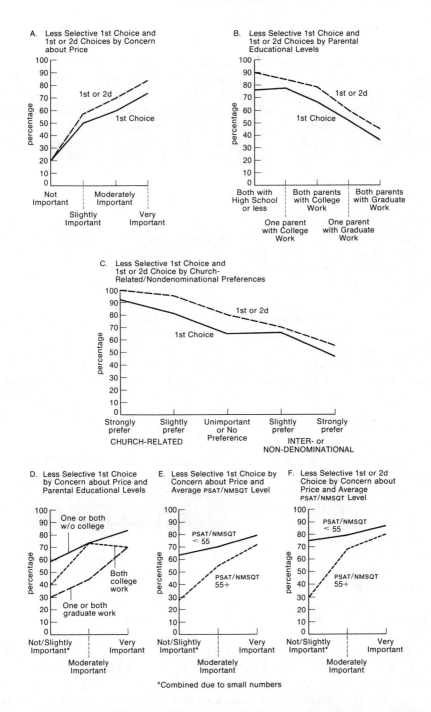

Figure 4-5. Erosion of High-Ranked Applications to Very Selective Institutions among Students Who Prefer an Academically Select Student Body by Concern about Price, and Preference for a Church-Related Institution.

A concern about price is a deterrent to applications to very selective institutions among students who desire them, *even when
their parents are highly educated.* Figure 4-5.B shows that the incidence of less-than-very-selective first-choice institutions rises with
the level of concern about price both for students from families
where at least one parent has had graduate work or where both are
college graduates, and for students where neither parent has been
to college or only one parent has a college education (these latter
groups were combined because of small numbers); the flight from
selective institutions shows approximately the same association
with concern about price in both these groups.

As with the choice of private institutions among students who
prefer them, a concern about price lowers the incidence of very
selective institutions among the top-choice applications for students who prefer selective institutions, *regardless of the students'
tested academic abilities* (Figure 4-5.E and F). Again, the negative
effects of financial concerns on the realization of such preferences
are stronger among the higher-ability group than among students
in the lower half of the ability distribution. Also, once again, these
greater effects among the higher-ability students are due to the
high incidence of very selective choices among students who express *low* levels of concern about price; high-ability students with
very high levels of concern about price are more likely than their
less academically talented peers to choose very selective colleges,
but only slightly so.

This evidence of price sensitivity has a number of important implications for a relatively high-priced, selective, private college like
Carleton. Two principal options emerge, with several considerations relevant to each. One strategy would be for Carleton to
position itself as a selective, private college that is relatively less
expensive than its peers, especially those in the East. This might
attract students from the East who are looking for a bargain
(although travel costs might reduce much of the advantage) and
keep Midwesterners from traveling east for a similar type of educational experience. Such a strategy might prove especially advan-
tageous in the West, where, compared with those of Eastern colleges, Carleton's lower tuition costs might be combined with
generally lower travel costs as well (at least in an era without air
fare wars). Lower-priced positioning might also help outside the
East because of the relatively high regard in these geographic
areas for the *much* lower priced public options. What is unknown
at this point is whether any price differential that could be sustained within the constraints of the type of educational program

offered at Carleton would be sufficient to mark it as a *bargain* relative to private alternatives and as *affordable* relative to public alternatives for those who are oriented toward the latter. Also, to the degree that price is used by students as a proxy for quality (see Zeithaml 1981), there may come a point at which too great a discrepancy between Carleton's price and the price of the institutions with which it seeks qualitative association would lead people to identify Carleton with a set of lesser-quality schools (see Monroe and Petroshius 1981).

The second strategy would be to establish a price position similar to that of the expensive private colleges in the East and to cultivate the substantial group for which price is of slight or no importance. (Among students who prefer private institutions, the group with a low concern for price is about half as large as the group that says price is very important; Carleton, however, is a small college, which requires a relatively small applicant pool, even to remain highly selective.) In the East, then, Carleton could position itself as an institution that offers the highest-quality education, with a different type of ambience, a distinctive *cultural* experience, and a chance to get away from home. In the Midwest Carleton could exploit a position as one of a handful of high-quality price leaders located between the Alleghenies and the Rockies. It could become an opportunity for an intellectual experience comparable with that of high-priced competitors in the East for students who do not wish to go so far from home or enter an Eastern cultural milieu. The high-price and different-location position would permit sufficient income (if demand is sustained) to assure quality equal to (or perhaps greater than) competitors, which are often in more expensive areas. Details of these two strategies are examined further in Chapters 6 through 9.

CONCLUSIONS

We have found highly distinctive patterns of concern about colleges and preferences for types of colleges; we have also found other fairly universal dispositions on these matters. We have been able to identify correlates of a preference for Carleton's type of institution and correlates of movement away from preferences for some of Carleton's characteristics. Pricing phenomena appear to affect directly the demand for private institutions in pronounced ways. The importance of both price concerns and religious orientations in moving people away from very selective institutions is also of note. The importance of concern about price is especially provocative, particularly because it provides a perspective different from that of previous research, which had found income inelasticities in the demand for selective institutions (Spies 1978).[19]

With these general perspectives established, we proceed to investigate particular markets in greater detail, always using the marketing problems and opportunities of Carleton as the lodestar for keeping us on a course with a practical orientation.

---

19. The oft-cited Spies (1978) study reported that quality differences among institutions had more effect on high-ability students' propensities to apply than price differences did. For the most part, however, Spies deals with income elasticities (which were low) and not price elasticities (which were not so satisfactorily measured). Unfortunately, we have no measure of income (it was considered injudicious to ask such information at the point at which our questionnaires were administered in a survey sponsored by the College Board). We do believe, however, that the question of price elasticity is indeed an open one, and we suspect that such elasticity exists—especially in some markets.

5.

A Search for Attractive Markets (with an Exposition of Intermarket Differences in College-Related Values)

A fundamental principle in marketing is that because people differ in a variety of ways, organizations can prosper by relating their services to these differences. Although individualization (or customization) of services is an attractive ideal – and indeed has a very important role in the broad spectrum of marketing efforts – it is generally prohibitively expensive. Instead, organizations that market effectively frequently attempt to identify and serve groups of individuals with similar needs and preferences (i.e., market segments).

There are a variety of ways in which individuals can be grouped for efficient and effective marketing efforts. The most desirable segmenting phenomena may not be the most efficient, however. Consumers' subjective attitudes, preferences, and needs usually correspond most directly to the various specific benefits or characteristics that differentiate organizations. For example, people who seek many social or academic options are more likely to prefer large institutions over small ones, students with insecurities about leaving home are more likely to respond positively to highly parietal colleges than are more adventuresome and independent types. Subjective phenomena are difficult for the marketer to deal with directly, however. While it is possible to design a program or a product in order to appeal to people with certain subjective characteristics, it is another matter to identify them directly with sufficient precision or reliability to permit the efficient delivery of information about the marketer's particular services or products. Therefore, it is usually necessary to identify objective or behavioral correlates of the relevant subjective phenomena. Among the commonly employed objective identifiers of distinctive groups for marketing purposes are sex, place of residence, age, occupation, religion, and education (the first two are more readily ascertained than the others); among the behavioral correlates used frequently are life-style characteristics (activities, etc.) and media-usage habits.

Although several of these phenomena have high potential as segmentation bases for higher education, we have chosen to look primarily at geographic markets. For a number of reasons geography is an important basis for differentiating college markets, especially for an institution that seeks a broad geographic base. Colleges are closely tied to their locations, and these locations represent varying costs and benefits for students in different geographic markets. There is good reason to suspect that widely dispersed geographic markets have somewhat distinctive cultures, even in a nation as closely linked through national media and massive migration as the United States (see, for example, Garreau's *The Nine Nations of North America*, 1981). This is especially true in higher education, since different regions of the country have very different academic traditions and distinctive mixes of institutional types and prestige patterns. Furthermore, it usually makes sense for colleges to treat a specific geographic market as a unit when they are planning and implementing recruiting activities – travel and communications costs and efficiency are geographically related; alumni can be mobilized and their activities supported through locally based clubs. The proximity of a market to a college also affects the amount and accuracy of the public's information about the college and the ways in which it is evaluated. Finally, as we saw in Chapter 2 and will see in greater detail below, the structure and the nature of the competition differ among geographic markets.

The six markets in which this research was conducted were originally identified on the basis of objective and subjective criteria that included current sources of Carleton students, concentrations of Carleton alumni, demographic and economic growth projections, and their attractiveness as a source of students and of marketing insights. The objective data were collected initially for many metropolitan areas. (These data are shown for the six markets in the study in the discussion of a Market Attractiveness Index below.) Minneapolis/St. Paul and Chicago were the two metropolitan markets that provided the largest numbers of Carleton students and had the largest concentrations of alumni. The Baltimore/D.C. area was a market in which the most prestigious institutions in the country were strong (but which does not, as do Boston and Philadelphia, contain a large concentration of these same institutions); it had also been a relatively good Eastern source of students for Carleton, and it was attractive because of a relatively large and regular influx of people from the Midwest who might know Carleton (compared with other Eastern cities, which do not contain the national political functions of this market). The three other markets used in the project were all areas with promising demographic and economic projections.

In sorting through many options that involve numerous or complex considerations, it is often helpful to develop indexes that reflect the relative attractiveness of each option. We did this to select the six markets in the study; we did it again, with an expanded set of data from the survey, to establish priorities among the six for detailed examination that could lead to tentative marketing strategies and, where necessary, to the design of additional research. This chapter reproduces this Market Attractiveness Index (MAI), which included the following groups of data:[1]

1. Demographic and economic conditions and projections (from published data).

2. Carleton-specific data —
From institutional records: applications, alumni, matriculating students.
From Six-Market survey data: applications, recognition, nominations as "best," average ratings.

3. Subjective orientations (from Six-Market survey data): patterns of preference for Carleton's generic characteristics.

4. Objective and behavioral indicators and the competitive picture (primarily from Six-Market data): institutional types chosen, unrealized preferences for institutions like Carleton, and distance from Carleton.

The six cities were ranked (from 1 to 6) on each of the specific indicators we examined in each of these four data sets. Then the ranks on each indicator were summed into a total for each of the four sets. The cities were in turn ranked according to each of these four totals; the four resulting rank orderings were again summed, and these final sums were ranked. In each case the cities with the lowest rank-order numbers were considered the most attractive for continued or expanded cultivation (i.e., 1 = most attractive).

Certainly there is an uncomfortable level of arbitrariness in such a mechanistic approach to market analysis. It would have to be supplemented by additional insights and judgments before an institution implemented specific marketing tactics for a given market or devised a strategy for different levels of effort across markets. In each market the specific nature of an institution's competition, the character of the particular alumni group and its leadership, the

---

1. The data in Part 1 of the MAI and the institutional data in Part 2 are the same as those used earlier to develop a preliminary evaluation of a large number of markets as potential research sites.

Table 5-1. Market Attractiveness Index, Part 1: Demographic and Economic Indicators*

	San Francisco	Denver/ Boulder	Chicago	Twin Cities	Dallas/ Ft. Worth	Baltimore/ D.C.
a Estimated population with our sample specs	1,600 ④	1,500 ⑤	4,900 ①	2,500 ③	1,100 ⑥	3,400 ②
b Total population, SMSA, 1980 (000)	3,228 ②	1,562 ⑥	7,104 ①	2,099 ⑤	2,816 ③	2,172 ④
c Per capita income, 1980 (PCI)	$7,076 ①	$6,179 ③	$6,360 ②	$6,021 ④	$5,892 ⑤	$5,292 ⑥
d Population projections (to 1985)	3.4% ⑤	9.7% ①	2.7% ⑥	3.5% ④	8.7% ②	6.0% ③
e PCI projections (to 1985)	11.1% ③	14.1% ①	9.3% ⑤	11.5% ②	10.8% ④	5.6% ⑥
f Sum of ranks (a–e)	15	16	15	18	20	21
g Rank order of summed ranks (f)	1	3	1	4	5	6

* In the tables on Market Attractiveness Index in this chapter, the numbers at the left of circled numbers are absolute or percentage figures; numbers *in* the circles are rank orders among the six markets (lowest numbers indicate most attractive markets on each indicator.
Note: Projections for line *a* are Volume Projection System estimates from the Student Search Service of the College Board, based on 1980–81 PSAT/NMSQT registrants. Projections for lines *b–e* are from Thomas B. Sivia, *U.S. Regional Projections, 1980–2000. Regional Economic Projections Series. Volume II. Population, Employment, and Income Detail for: Regions, States, Economic Areas, SMSAs.* Washington, D.C.: National Planning Association, 1980.

quality of the local secondary school counseling programs and personnel, the specific financial aid environment – for example, portable state scholarships (+), level of nonportable scholarships (–) – and other considerations would definitely need to be taken into account. The researcher or the marketer might also wish to weight certain considerations more heavily than others, or differently than we have in our present index. For example, if an institution wished to promote its selectivity, preferences for a selective institution might receive more value in the index than do the other components; or the researcher might weight the general projections of demographic and economic data lower than the other parts of the index that relate more directly to higher education preferences and an institution's current market position. These more complex marketing considerations notwithstanding, our index provided a useful foundation for ordering our inquiry.

The general nature of a given market and its future are important in assessing its potential. Growing markets present more potential for development than do stagnant or declining markets; in the latter, competition among institutions that already have a share will only increase, whereas in growing markets an institution has an opportunity to tap some unclaimed new members of the market. Similarly, a larger market is usually less crowded than a small market, or at least offers more opportunity to carve out a distinctive market niche of sufficient size to warrant the expenditures required to establish a position. Table 5-1 examines some of these more general measures of market size and growth. Five demographic and economic indicators are shown. The sum of each market's rankings on the indicators is recorded in line f, and the rank order of the sums in line f is shown in line g; the latter indicates each market's overall ranking on this type of market attractiveness data, ranging from most attractive (1) to least attractive (6). Unfortunately, population projections were not readily available for 18-year-olds or high school graduates for our specific geographic units, so we had to use projections for Standard Metropolitan Statistical Areas.

For the most part, growth is expected to be greatest in the markets that are presently the smallest. The Denver/Boulder market has the strongest growth indicators but has a very small existing population base. Both its existing and projected economic indicators are highly attractive. The Baltimore/D.C. market has moderate population indicators but relatively poor economic conditions, both present and projected. The Chicago market is currently a very large and prosperous market, but it has poor economic and demo-

Table 5-2. Market Attractiveness Index, Part 2: Current Carleton Market Share, Applicant Pool, and Recruiting Resource (Alumni) Indicators*

	San Francisco	Denver/ Boulder	Chicago	Twin Cities	Dallas/ Ft. Worth	Baltimore/ D.C.
From institutional records						
a Total applications†	32 ⑤	35 ④	197 ②	306 ①	7 ⑥	54 ③
b Total matriculants†	7 ⑤	9 ④	43 ②	109 ①	1 ⑥	12 ③
c Alumni	558 ③	331 ⑤	1,394 ②	2,975 ①	75 ⑥	488 ④
From Six-Market survey data						
d Carleton first choice	.4% ③	0 ⑥	1.5% ②	4.9% ①	0 ⑥	0% ⑥
e Total Carleton applications	1.31% ③	.4% ④	2.1% ②	8.5% ①	0 ⑥	.4% ④
f % know Carleton	25% ⑤	30% ③	34% ②	92% ①	14% ⑥	29% ④
g Average rating (known only)	4.1 ⑤	5.2 ③	5.7 ①	5.5 ②	3.8 ⑥	4.5 ④
h Listed as "best"	1.7% ④	2.0% ③	3.9% ②	26.8% ①	0 ⑥	.4% ⑤
i Sum of ranks	33	32	16	9	48	33
j Rank order of summed ranks	4	3	2	1	6	4

* Numbers at the left of circled numbers are absolute or percentage figures; numbers in the circles are rank orders among the six markets.
† Average figures for 1979–80 and 1980–81 (rounded up).

graphic growth projections. Because we have more indicators of current scale than growth indicators (3 to 2), Chicago emerges tied with San Francisco as most attractive overall on the basis of this set of indicators; Denver/Boulder follows as a very close third. Since marketing is a future-oriented activity, it might well be desirable to weight the future-oriented indicators somewhat higher than the others. This would move Denver up to the front of the pack and drop Chicago back considerably.

Carleton's current share of each market and the relative importance of the market in Carleton's applicant and matriculant pools are tabulated in Table 5-2 of the MAI calculations. We have included data both from Carleton's institutional records and from the Six-Market survey.

The Twin Cities' role as a primary market for Carleton stands out dramatically in these data, as does Chicago's role as a major secondary market. Indeed, Chicago has approximately two-and-one-half times as many alumni as the third-ranked market and contributes almost four times as many applicants; the Twin Cities area contains twice as many alumni as Chicago and is the source of half again as many applicants.[2] Running a distant third in the summary rank order is the Denver/Boulder market, with the markets on either coast almost indistinguishable from Denver/Boulder and from each other. The Dallas/Ft. Worth market scores a consistent last on every indicator. It is worth noting that in this institutionally specific part of the MAI, each market scores quite consistently on each of the indicators.

In the third part of the MAI we turn to a set of subjective indicators of students' orientations toward colleges (Table 5-3). General preferences for particular types of institutions (Question 10 in the survey questionnaire) and the institutions listed as the best (Question 7) were examined, with the specific characteristics of Carleton used as a frame of reference. Eight characteristics were chosen,

---

2. Alumni are particularly important carriers of institutional goodwill, even though they may not be used effectively or even work well directly in institutional recruitment programs. When dealing with an "experience" or "credence" product (as almost all services are), where intangibility is high, alumni provide some of the most complete and credible evidence regarding the character, quality, and benefits of the "service" rendered by a college. Services marketing theory has become aware of the importance of personnel in such marketing (Guseman 1981). Alumni are even better than most personnel; they are quasi products.

Chicago has more applicants per alumnus than the Twin Cities area does, even though the latter market presents considerable apparent advantages because of proximity.

Table 5-3. Market Attractiveness Index, Part 3: Preference Patterns (favorable to Carleton)*

Preferences	San Francisco	Denver/ Boulder	Chicago	Twin Cities	Dallas/ Ft. Worth	Baltimore/ DC	Δ**
a Private	34% ⑥	43% ④	54% ②	47% ③	43% ④	57% ①	23
b College	7% ⑤	17% ②	11% ④	33% ⓪‡	7% ⑤	15% ③	26
c Ecumenical	73% ①	69% ②	52% ⑤	54% ④	47% ⑥	65% ③	26
d Selective	54% ⑤	60% ④	62% ②	53% ⑥	61% ③	65% ①	12
e Liberal arts	59% ⑥	71% ④	72% ③	77% ①	65% ⑤	75% ②	18
f Studious	46% ⑥	55% ①	54% ②	50% ④	52% ③	50% ④	9
g Rural	34% ③	37% ②	27% ④	26% ⑤	24% ⑥	38% ①	14
h Small	20% ⑤	27% ②	20% ⑤	36% ①	22% ④	25% ③	16
i Prefer or indifferent to a–g	6% ④	7% ③	5% ⑤	8% ②	5% ⑤	12% ①	7
j Sample Population × i	90.2 ⑤	104.8 ④	228.2 ②	202.9 ③	61.9 ⑥	400.9 ①	—
k Best list more than 50% private(+)	57% ⑥	73% ②	73% ②	71% ④	66% ⑤	84% ①	27
l Best list more than 50% very selective(+)	49% ④	50% ③	58% ②	42% ⑤	39% ⑥	74% ①	35
m Average rating of Minnesota	2.70 ④	2.97 ③	3.02 ②	4.17 ①	2.53 ⑥	2.68 ⑤	—
n % rating Minnesota positively	9% ④	23% ②	21% ③	78% ①	5% ⑥	8% ⑤	—
o Sum of ranks	64	38	43	38	58	32	—
p Rank order of summed ranks	6	2	4	2	5	1	—

* Numbers at the left of circled numbers are absolute or percentage figures; numbers in the circles are rank orders among the six markets.
† Percentage point difference between highest and lowest markets.
‡ Difference between next closest market exceeds 10%; additional "point" subtracted.

and ratings of "indifferent" were excluded (*a–h*); the dimensions were those that correlated with ratings of Carleton in those cities where Carleton was known to some extent (Twin Cities, Chicago, Baltimore/D.C., and Denver/Boulder).

Substantial intermarket differences can be seen on some of the attributes. The greatest differences are on preferences for private institutions (versus public), for colleges (versus universities), and for a nondenominational or an ecumenical religious atmosphere (versus a denominational institution). The incidence of preferences for private institutions ranged from about one-third of the students in San Francisco to over one-half of the students in the Chicago and the Baltimore/D.C. markets. One-third of the Twin Cities students indicated a preference for a college over a university, with fewer than 1 in 10 in California or Texas so disposed. Almost three-quarters of the students in the San Francisco area exhibited a preference for a nondenominational atmosphere, whereas fewer than one-half of the students in the Texas market reported the same preference.

The ranking of a given market varied considerably according to the specific characteristic being rated; for example, students in the San Francisco area market were the *most* likely to indicate a preference for a nondenominational over a denominational institution, but the *least* likely to prefer a private over a public institution or a studious over a social atmosphere. (In many cases, however, the percentage differences between markets are quite small, even though the rankings are always whole numbers ranging from 1 to 6.)

Line *i* shows the percentage of students in each market who preferred or were indifferent to seven of these characteristics (another index of "openness to Carleton").[3] Taking all of these characteristics together, the Baltimore/D.C. market had the highest incidence of students who were not opposed to Carleton's characteristics; it was followed by the Twin Cities and Denver/Boulder. Preference patterns were least favorable for Carleton in the San Francisco and Dallas/Ft. Worth markets.

Applying these percentages to the relevant populations of each city, a different picture emerges. Line *j* of Table 5-3 was derived by multiplying the percentage of students in each market who pre-

---

3. Size was eliminated because of the floating boundary between "small" and "medium-sized" (the point at which students defined small in Question 3 ranged from fewer than 1,500 for 25 percent of the students to fewer than 5,000 for 75 percent of them).

ferred or were indifferent to all eight characteristics listed in lines *a* to *h* by the size of the population in the market who possessed the personal characteristics that defined our sample (see Chapter 3). Baltimore/D.C. continues to rank first by this measure. Chicago and Denver/Boulder change places, however. Although the latter had a relatively high percentage who were not ill disposed toward Carleton's characteristics, it also has a relatively small population. The Texas and California markets continue to look relatively unattractive from this perspective.

In addition to stated preferences, we included some summary measures of the kinds of institutions that were listed as the "best" institutions (Question 7), because of the limitations of abstractly stated preferences discussed in Chapter 4 in the section on Preferred Characteristics. The incidence of private and very selective institutions on students' lists of best colleges and universities was interpreted as favorable for Carleton. For the most part, rankings on these two indicators paralleled each other. It is worth noting, however, that both by this measure of an orientation toward selectivity and by students' stated preferences, the Twin Cities market is not well disposed toward such institutions. Although this market scores well on most of the other characteristics Carleton offers, selectivity does not appear from these data to be something these Twin Cities students strongly desire (we return to this phenomenon in Chapter 6).

Finally, we included students' ratings of Minnesota in this portion of the index. Location has consistently emerged as a primary determinant of institutional attractiveness (regardless of the specific measure employed), and it is a relatively immutable characteristic of an institution (although it can be marketed well or poorly). For these reasons we even gave it additional weight by using two measures of students' evaluations of this attribute. As would be expected, Minnesota rates most highly among its own residents, with students in the other two markets that are closest — Denver/ Boulder and Chicago — runners-up. Although Baltimore/D.C. appeared very attractive on the other measures in this part of the index, students there have a negative orientation toward Minnesota.

Part 4 of the MAI (Table 5-4) includes indicators of competitive advantages and disadvantages. It includes a rather eclectic collection of indicators, which differ from those in Table 5-3, for the most part, by their behavioral or objective natures. Markets with large percentages enrolling in private institutions were considered more attractive than those where students attend public institutions in

Table 5-4. Market Attractiveness Index, Part 4: Competitive Advantages (+) and Disadvantages (−)*

	San Francisco	Denver/ Boulder	Chicago	Twin Cities	Dallas/ Ft. Worth	Baltimore/ D.C.
a Private first choice (+)	43% ⑥	50% ⑤	64% ②	55% ③	51% ④	68% ①
b % out-of-state first choice (+)	22% ⑤	44% ②	44% ②	37% − †	26% ④	58% ①‡
c Prefer Carleton-type institution§ (+)	2.8% ②	5.6% ①	1.2% ⑥	2.8% ③	2.3% ⑤	2.7% ④
d % line c who list Carleton-type institution as first choice (−)	0 ①	66% ⑥	0 ①	57% ⑤ ‖	25% ④	14% ③
e COFHE share of best (+)#	53% ②	51% ③	49% ④	39% ⑤	37% ⑥	66% ①
f COFHE share of applications (−)#	26% ⑤	17% ③	24% ④	12% ①	16% ②	37% ⑥
g Average no. of applications (−)	2.5 ④	2.4 ③	2.5 ④	2.1 ①	2.3 ②	2.9 ⑥
h Distance from Carleton (−)	1,595 ⑥	715 ③	360 ②	40 ①	850 ④	935 ⑤
i Sum of ranks	31	26	25	19	31	27
j Rank order of summed ranks	5	3	2	1	5	4

* Numbers at the left of circled numbers are absolute or percentage figures; numbers *in* the circles are rank orders among the six markets.
† Minnesota excluded because out-migration works to Carleton's disadvantage; although this contributes to a lower score for this market, the differences on the sum of ranks (*i*) are great enough to keep the Twin Cities in first place, regardless of how this variable was scored.
‡ Defined as not in Maryland, D.C., or Virginia.
§ Students who indicate a preference for nondenominational, rural, selective, coed, private, small institution.
‖ Three of the seven listed Carleton.
Carleton excluded from these calculations.

greater proportions (the price competition will be less severe); likewise, except for Minnesota, markets where students were relatively likely to travel out of state were also likely to be more receptive to Carleton than were more parochial markets.[4] Another more exacting indicator of preferences for Carleton-type institutions was constructed (fewer dimensions than the indicator used in Table 5-3, but with indifferent ratings excluded); relatively high levels of this preference pattern were considered a plus (no market made a very impressive showing), but markets where students with such preferences were already seeking admission to such schools were considered relatively closed to Carleton (it would have to outcompete similar institutions directly instead of simply creating an awareness of its existence and accessibility). Esteem for selective, high-priced institutions was treated as a desirable indicator. (We used the members of the Consortium on Financing Higher Education, COFHE, as a ready reference in the context of the institutional coding scheme we had devised to serve several purposes, although COFHE is not exhaustive of all such institutions.) But if a market's students already show a strong propensity to apply to such institutions, this was viewed as an offsetting liability for Carleton (again, it would have to capture market share from highly attractive institutions). Markets where students now submit large numbers of applications were judged to be more difficult to crack than markets where Carleton might be added to the small set under serious consideration, and then work to increase its relative attractiveness between the point of application and the point of decision. Finally, distance from Carleton was considered to be a negative phenomenon because of increased costs (financial and psychological — e.g., distance from family).

This is the most problematic set of indicators in our index. Wide variations in a given market's rankings across the several indicators in this heterogeneous set are evident. We have taken each indicator at unit value. However, depending on potential marketing strategies (e.g., the kind of position an institution sought or the kinds of resources available to it), certain indicators might well be given more weight than others; indeed, some of our assumptions about the "attractiveness" associated with certain dimensions might even be reinterpreted. For example, it might be more difficult to get students in markets where the norm is one or two ap-

---

4. This is a crude indicator, however. Going out of state in Texas can involve considerably more distance than going from Baltimore to Pennsylvania, or even New York; or from Chicago to Indiana, Wisconsin, or parts of Michigan.

Table 5-5. Market Attractiveness Index, Part 5: Overall Ranks

	San Francisco	Denver/ Boulder	Chicago	Twin Cities	Dallas/ Ft. Worth	Baltimore/ D.C.
Part 1	1	3	1	4	5	6
Part 2	4	3	2	1	6	4
Part 3	6	2	4	2	5	1
Part 4	5	3	2	1	5	4
Sum of ranks on MAI components . .	16	11	9	8	21	15
Rank order of summed ranks	5	3	2	1	6	4

plications to add Carleton to their list of schools being considered than it would be to get students where the norm is three or four applications to substitute Carleton for their third or fourth choice – and then work on their preference rankings.

Overall, the Twin Cities area emerges as the most attractive market on this set of indicators; this would have been true even if we had scored it down because it was "too close to home" for high-ability students. Chicago follows as a relatively close second, with our Rocky Mountain and Eastern markets close on its heels.

The summary values on the Market Attractiveness Index are presented in Table 5-5; these were derived by summing the overall ranks on each of the component parts. By these formulas the Twin Cities area edges out Chicago on the basis of overall attractiveness. The Twin Cities area, however, as revealed in Table 5-2, is truly a *primary* market. Carleton will have to maintain its strength in this market. Should hard times emerge as forecast, this will be an important market in which to seek an expanded share in order to preserve Carleton's institutional size, its financial base, and its existing level of program richness (albeit at the sacrifice of some of its most cherished characteristics – e.g., geographic diversity). Chicago comes through as a very important secondary market for Carleton College, and perhaps an area with some possibilities for expansion. The Denver/Boulder, Baltimore/D.C., and San Francisco areas appear to be reasonably attractive markets, but for different reasons. The data presented in this chapter provide only hints of how an institution might tap the potential in these various markets or why some of them are particularly unpromising for institutional efforts (from Carleton's perspective). The following chapters examine several of these markets in greater detail, focusing also on the development of marketing strategies for particular markets.

6.

Approaches to Understanding a Primary Market (the Twin Cities Market)

Clarity of marketing insights, we repeat, begins at home. We initiated our market research foray into the world beyond the Carleton applicant and inquiry pools with an analysis of Carleton's primary market—the Twin Cities; 19 percent of Carleton's applicants come from Minnesota, and 78 percent of its Minnesota applicants come from the metropolitan area of Minneapolis/St. Paul. Although Carleton College has a broader geographic base than do several more selective institutions with greater national visibility (confidential market research data from the Consortium on Financing Higher Education), the local Twin Cities market always has been, and will continue to be, a major source of its applicants.[1] It is imperative, therefore, that this market is well understood, that Carleton's market share is protected, and, perhaps, that its position is strengthened.

Our investigation starts with consideration of the general "culture" of the Twin Cities market as it relates to academic preferences and concerns, and of the structure of the market (with regard both to esteem for colleges and to application patterns). This is followed by an exploration of factors that lead to an application to Carleton and how Carleton might appeal to students who are well disposed toward the college but don't apply. Finally, we consider issues of positioning the institution in relation to its principal competitors.

---

1. Data from the Cooperative Institutional Research Program indicate that two-thirds of the freshmen in American colleges and universities are attending school within 100 miles of their homes.

THE GENERAL ACADEMIC CULTURE

Important Attributes and Preferred Characteristics

In general, the important attributes and preference patterns exhibited by students in the Twin Cities mirror the patterns reported for the total sample (Chapter 4). There are several noteworthy, although minor, deviations, however. Among the ratings of important attributes, Twin Cities students had the highest proportions who indicated that financial attributes are very important—64 percent for net cost (10 percentage points above the figure for the total sample) and 58 percent for financial aid (12 percentage points above the total sample).[2] In their reported preferences for specific characteristics in institutions, the Twin Cities students manifest marginally distinctive patterns; some are favorable to Carleton and some are not. They are more likely than students elsewhere to report a preference for a college over a university; Twin Cities students are almost equally likely to prefer a college to a university, whereas in the total sample, the preference rate for universities is four times the incidence of preference for colleges. Twin Cities students are more likely than their peers to report a preference for small over medium-sized institutions; in the Twin Cities medium-sized is preferred by one-and-one-half times as many students as the proportion that prefers small size, whereas in the total sample the medium-size-oriented group is two-and-one-half times as large as the group that prefers small institutions. Also favorable to Carleton is the relative lack of interest in geographic mobility among Twin Cities students. In the total sample the proportion who prefer to be close to home is approximately half the proportion who would like to be a moderate distance from home (on the close or moderate pair); in the Twin Cities 39 percent would prefer to be close to home, with 47 percent preferring to be a moderate distance away. In the total sample preference for an institution a moderate distance away is almost four times the incidence of preference for an institution far away (on the moderate or far pair); in the Twin Cities preference for moderate distance over far away is greater by more than five times. Working against Carleton (although it might be overcome somewhat by appropriate marketing developments) is

---

2. Since Twin Cities students constitute 17 percent of the total sample, these comparisons understate their distinctiveness.

the relative penchant among Twin Cities students for an urban environment. Among Twin Cities students an urban environment is preferred over a rural situation by 2 to 1; in the total sample the size of the segment with urban preferences is only one-and-one-half times the size of the group that prefers a rural location. Also, Twin Cities students prefer a nondenominational college over a church-related institution by about 2 to 1, whereas in the total sample the ratio is over 3 to 1.

Parents in the Twin Cities are more distinctive from their peers than the student group is from other students. They exhibit a slight antielite and anti-intellectual bias. These parents are the most likely of those in any of the markets to rate an institution's price, financial aid, and career outcomes as very important (differing from the Six-Market average by over 10 percentage points on the first two and 7 points on the last). They are the least likely to prefer a selective institution or to rate the library collection, average test scores, or faculty doctorates as very important (differing from the Six-Market *average* by over 10 percentage points on the first two measures and by over 5 points on the last two). They were 15 percentage points less likely than the total sample to rate the pursuit of excellence very positively. On all these measures the Twin Cities parents stand in marked contrast to the parents of the Baltimore/D.C. area, which occupies the other end of the distribution among the six markets.

These data point quickly to some marketing problems Carleton has within its primary market. Twin Cities students appear more likely than other students to prefer a college over a university, a small institution, and one that is close to home – all of which Carleton can provide – but they seem more than students elsewhere to want their small college to be inexpensive, in a city, or to have a religious affiliation (or some combination of these characteristics). To the considerations just noted, Twin Cities parents add their relatively negative reactions to selectivity and to other values with which Carleton is identified.

Patterns of Esteem and Choice

The next step in the analysis of the Twin Cities market was an examination of the general market structure along two dimensions – esteem (the institutions listed as the "best") and choice (the institutions to which applications were submitted). Again, we used a multidimensional scaling (MDS) program to perform these analyses of market structure.[3]

The "Best" Institutions. A preferred market position for Carleton is to be counted among the best small colleges in the nation and to have solid recognition of such a status within its region. We therefore analyzed the lists of best institutions that students reported in response to Question 7 on the Six-Market questionnaires. The purpose was to determine where Carleton stands in relation to this set, who the competition for high esteem is, and what the structure of this competition is.

Finding out which schools dominate the market on this dimension and whether Carleton is among them is an easy task. We simply counted the number of times particular institutions were mentioned in this free-response item (it was asked well ahead of the point in the questionnaire where specific institutions were mentioned, and the respondent was instructed not to return to this item after proceeding through the questionnaire). Table 6-1 lists the institutions cited most frequently as best by students in the Twin Cities. These students gave 817 responses, naming a total of 121 different colleges and universities as best. The top 5 percent of the institutions specified received 47 percent of all the mentions, showing the dominance of a relatively small number of institutions on this measure of prestige. (One way of considering the structure of a market and openings in the market is to examine the degree to which esteem or applications are concentrated or diffused. It may be easier to carve out a differentiated niche in a market where a few institutions dominate than in one where a large number of dif-

---

3. See Developing a Broader Market Perspective in Chapter 2 for a discussion of how MDS works. We used the SCALAR program from the University of North Carolina. The program for generating incidence of cocitations for pairs of institutions, which is used as input into the SCALAR program, was written by Daniel Sullivan and David Brodigan at Carleton.

Other researchers have used factor analysis to accomplish similar objectives (Rowse and Wing 1982). We experimented with this method, but the small number of cases in our sample made the results very difficult to interpret. Our Twin Cities sample had an N that was one-eighteenth as large as the New York state sample used by Rowse and Wing. The reader is referred to this excellent paper, however, for an alternative approach to market structure analysis.

Yet another approach to examination of market structure is found in the work of Robert Zemsky and his colleagues (1983); the data used by this group of University of Pennsylvania researchers come from students' requests that their SAT scores be sent to colleges and universities.

ferent institutions each have a small share; in the latter market, all viable positions might well be taken.)

In the Twin Cities Harvard squeaks in just ahead of the University of Minnesota on this esteem dimension; Carleton comes in as a somewhat distant third. Among the institutions listed by at least eight students, 32 percent of the citations were Ivy League. An additional 47 percent were other private institutions, giving a total of 79 percent to the private sector. Forty-nine percent of the mentions went to Minnesota institutions. Carleton clearly has a strong market position on this dimension, as does its crosstown competitor, St. Olaf College.

To understand an institution's current position in a market and to determine opportunities for repositioning (where desirable), the market structure needs to be assessed. We chose to examine the structure of esteem by analyzing which institutions were named together on these best institutions lists. The lower portion of Figure 6-1 presents a two-dimensional MDS plotting of these relationships between institutions named frequently. The institutional code letters are decoded in Table 6-1. The closer two institutions' points are, the more frequently they were cited together as best institutions. Thus, institutions that cluster on such a plot are considered to be more similar along some dimension (or dimensions) than are more distantly placed institutions; in the questionnaire we defined the referent(s) only loosely as best "for students with high academic potential."

There is a fairly large level of "stress" in these maps, so that great precision in the placement of a given point cannot be assumed and minor differences in proximity should not be overworked.[4] Nevertheless, the plots are highly suggestive: institutions cluster in intuitively meaningful ways. The national private colleges and universities are located on the left side of the map, generally in the lower left quadrant. Carleton is placed closest to Harvard, and St. Olaf is near this grouping, although the latter is drawn toward the Minnesota institutions that dominate the right side of the map.

When viewed this way, Carleton's position in this market is illu-

---

4. These plots represent a "compromise" mapping of all paired relationships. "Stress" is a technical measure of the goodness of fit between the interpoint distance as plotted on the maps and the actual proximity measures between pairs of institutions. In these plots stress ranges from .59 to .68. Occasionally, institutions not cited frequently together appear within a cluster because they were both mentioned frequently with a third institution.

Table 6-1. Institutions Named "Best" by Twin Cities Students

Code*	Institution	Times Named
H	Harvard University	90
UM	University of Minnesota	89
C	Carleton College	61
SO	St. Olaf College	54
Y	Yale University	52
S	Stanford University	42
P	Princeton University	30
MIT	Massachusetts Institute of Technology	29
N	Northwestern University	20
SCS	St. Cloud State University	16
G	Gustavus Adolphus College	13
M	Macalester College	13
D	Dartmouth College	11
MS	Mankato State University	11
LA	University of California at Los Angeles	11
SJ	St. John's University, Minnesota	11
B	Brown University	10
A	Augsburg College	10
ST	College of St. Thomas	9
ND	University of Notre Dame	9
BU	Boston University	8
SC	College of St. Catherine	8

* Codes used in Figure 6-1.

minated, not simply according to Carleton's own perceptions or desires, but according to the way that high-ability students view it. Objective institutional characteristics can help interpret such a plot. For example, Carleton College is the only Minnesota institution in the highest two categories of selectivity reported by Cass and Birnbaum, and 81 percent of its students come from out of state. It is a highly selective, national institution, and Twin Cities students seem to place it in that category.

The upper part of Figure 6-1 — the hill diagram — is a synthesis of the information contained in the two-dimensional plot and the frequency-of-mention table. The plane at the base of the hills is the two-dimensional plotting of the lower diagram, viewed from 11 degrees above the horizontal. The shaded spikes, or bumps, on this plane, with the letter codes, represent the individual institutions; the heights of the spikes are roughly proportional to the number of citations reported in Table 6-1. The darkly outlined larger hills on this map represent the aggregate level of esteem (the summed number of mentions) for each of the institutions grouped together

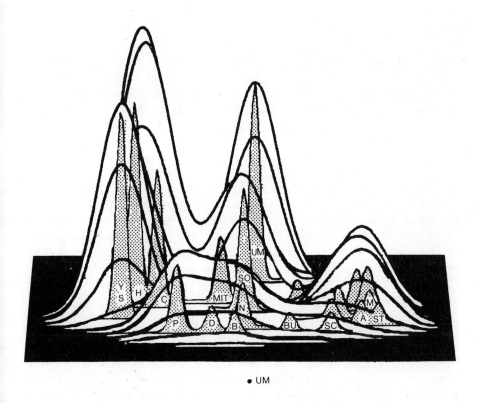

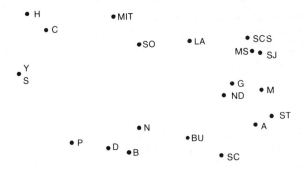

Figure 6-1. Structure of College Esteem among Twin Cities Students (Best Institutions)

in the area over which the hill rises.[5] In the picture that emerged for the Twin Cities students, there are six major hills. The tallest is the Harvard-Carleton hill, to the rear in the west. Before it is the slightly smaller hill formed by Yale and Stanford, with the other selective, national institutions gathered in the ridge in the center foreground. The St. Olaf hill stands behind this selective, national ridge, and the University of Minnesota peak looms behind Mt. St. Olaf. On the right are the foothills of the Minnesota private and state colleges. This picture is a dramatic topographic portrayal of the structure of esteem in the Twin Cities market. The overall dominance of several groupings of private institutions is clearly revealed, along with the University of Minnesota's strong position in this realm. Carleton occupies a position of high esteem, offering a local alternative to some of the most highly regarded institutions in the nation. St. Olaf, on the other hand, has an alternatively enviable position; it is centrally located because it is found both on the lists of students who are inclined toward local institutions and on those of students who are more cosmopolitan in their orientations.

The Applications Submitted. Although "respect" is a major objective of colleges and universities (Garvin 1982), they survive and prosper only if they have students. Therefore, we also asked students to list the institutions to which they had applied or intended to submit applications (Question 13). We coded the first four entries that were listed in response to this question (remember that it was asked in midwinter) and subjected the answers to the same type of analysis used on the lists of best institutions. As noted in Chapter 4, lists of best institutions can differ substantially from the institutions chosen for applications. It is important to know both when and why esteem does not translate into applications.

The University of Minnesota rises to the top of the applications list in Table 6-2 by a commanding lead; the second-place institution, St. Olaf, receives only about one-fourth as many applications. Ap-

---

5. These hills are actually bivariate normal distributions — bell-shaped curves — whose heights are proportional to the cumulative incidence of mentions for each of the institutions they contain. Their widths (standard deviations) can be varied arbitrarily to accentuate individual institutions or groups of institutions (when individual institutions are accentuated, the plot will have many smaller, narrower hills). Setting the standard deviation is analogous to using microscopes of varying powers. We have chosen to give primary attention to the aggregate demand for groups of institutions, since institutions did group together in this plot according to readily apparent similarities. The programs to produce these diagrams were written by Les LaCroix and David Brodigan.

plications are somewhat more widely dispersed than is esteem—these students submitted 462 applications to 110 institutions, with 11 percent of the institutions receiving 50 percent of the applications. Among the 20 institutions that received 5 or more applications, 85 percent of the applications went to Minnesota institutions (we have combined all community colleges into one "institution" for these purposes), and 45 percent went to private institutions; only 4 percent went to the Ivy League institutions that dominated the list of top institutions on the esteem dimension.

The groupings revealed in the lower part of Figure 6-2 differ from those we observed for the lists of best institutions. The Minnesota public institutions, except for the University of Minnesota, are grouped apart (upper left) from the local private colleges (midright area). In a grouping of Midwestern universities, two out of three are public (lower right). A trio of highly selective, national universities is situated in the lower left corner. Carleton occupies a position between these high-prestige universities, the University of Minnesota, and the Minnesota private colleges, with apparently closer linkages to the Minnesota institutions than to the national set.

Again, in the hill diagram of Figure 6-2 the two preceding perspectives are combined in bold relief. A single hill dominates this picture; it is composed of the University of Minnesota. Behind the University of Minnesota, and mostly obscured, is a large peak composed of the Minnesota public institutions, and the local private institutions sit off in a hill to the right. When it comes to applications, the national, selective universities are completely overshadowed by the local competition; the former constitute a small mound in the left foreground.

As noted above, the application picture is more diffuse than the esteem plotting. Students spread their applications across various sectors. Among students who applied to two or more institutions, 33 percent applied to both public and private institutions, 40 percent applied to institutions both within and outside Minnesota, and 78 percent applied to institutions that differed in their selectivity (as rated by Cass and Birnbaum 1977).

The major inference to be drawn from this analysis of applications of Twin Cities students is that when they apply to colleges, they are relatively idiosyncratic in their choice patterns and may have fairly complicated strategies in mind. Schools both near and far from home, schools with differing levels of selectivity, and schools in both the public and the private sectors will all be taken as options at this stage of the college-selection process. The motiva-

Table 6-2. Applications Submitted by Twin Cities Students

Code*	Institution	Times Named
UM	University of Minnesota	83
SO	St. Olaf College	23
MC	Minnesota Community Colleges	21
C	Carleton College	19
G	Gustavus Adolphus College	19
UMD	University of Minnesota, Duluth	16
SCS	St. Cloud State University	14
MS	Mankato State University	12
ST	College of St. Thomas	11
UW	University of Wisconsin	11
M	Macalester College	10
SJ	St. John's University, Minnesota	10
H	Harvard University	7
A	Augsburg College	7
P	Princeton University	6
SB	College of St. Benedict	6
S	Stanford University	6
L	Lawrence University	6
I	Iowa State University	5
ND	University of Notre Dame	5

* Codes used in Figure 6-2.

tions behind this behavior are undoubtedly complex: some students may not yet have made critical decisions about the distance from home they are willing to travel; others may apply to certain colleges because parents want them to; some will have doubts about being admitted to a highly selective institution and will send applications to backup schools; and some may be contemplating costs and waiting for financial aid offers before making final decisions.

For Carleton there is both good and bad news in this picture. Its position on the edge of the grouping of Minnesota's strongest private and public schools, facing toward the national grouping, can only be considered fortunate. Clearly there are students within the Twin Cities who see Carleton as prominent among the many good local educational opportunities; it is placed close to the institution that enjoys a commanding share of the market in this mapping of application overlap. On the other hand, Carleton is not in as good a position as might be desired among the Twin Cities students who lean toward the most selective colleges and universities, especially those located in the East. There may be marketing potential here by moving Carleton to become known better locally as an accessible college with a national character and many of the same attributes that are so attractive in those distant institutions. That Carleton occupies a strong overall position in a relatively diffuse application

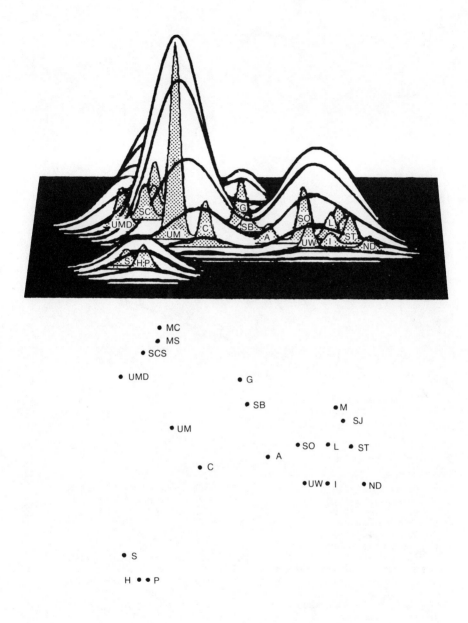

Figure 6-2. Structure of College Choice among Twin Cities Students (Applications)

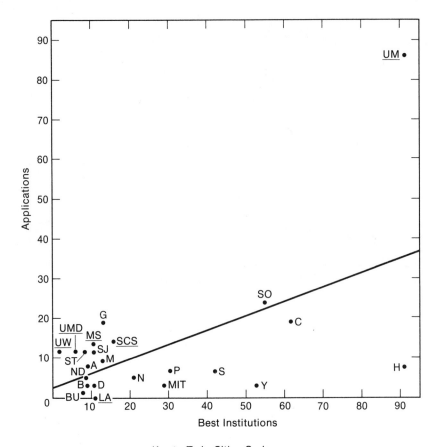

Key to Twin Cities Codes

A — Augsburg College
B — Brown University
BU — Boston University
C — Carleton College
D — Dartmouth College
G — Gustavus Adolphus College
H — Harvard University
LA — University of California at Los Angeles
M — Macalester College
MIT — Massachusetts Institute of Technology
MS — Mankato State University
N — Northwestern University

ND — University of Notre Dame
P — Princeton University
S — Stanford University
SCS — St. Cloud State University
SJ — St. John's University, Minnesota
SO — St. Olaf College
ST — College of St. Thomas
UM — University of Minnesota
UMD — University of Minnesota, Duluth
UW — University of Wisconsin
Y — Yale University

Note: Plot is limited to institutions with eight or more citations on at least one dimension. Public institutions are underlined.

Figure 6-3. Institutions Named Best and Institutions Receiving Applications among Twin Cities Students

market suggests that Carleton is respectably in the running while issues such as distance from home, admissions prospects, and financing options are still being sorted out by Twin Cities students and parents. It also suggests that there may be opportunities for repositioning the college, cashing in on its esteem, gaining an advantage on a major competitor, or a combination of the above.

Applications Compared with Esteem. The esteem-choice matrix in Figure 6-3, combining the volume data in Tables 6-1 and 6-2, shows that some colleges receive more applications than their relative incidences of esteem would predict. Esteem is clearly not the only basis for application generation; Chapter 4 reported a number of other considerations that can serve as alternative bases for choice or as obstacles to the conversion of respect into applications. This figure brings these phenomena into focus at the institutional level. Some institutions exhibit greater esteem-choice discrepancies than do others, and some have reservoirs of goodwill into which they might dip if they could undertake marketing initiatives that would reduce obstacles or complement general respect with particular benefits.

The regression line in Figure 6-3 is the best estimate of the number of applications a given institution would receive based on the general pattern of esteem and choice. The Ivy League institutions receive substantially fewer applications than would be predicted simply on the basis of their high levels of esteem; local institutions receive larger shares of the applications than their nominations as best institutions would predict. For example, Gustavus Adolphus College does considerably better in eliciting applications than its incidence among the best-institution listings would predict. Carleton College does less well on applications than would be predicted, while St. Olaf College does slightly better. The University of Minnesota is in a league by itself. In this market Princeton and Stanford have done considerably better in converting esteem into applications than have Harvard or Yale.

CARLETON APPLICANTS AND WELL-DISPOSED NONAPPLICANTS

To understand more clearly Carleton's position in this market in general, and the particular market segments in which it is currently strong and those where it might be strengthened, we performed two analyses. In one approach we sought to determine what variables might predict an application to Carleton from among the students who rated Carleton as a desirable institution for them; in the second approach we examined Carleton's market share in relation to two of its principal local competitors and analyzed the nature of their respective applicant pools. These two analytic approaches essentially relate to tactics associated with strategy number 2, as discussed in Basic Marketing Strategies in Chapter 1 (win students from principal competitors). The high incidence of familiarity with Carleton in this market effectively precludes use of strategy number 1, the awareness-increasing strategy (unless, of course, Carleton is substantially misunderstood; we did not delve deeply enough in this survey into matters of misperceptions to know much about this potential problem — it would take a more geographically focused study to deal with these matters effectively).

In our first analysis we selected only the 149 students who rated Carleton 6 or greater as a personally desirable school on our 8-point rating scale in Question 20 (60 percent of the Twin Cities sample). Note should be made here that whenever we deal with Carleton applicants, we are saddled with very small numbers (19 applicants, 11 with Carleton as first choice). All findings that relate to this group are highly tentative but are presented to demonstrate analytic approaches and marketing implications that might flow from such evidence.

Multiple discriminant analysis was again used to predict a first-choice Carleton application from within this group. A 10-variable classification function permitted successful assignment of 83 percent of the students (10 out of 11 Carleton applicants were so identified; 83 percent of the 128 nonapplicants were classified as nonapplicants via the statistically derived classification model).[6] The variables that figured most prominently in the prediction function were preference for a nondenominational atmosphere over a denominational college, preference for a private over a public institution, verbal PSAT/NMSQT score, and preference for a high-priced over a medium-priced institution.[7]

---

6. Ten cases were excluded from the analysis because of missing values on the independent variables.

7. The following variables figure in the predictive function: church/nondenominational preference (.58), public/private preference (.49), verbal PSAT/NMSQT score (.41), preference for high price over moderate (.39), professional father (.31), preference for no fraternities (.28), father a *college* alumnus (.27), student a Protestant (.20), preference for medium-sized over large institutions (.20), and father a doctor (.19). Thirty-five additional background and preference variables were included in the analysis, but they did not make a statistical contribution to the prediction function. In another analysis the measures of attribute importance (Question 4) were also included, but the analysis failed to find combinations of variables that permitted successful prediction of Carleton applicants, and it was abandoned.

We examined a wide variety of data for clues to ways in which we might approach the group of students who rate Carleton highly but who don't apply (we called them the well-disposed nonapplicants). They were compared with the small group that does submit applications. The results of the inquiry showed that the two groups were similar on most counts, but that there were hints of some promising steps — and of some tactics that would probably fail.

We started with the student responses to a variety of college-related phrases listed in Questions 1 and 2. Majorities of both groups responded positively to phrases like the pursuit of excellence, concern for the whole person, character building, international programs, and independent study. The major difference between the two groups was their reaction to the word "traditional" — over 50 percent of the Carleton applicants reacted positively versus 30 percent of the nonapplicants; 25 percent of the nonapplicants reacted negatively versus 5 percent of the applicants. Cultivation of a traditional image may help attract more students like those who now apply to Carleton (if they are out there), but it might repel, or fail to move, a substantial number of nonapplicants who are otherwise well disposed toward Carleton as they now perceive it. Market research can be as useful in indicating what to avoid as in moving an institution toward positive actions.

The principal positive and negative images associated with some of these phrases by the two student groups provide additional marketing hints and clues for further research (Table 6-3). These specific images were coded into broad categories from free re-

Table 6-3. Images of College-Related Phrases for Twin Cities Carleton Applicants and Well-Disposed Nonapplicants

Phrases and image	Applicants*	Well-Disposed Nonapplicants*
Small college		
Positive: small classes, etc.	79%	53%
Liberal arts		
Positive: broad opportunities, etc.	42	24
Private colleges		
Negative: expensive	54	53
Positive: selective	26	11
prestigious	16	3
Public university		
Negative: large, etc.	53	44
N =	19	114

* Percentage of students mentioning phrases.

sponses (each coding was "verified" by a second coder). For a number of phrases both groups reported similar negative and positive images. On several counts the applicants were more likely than the nonapplicants to see positive aspects. These data do not tell, however, whether the nonapplicants' tendencies not to mention something as a positive image for a particular phrase are due to their failure to associate the image with the phrase, or a failure to view the particular image positively (additional clues are examined below).

Both groups were likely to mention large size as a negative aspect of public universities; the applicant group, however, was more likely to list small classes, low student-to-faculty ratio, and good student-faculty relations as positive associations with small colleges. If Carleton is to exploit these perceptions, documentation of its small classes should serve to attract more students like the current applicants. To use these phenomena and perceptions to advantage with the well-disposed nonapplicant, however, it appears that Carleton would have to draw more explicit attention to the benefits afforded by small classes, low student-to-faculty ratio, and good student-faculty relations and relate these benefits of a small college specifically to the negative aspects of large size.

Both groups saw a variety of "limitations" (social, curricular, general) as the major negative aspects of small colleges (data not shown), but the applicants are more likely than nonapplicants to associate the idea of "broad opportunities" or "variety" with the phrase liberal arts, possibly providing an offset to the negative images associated with "small." Again, either the breadth aspects of liberal arts will have to be more clearly spelled out for the well-disposed nonapplicant, or other benefits associated with small (depth, etc.) will have to be emphasized—and the positive images associated with these concepts will have to be linked specifically with Carleton.

Finally, both groups were likely to associate "expensive" as a negative image with private college; the applicants were more likely than the nonapplicants to mention "selective" or "prestigious" as a positive aspect of private colleges. The applicant seems to expect more bang for his or her buck from a small or private institution. Nonapplicants will need to be made more aware of the selectivity and prestige aspects of private colleges or, more likely, to be shown the positive benefits that can flow from such characteristics (e.g., a richer educational environment through the input control that selectivity affords; a greater geographic mobility or career advantages from the visibility or prestige aspect). In each case, along with the basic educational effort regarding specific characteristics and their benefits, Carleton would have to demonstrate that it offers the particular characteristics and benefits being promoted—perhaps more effectively or at relatively lower cost than do other institutions (especially compared with those in the East).

The college attributes that applicants and well-disposed nonapplicants rated as "very important" in Question 4 were quite similar (Table 6-4). Fields of study, teaching reputation, career outcomes, and scholarly reputation of the faculty were rated very important by a majority in each group. Applicants are slightly more likely than nonapplicants to be oriented toward scholarly concerns—scholarly activities, faculty doctorates—although their expressed interests may compensate for our failure to include prestige on the list and may reflect this interest instead. Applicants show a curiously lower level of interest in the library. Well-disposed nonapplicants show a greater incidence of high interest in financial aspects. [Although it is a minority in both cases, nonapplicants are slightly more likely to rate campus appearance as very important. We will simply note the financial concerns of nonapplicants again here and return to them later. Carleton might meet the concerns of nonapplicants regarding appearance by sustaining the campus beautification program, which is under way, and by liberally incorporating pictures of the campus that include some of the modern buildings by noted architects, the historic landmark buildings of

Table 6-4. College Attributes Rated Very Important by Twin Cities Carleton Applicants and Well-Disposed Nonapplicants

	Applicants*	Well-Disposed Non applicants*
Fields of study	89%	79%
Teaching reputation	68	75
Career outcomes	68	74
Scholarly reputation of faculty	57	50
Social atmosphere	53	46
Net cost	47	61
Price	47	55
Graduate/professional school acceptance rate	47	51
Residential life	42	49
Faculty doctorates	36	12
Appearance of campus	32	46
Library collection	21	36
N =	19	114

* Percentage of students rating selected attributes very important.

Table 6-5. Most Important College Characteristics Sought by Twin Cities Carleton Applicants and Well-Disposed Nonapplicants

	Applicants*	Well-Disposed Nonapplicants*
Coeducational	26%	42%
Residential	52	20
Small size	37	15
Liberal arts	32	26
Close to home; moderate distance; not too far	21	36
N =	19	114

* Percentage of students giving most frequently cited characteristics. Respondents could list up to 4 characteristics, so percentages do not add to 100.

great character, and the lakes and woods on campus. Improvement in the communication of information about its appearance might increase its attractiveness to nonapplicants, probably without alienating current applicants who appear to be somewhat less interested in such matters.]

When limited to specific characteristics (instead of important attributes) and constrained to the *four most important* characteristics (Question 11), the two groups have rather different profiles. The most frequently cited characteristics are listed in Table 6-5. The applicants show a much greater incidence of interest in residential colleges and in institutions of small size; nonapplicants are relatively more concerned that their colleges be coed and relatively close to home.

The data in Table 6-6 on the most important kinds of information students want (Question 5) underscore some of the themes that have been emerging to this point. Nonapplicants are slightly more likely than applicants to report concern about financial aspects and less likely to cite information about size, academic standards, or general reputation as among the most important kinds.

Table 6-6. Most Important Information about Colleges Listed by Twin Cities Carleton Applicants and Well-Disposed Nonapplicants

	Applicants*	Well-Disposed Nonapplicants*
Price	31%	43%
Size	21	9
Academic standards	26	16
General reputation	26	17
N =	19	114

* Percentage of students listing most frequently cited items of information. Three responses could be given, so percentages do not add to 100.

All of these data suggest that Carleton may have to be cautious in its price increases and price differentiation from the competition or do an even better job of acquainting people with the benefits associated with its costs and of documenting its "bargain" prices relative to other institutions with which it is compared. (See Solmon and Astin[1981] for a listing of the "peer group," in addition to the market structure and application overlap data discussed in our volume.) The data also suggest that Carleton may have to engage in some education about the benefits that can come from the generic characteristics of small size, selectivity, and residential campuses. In answer to the question posed above about whether nonapplicants fail to associate given benefits with small, private colleges or, rather, fail to appreciate them as benefits (relative to the appreciation levels among applicants), the latter seems to be the more plausible hypothesis. Small size, residential nature, selectivity, and high prestige simply aren't mentioned so often by the nonapplicants as important characteristics or types of information.

The principal images that Twin Cities students associate with Carleton give some further clues regarding its strengths and its marketing problems, current and potential. Just under one-third of the 103 well-disposed nonapplicants who gave an image of Carleton wrote something to the effect that it was a good or an excellent institution. Fifteen percent indicated that they considered it an intellectual or a stimulating place, and an equal number noted that their image of Carleton was "expensive." Twelve percent suggested that Carleton was difficult, rigorous, tough, or competitive. These images indicate that Carleton has substantial recognition for its quality; it is also recognized as an expensive institution (which, by local standards, it is). Should the demographic decline mean that eventually Carleton has to dip deeper into its Minnesota pool to sustain its size, it might be preferable to persuade some of these highly qualified nonapplicants that it is not as difficult to get into Carleton as they might have thought, instead of taking less-qualified members of the current applicant pool.

We have previously examined the general structure of the Twin Cities market for colleges and universities; where does this particular group of students who are well disposed toward Carleton, but who don't apply, submit their applications? Just over 50 percent of their first-choice applications go to private institutions, with St. Olaf College dominating this set (12 percent of all first-choice applications in this group go to the college across the Cannon River from Carleton); the University of Minnesota has a commanding position among the public institutions (17 percent of all first-choice applications are directed there). Collectively the Ivy League institutions garner 6 percent of the first-choice applications, with none of them obtaining more than 2 percent. Counting all the applications submitted (within our limit of four per person), almost two in five of these well-disposed nonapplicants (to Carleton) sent an application to the University of Minnesota.

We have noted a number of actions that might be taken to enhance Carleton's attractiveness to a particular kind of student, or to address weaknesses in its image or the appreciation of its benefits. Such suggestions cry out for further research. The findings on which they are based would need to be replicated with a sample that included a larger number of applicants. Furthermore, we have not addressed the cost-effectiveness of these moves—the costs of making the changes (especially where they require changes in the institution and not just promotional focus) and the responsiveness that different types of students might exhibit to specific marketing initiatives.

A DETAILED ANALYSIS OF COMPETITIVE POSITION: CARLETON, ST. OLAF, AND THE UNIVERSITY OF MINNESOTA

In both the general analysis of the competition and our analysis of the competition for students who rate Carleton College very positively, two institutions stand out. Although an institution might try to make gains against the competition by attracting students from a number of minor competitors, the diffuseness of such a target creates some substantial problems for marketing planning. (Unlike some institutions, Carleton is not a promising candidate for attracting students who now are unlikely to attend college, because of the rigor of its academic programs; its location makes serving older or returning students a risky prospect.) It may well be more efficient to develop a marketing plan that seeks to attract students in a particular market segment (or segments) away from a major competitor. We explore this line of inquiry here.

St. Olaf is Carleton's closest competitor in the Twin Cities market (the most overlap in applications from a similar institution).[8] The University of Minnesota (hereinafter referred to as Minnesota) dominates the market and is a major competitor. These are also the two institutions that receive more applications in this market than Carleton does. We decided, therefore, to perform some extensive

---

8. It is also closest in another sense: both institutions are located in Northfield. This led one observer to note that Northfield may be the only town in the nation with twice as many colleges as movie theaters.

analysis of the market shares and sources of applicants for these two institutions, along with an analysis of the sources of applicants and market share for Carleton.[9] Such an analysis provides not only an important perspective on Carleton's marketing strengths and weaknesses, it also provides some clues to opportunities for competitive improvements. We have already noted the analytic problems created by the small number of Carleton applicants; although it had more applicants in our data, the St. Olaf number is also very small. Again, all our findings are highly tentative.

Once again we started with a multiple discriminant analysis (MDA) of variables that might predict a student's listing one of these three schools as a first-choice application. The predictor variables consisted of personal, academic, and family background variables plus the set that indicated preferences for different types of colleges (Question 10). Using 17 variables, the analysis was able to classify successfully 62 percent of the 230 cases for which complete data existed. This is a 49 percent improvement over the classification of cases simply by random assignment among the four categories (Carleton, St. Olaf, University of Minnesota, and the residual group).[10] Table 6-7 shows the number of students who listed each institution as their first choice who were correctly identified on the basis of the combinations of variables the MDA model used for mak-

Table 6-7. First-Choice Application Classification Results (Based on Multiple Discriminant Analysis of Twin Cities Sample with 17 Variables)

Actual Group	N	Predicted Group			
		Carleton	St. Olaf	U. of Minnesota	Other
Carleton.	11	82%*	9%	0	9%
St. Olaf	15	13%	67%	13%	7%
University of Minnesota . .	42	0	5%	76%	19%
Other	162	13%	13%	18%	56%

* Underlined percentages are correct classifications of students.

---

9. Since St. Olaf was specifically named in the questionnaire, we asked their permission to publish the following findings; they graciously consented. Other data in this volume that pertain to specific institutions come from the free responses of the students.

10. A greater percentage of successful classifications was obtained by using the actual proportional size of the groups that chose each institution as first choice as the base against which the successful MDA assignment of cases was compared. However, the percentage of successful assignments to each of the institutional groups in which we have an interest was lower. The improvement came because there were fewer errors in assigning the members of the residual group, the largest of the four groups.

ing predictions. The diffuse residual group was understandably the most difficult to classify; they actually applied to a wide range of specific institutions, some of which are very similar to the institutions we were examining. The Carleton group was the most successfully identified, with 9 out of 11 correctly classified. St. Olaf's applicants were the least successfully classified, suggesting that it may have a somewhat more diffuse appeal in the Twin Cities market than Carleton does.

The most powerful predictor of a Carleton first-choice application was a set of variables that included as its principal components the following: verbal PSAT/NMSQT score, parental education, preference for a college over a university, preference for a medium-sized over a large institution, and preference for a high-priced over a moderate-priced institution. Another set of variables (a second function) also had some predictive power in identifying the Carleton student. Principal among these were the following: preference for a nondenominational atmosphere and preference for a private over a public institution.

The most powerful predictor of a first-choice application to the University of Minnesota among our high-ability Twin Cities students was the same set of variables that predicted Carleton students, except that it worked in reverse. The University of Minnesota students were more likely to have lower PSAT/NMSQT scores, parents with lower levels of education, and so forth (within our highly selected sample).

The set of variables that did the best job of predicting St. Olaf choices was second in effectiveness for predicting the Carleton student, except that it was reversed. St. Olaf students appeared more likely to prefer a church-related college over a nondenominational institution but were less likely to state a preference for a private over a public institution.

Multiple discriminant analysis is an efficient way to begin to explore the effects of a large number of variables on specific types of behavior. Since it looks for the best *combinations* of variables to develop one or more mathematical functions that can be used in such predictions, it also tends to obscure some specific relationships that can be of interest to the marketer. Therefore, we proceeded to examine separately some of the variables that emerged from the MDA results and their relationships to selection of each of these three institutions as first choice.

Our analysis proceeded in two directions simultaneously. Social scientists (and philosophers) speak of two types of relationships — those that indicate necessary conditions for a certain type of behavior (or approach such conditions) and those that show sufficient conditions (or approach such conditions). We examined a number of market segments as defined by the selected variables and determined the market share enjoyed by each of our three institutions. If a given institution captured all of a given market segment (an unlikely event, given the complexity of educational institutions and educational decision-making processes), membership in that group would be a sufficient condition for attraction to that particular institution. Even short of absolute domination, it is still of interest to the marketer to identify institutional dominance or a major share in a given market segment. This tells the marketer where the hunting is most likely to be rewarding and, by inference, something about the aspects of the institution that enhance its attractiveness.

We also looked at the ways in which first-choice applicants to each institution are distributed among the various market segments (a matter of calculating the percentages in the opposite direction from the way in which they were calculated for market-share analysis). Thus, if all the students who name a given institution as their first choice come from a particular market segment, membership in this group is a necessary condition for attraction to this institution. Again, even short of the extreme case, it is still of interest to the marketer to know if the students at a given college exhibit a strong propensity of one sort or another in order to understand the particular appeal the college may have.

It is conceivable, but highly unlikely, to have conditions that are both necessary and sufficient — all the students in a given group attend a particular college and all the students at that college come from a particular group (demographically, economically, or subjectively defined). If such were the case, all the marketer would have to worry about is the social and economic survival of that group, the possibility of another institution's developing a combination of characteristics that have greater appeal to this group, and the educational viability of the college (since homogeneity is a mortal enemy of effective education); these, however, are hardly concerns of little consequence.

To avoid extremely dense and complex tables, we have presented only the second set of percentages (based on each institution's first-choice applicants) in the tables that accompany the text; market-share data, which tend to show smaller differences because of the small total shares enjoyed by each institution, are given in similar tables in Appendix F. Observations that involve data shown in Appendix F have been placed in parentheses. As a benchmark, we should repeat that in our Twin Cities sample Carleton received first-choice applications from about 4.5 percent of the students, St. Olaf was first choice for about 7 percent, and the University of Minnesota was listed as first choice by almost 18 percent of the students. The small number of students who list Carleton or St. Olaf as first choice render their data especially tentative.[11] These results are partially supported, however, by other types of analysis we have conducted that involve larger numbers in each institution's group, but that have a more ambiguous measure of market behavior or orientation — the relative ratings of the three institutions. These supportive findings are mentioned briefly below.

Table 6-8. Ability and Educational Characteristics of First-Choice Applicants

	Carleton	*St. Olaf*	*U. of Minnesota*
Verbal PSAT/NMSQT			
Less than 50	0%	29%	35%
50–54	36	18	37
55–59	18	23	12
60 or greater	45*	29	16
	99%	99%	100%
Family educational level			
Both parents high school or less	9%	18%	35%
One with college work/degree.	9	12	21
Both with college work/degree	18	29	30
One with graduate work/degree	36*	29	14
Both with graduate work/degree	27*	12	0
	99%	100%	100%
$N=$	11	17	43

* Carleton/Minnesota difference statistically significant at .05 level or less.
Note: See also Appendix F-1.

Table 6-8 shows why verbal PSAT/NMSQT scores were such an important predictor of applications to Carleton and the University of Minnesota. Almost two-thirds of the applicants whose first choice was Carleton had scores in the upper ends of our ability range, and almost three-quarters of the applicants to the University of Minnesota (also first choices) had scores at the lower end. None of the Carleton applicants came from the lowest group. St. Olaf first-

11. In the tables that follow we have selectively applied tests of statistical significance to the differences in proportions for the measures that had particular strategic relevance for our case. Most of the differences failed the test because of the small numbers of applicants on which they were based. In the tables we have indicated Carleton/St. Olaf and Carleton/Minnesota differences that are statistically significant at the conventional .05 level or less.

choice applicants were fairly evenly distributed across the ability groups in this high-ability sample. (Indeed, Appendix F-1 shows that Carleton's share of the highest-ability pool was equal to St. Olaf's, which is one-and-one-half times as large, and only 5 percentage points smaller than the University of Minnesota's, which is 25 times larger. Despite the impressive achievements of the two small colleges among students with extremely high ability, it should be noted that the university receives more first-choice applications from this group than either of them do. Together these three institutions capture almost two-fifths of the market of students with extremely high ability in the Twin Cities.)

Table 6-8 also shows the relationships between parental education and selection of our three institutions. Carleton's applicants were the most likely among the three institutions to come from very highly educated families. (Carleton edges St. Olaf as the institution of choice among students from very highly educated families, although the two institutions have equal market shares for students from families where at least one parent has education beyond the bachelor's level. In data not shown, Carleton is the only institution among the three to receive a first-choice application among the small set of five students who have mothers with doctorates.)

Table 6-9 examines the relationships of these three institutions to several preference segments. In the Twin Cities a stated preference for a private institution is a necessary condition for the selection of Carleton as a first choice. On the other hand, almost two-thirds of the students for whom Minnesota is their first choice indicate a preference for public institutions, and it garners almost one-third of the students who express such preferences.

St. Olaf and Carleton are heavily dependent on students who declare a preference for colleges over universities, and the university relies as heavily on students who prefer a university. (Indeed, Minnesota captures over two-thirds of the university-oriented students in the Twin Cities. No one who preferred a university chose St. Olaf; on the other hand, among Carleton's applicants, about one-quarter actually preferred a university over a college.)

The University of Minnesota applicant comes largely from among students who prefer an urban environment; St. Olaf applicants are predominantly rural-oriented. (Indeed, St. Olaf is the first-choice application of almost one in six Twin Cities students who prefer a rural college.) Carleton applicants, on the other hand, are a much more diverse lot on this dimension; they are almost equally divided among the rural-oriented, the urban-oriented, and the indifferent.

Table 6-9. Preference Orientations of First-Choice Applicants

Preferences	Carleton	St. Olaf	U. of Minnesota
Private	100%	71%	14%
Indifferent	0	12	23
Public	0	18	63
	100%	101%	100%
College	73%	71%	8%
Indifferent	0	29	21
University	27*	0	70
	100%	100%	99%
Rural	36%	59%	12%
Indifferent	36	29	16
Urban	27	12	72
	99%	100%	100%
Selective (academic)	91%†	82%	40%
Indifferent	0	0	20
Diverse	9	18	41
	100%	100%	101%
Studious atmosphere	73%†	59%	40%
Indifferent	0	12	28
Social	27	29	33
	100%	100%	101%
Mostly Caucasian	18%	29%	21%
Indifferent	27	41	47
Racial diversity	55	29	33
	100%	99%	101%
Church-related	9%	50%	9%
Indifferent	0	31	28
Nondenominational	91*	19	63
	100%	100%	100%
N =	11	17	43

* Carleton/St. Olaf difference significant at .05 level or less.
† Carleton/Minnesota difference significant at .05 level or less.
Note: See also Appendix F-2.

Carleton and St. Olaf applicants are very likely to report a preference for a selective institution; the students headed for Minnesota divide equally among those who seek academic selectivity and those who prefer academic diversity. (Among students who have a strong preference for selectivity, Carleton has a commanding position, given its small size.) Similarly, about three-quarters of the Carleton applicants prefer a studious atmosphere; slightly fewer than half of Minnesota's applicants (although it's still a sizable proportion) reveal such preferences. The St. Olaf applicants fall in between, somewhat closer to the profile of the Carleton applicants.

In addition to its distinctive position among students who prefer a rural location, St. Olaf distinguishes itself from the other two schools among students who prefer a church-related institution (it is the only one of the three with such affiliation). Almost all of Carleton's applicants prefer a nondenominational institution or an ecumenical religious atmosphere; almost two-thirds of Minnesota's applicants prefer the same. Half of the St. Olaf applicants, on the other hand, indicate a preference for a religious college.

In Table 6-10 additional evidence is examined, drawn from the questions that deal with the importance of various attributes of colleges. The relative importance of scholarly and academic attributes to the Carleton applicant (scholarly reputation, faculty doctorates) and the relative importance of campus activities to St. Olaf applicants are notable. Carleton applicants are slightly less likely than are applicants to the other two institutions to be concerned about the career outcomes of their undergraduate educa-

Table 6-10. Attribute-Importance Orientations of First-Choice Applicants

Attribute Importance	*Carleton*	*St. Olaf*	*U. of Minnesota*
Scholarly reputation			
Slightly/not important	0%	12%	12%
Moderately important	18	35	33
Very important	82	53	56
	100%	100%	101%
Faculty doctorates			
Slightly/not important	27%	47%	37%
Moderately important	27	35	56
Very important	45*	18	7
	99%	100%	100%
Career outcomes			
Slightly/not important	18%	6%	0%
Moderately important	18	19	14
Very important	64	75	86
	100%	100%	100%
Graduate school acceptance			
Slightly/not important	18%	12%	19%
Moderately important	27	29	36
Very important	55	59	45
	100%	100%	100%
Campus activities			
Slightly/not important	18%	24%	33%
Moderately important	64	35	44
Very important	18	41	23
	100%	100%	100%
N =	11	17	43

* Carleton/Minnesota difference significant at .05 level or less.
Note: See also Appendix F-3.

Table 6-11. "Very Positive" Ratings of Selected Phrases by First-Choice Applicants

Phrases (Very Positive)	Carleton	St. Olaf	U. of Minnesota
Character building	36%	47%	20%
Concern for the whole person	27	53	36
International programs	36	35	26
Independent study	36	35	27
N =	11	17	43

tions. The importance of graduate school acceptance rates is about the same for the three institutions, with Minnesota trailing slightly.

Finally, we examined market share and applicant pool traits in relation to students' ratings of certain college-rated phrases (Question 1). These results, shown in Table 6-11, cast further light on the positions these three institutions hold in the Twin Cities market. (There was little difference among the three in their shares of the market among students who react very positively to the phrases international programs or independent study, beyond the institutions' overall differences in market share.) The concepts of character building and concern for the whole person, however, stand out as more important among St. Olaf applicants than among students who select the other two institutions. Carleton applicants are second in their disposition toward "character"; the applicants to the university rank second in their desire for "concern."

Although some striking patterns emerge from these data, the risk of unreliable findings is severe with such small numbers. Fixed-response options on a questionnaire or the need to code open-ended responses into manageable numbers of categories exacerbate the problems presented by small numbers. Indeed, as we carefully examined the questionnaires of the students who listed Carleton as their first choice, we found evidence of idiosyncratic behavior. Of concern to most institutions conducting this type of research is the problem of particular pressures that may play upon a given student, especially children of alumni. We found one Carleton applicant who reported that Carleton ranked ahead of his second choice (Williams) because "My mother graduated from Carleton; it is much closer to home and in an area I have grown to love by living only 14 miles from Carleton for two years." It is difficult to determine from this response exactly where the legacy aspect fit in his decision, but it was undoubtedly important. Another questionnaire had an even more unusual set of reasons for ranking Carleton over the student's second choice

(Bemidji State): "Carleton has more to offer academically—and the running programs are exactly what I am looking for." Carleton College is not generally known as an athletic powerhouse, but it does have a nationally ranked cross-country program (Division III). (In recent years, it has also developed a nationally ranked ski program, Nordic and Alpine, a move that directly addresses one of its most severe marketing problems—the Minnesota winter.)

Because the numbers, especially in the Carleton and St. Olaf groups, were so small, we compared some of the findings just reported with work performed early in our analysis, which used institutional ratings as the basis for comparison. As we have seen previously, ratings and esteem are cheaper for the respondent than are applications and therefore easier for an institution to acquire. By the same token, however, they afford larger data bases with which to work. We compared the ratings given to Carleton and St. Olaf in Question 20, which asked students to rate each of 11 institutions. We classified students into three groups: (1) Carleton rated superior to St. Olaf (31 percent), (2) St. Olaf rated over Carleton (38 percent), and (3) equal ratings given to both institutions (31 percent). These figures show that just as in the applications arena, St. Olaf has a slight edge in this aspect of the ratings game. We will consider only (1) and (2), calling the first group the Carleton-oriented and the second the St. Olaf-oriented.

Among students who gave a very positive rating to the phrase private college, 47 percent were St. Olaf-oriented versus 32 percent who were Carleton-oriented. Among students who gave a very positive rating to the phrase small college, 47 percent were St. Olaf-oriented versus 28 percent who were Carleton-oriented. This latter fact was surprising because St. Olaf is over half again as large as Carleton. Similarly, although Carleton and St. Olaf are in the same town, among students who reported a preference for a rural institution, 45 percent were St. Olaf-oriented and 22 percent were Carleton-oriented; among students who prefer an urban environment over a rural campus, Carleton came out ahead (45 percent to 35 percent). And finally, although both institutions are colleges, among students who prefer a college over a university, 46 percent were St. Olaf-oriented versus 31 percent who were Carleton-oriented; students who prefer universities came out in favor of Carleton (40 percent to 30 percent). Clearly, St. Olaf has images that distinguish it from Carleton, some of which even run counter to objective indicators. "Small" means something more than size; "rural" involves something more than location.

Two other results should be mentioned briefly. The greater the education of the parents, the more Carleton-oriented the students are; and the higher the student's combined PSAT/NMSQT scores, the more a Carleton orientation is found.

The comparison of Carleton with St. Olaf used the results from a survey question that explicitly asked for a rating of the two schools (Question 20). An analog for the ratings had to be manufactured for the University of Minnesota from Question 7, in which students were asked to name up to four schools that "present the best opportunities for students with high academic potential." A total of 27 percent of the students named Minnesota and not Carleton, 18 percent named Carleton and not Minnesota, 8 percent named both, and 47 percent named neither. When Minnesota was named and not Carleton, we infer that in a direct rating the student would be likely to rate the university over Carleton; in the second group Carleton would be rated over the university. We will consider only these two groups.

Students who react very positively to the phrase private college are less likely to mention Minnesota as a best institution (11 percent) than they are to mention Carleton (30 percent). Students who rate the phrase racial diversity positively are about equally likely to mention the two institutions (20 percent Minnesota, 23 percent Carleton); among students who react negatively to this phrase, or who are indifferent to it, however, Minnesota outdraws Carleton by over 2 to 1 (35 percent versus 15 percent).

When size of student body is rated as a very important attribute, Carleton receives more mentions as best (27 percent) than Minnesota does; when size is not important or only slightly important, Minnesota is mentioned five times as often as is Carleton. The results are similar for the ratings of campus activities and setting (neighborhood, etc.). Very important ratings for campus activities result in Carleton's being mentioned 20 percent of the time and Minnesota 18 percent; not important or slightly important ratings give Minnesota the edge, 37 percent to 14 percent. When setting is very important, Carleton and Minnesota are equally likely to be listed as best institutions; when setting is unimportant or only slightly important, Minnesota has a commanding position (40 percent mention Minnesota, 13 percent mention Carleton).

There are several other situations where students strongly differentiate between the University of Minnesota and Carleton, but the distinctions are obvious and there is not much either Carleton or Minnesota can do to change things except stress the positive aspects when they fit. For example, when students greatly prefer a rural atmosphere, they mention Carleton 20 percent more often than when they prefer an urban environment. Carleton can offset some of the disadvantages of its location while preserving its advantages by continuing to facilitate student access to the Twin Cities. Minnesota is also vulnerable when students prefer an academically select student body – as 53 percent of the respondents do – rather than more open admissions, and Carleton benefits to a degree from this distinction.

On the other hand, Minnesota has a strong position when price is very important. Carleton is not so badly *hurt* by a concern about price as Minnesota is *helped* (as measured by mentions as a best institution). Among students who report that price is very important, Minnesota is mentioned by twice the proportion (36 percent) as it is among students for whom price is not important or only slightly important (17 percent); among the highly price-conscious group Carleton is mentioned by 18 percent, while among those who care less about price, Carleton is mentioned by 24 percent.

Finally, in this detailed analysis of Carleton's position, it should be noted that among the 11 students who listed Carleton as a first-choice application, the most frequently cited reason for choosing Carleton over the second-choice institution was its smaller size; 3 of the 5 students who gave this reason listed a Minnesota public institution as the second choice (one listed Harvard and the fifth listed no specific institution).

TOWARD A TWIN CITIES STRATEGY AND THE RESEARCH TO VALIDATE AND REFINE IT

While many of the results discussed above seem, in retrospect, to be common knowledge, the implications for Carleton's recruiting strategy within the state may be profound. Certainly top priority is to validate these findings via research with larger samples, through more qualitative inquiry, or both. Let us consider some elements of a strategy that might emerge if these findings withstand further scrutiny.

St. Olaf appears strongly positioned within the state as a high-quality, small, warm, friendly college concerned with important religious values – indeed, it is seen as the best of this type of institution. Carleton, on the other hand, also appears to be considered of very high quality, but it has a harsher, more cosmopolitan, and more national image. It would probably be difficult for Carleton to supersede St. Olaf on the dimensions where St. Olaf is now dominant. Furthermore, it appears on at least three counts that it might be inadvisable for Carleton to try to do so. First, the closest very selective private *university* to the Twin Cities is in Chicago. Among the Minnesota private colleges, Carleton is the most selective, and it has some of the diversity (particularly geographic and racial) and the visibility more closely associated with universities than with colleges. It has a faculty that, for a *college*, is relatively active in scholarship and research, and it seeks to provide opportunities for undergraduate involvement in research in many of its departments. Despite its size, Carleton may well be able to provide some "private university benefits" for students who do not wish to travel very far to get them.

Second, St. Olaf's applicant pool is only a small fraction of the state pool, compared with the pool for the University of Minnesota, and Minnesota is vulnerable to competition in areas where Carleton is strong. A 1 percent improvement in Carleton's success competing against the University of Minnesota—which could be attempted via better promotion and appropriate pricing and financing policies, rather than by changing the character of the college—would yield as many more new applications for Carleton as would a much larger percentage gain against St. Olaf. Third, the kind of marketing necessary to compete better against Minnesota is congruent, by and large, with what is necessary to compete better nationally, whereas competing more effectively against St. Olaf might diminish Carleton's national attractiveness.

Within the state of Minnesota, the University of Minnesota is unquestionably Carleton's biggest competition. It is against the University of Minnesota that Carleton may well make the most progress in what will increasingly become a zero-sum admissions competition. The other private colleges in the state have rather specialized niches. To compete against one of them (by becoming more like that institution in order to attract its customary applicants) results in a reduced ability to compete against the others and against the University of Minnesota. Only the University of Minnesota tries to be a wide variety of things to a wide variety of students. It may well be vulnerable to an aggressive specialist or a more focused generalist. If or when Carleton chooses to expand its share of the Twin Cities market, it should address the University of Minnesota as its principal local competition.[12]

---

12. At present the percentage that students from the state of Minnesota constitute in Carleton's student body is considered a solid and appropriate base for a college that seeks to serve a national role and constituency. With a generally growing applicant pool, there is little reason to undertake targeted *expansion* in this particular market—except for the attraction of local state aid (direct and via student scholarships). The marketing initiatives of the University of Minnesota will also have to be monitored closely as a protection against application erosion.

Our examination of the University of Minnesota applicant pool gives us some clues about how Carleton might compete and about additional research that should be conducted to further refine our understanding of this market and Minnesota's place in it. It is obvious that a substantial published price difference exists between Carleton and Minnesota; the *net cost* difference after financial aid can be markedly less, however. The financial aid programs of Carleton will have to be marketed very well in the Twin Cities if it is to make gains against this major public competitor. Furthermore, a Carleton education will have to be promoted in a way that relates its additional costs for many students to commensurate benefits. Some benefits are relatively unique to Carleton (when compared with Minnesota)—for example, a broader national academic visibility (for a brief moment when it intellectualized its sports program by hosting the first metric football game, it even had broader athletic visibility), a more national and cosmopolitan mix of students (the direct educational benefits of the student body should be emphasized), and a smaller, more accessible campus and set of extracurricular activities.

University of Minnesota applicants were the most concerned about career outcomes among the three institutions whose applicant pools we examined. The career benefits of a Carleton education should be stressed when the college is competing for the Minnesota-bound student. The students who are headed for Minnesota appear likely to prefer a nondenominational religious atmosphere over a denominational campus; Carleton's singular position as a nondenominational private college in this market should be exploitable among these students.

In these data, Minnesota's applicant pool contained substantial proportions of students who seek two of the principal hallmarks of Carleton—selectivity (40 percent) and a studious atmosphere (40 percent). As marketing themes, however, these two characteristics do not appear equally promising for use in winning students from the University of Minnesota. We have noted earlier that perceptions of what constitutes "selectivity" may present some problems for Carleton—students appear to draw the line much lower than it would be drawn at Carleton. To promote selectivity, an educational program would have to be mounted regarding what selectivity is and what its benefits are for the student. Focusing on this attribute, however, in a market where selectivity is not generally as highly regarded as in other markets, and where Carleton is already seen as "difficult/tough/competitive," might not win very many more friends. Promotion of its studious atmosphere, and the benefits of such an atmosphere (along with some of the lighter aspects of Carleton), might well be more productive. We need to find out, however, more about what students mean by "studious" and what kinds of evidence they would respond to concerning a desirably studious atmosphere. It seems likely that it will not be pictures of students grinding away in a library; more likely it will be accounts and pictures of students working together on exciting research projects or being rewarded for exceptionally fine pieces of student scholarship—or events such as the metric football game and Carleton's campuswide *international* Monopoly game (played with multinational boards and foreign exchange, and where students speak in the language of the country they are "in").

When students who listed the University of Minnesota as their first-choice institution reported why they chose it over their second choice (Question 14), one reason dominated all others—it was closer to home. (Although 58 percent of these students did not list a second-choice application, most of them answered the question anyway.) Why this is such an important reason is certainly a primary candidate as a focus for further research in this market. Is it for financial or psychological reasons? The answer to this question would give some important clues regarding whether the college should invest some marginal dollars in financial aid or in its transportation linkages to the Twin Cities, if it seeks to attract these students. It also suggests that Carleton should promote the fact that it is by far the closest to home of any institution in its class (national liberal arts colleges that approximate universities in many respects relevant to the undergraduate).

7.

Exploration of a Consortial Perspective and Examination of Three Distinctive Markets: Baltimore/D.C., Dallas/Ft. Worth, and Denver/Boulder

At several points in this book we have alluded to the value of market research for groups of institutions and the ways in which consortial efforts can contribute to the accomplishment of market research: comparative perspectives can be gained, costs (and risks) can be shared, and research efforts can achieve broader legitimacy. Although cooperation in this highly competitive arena can be difficult to achieve, the benefits can be considerable. In addition to cost-effective inputs for institutional marketing planning, the research can lead to suggestions for cooperative marketing efforts. Still more is made of these points in Chapter 9.

This chapter examines our data from a consortial perspective and explores some of the benefits of cooperative market research. Although the Six-Market Study was an institutional effort, we believe that its costs make consortial sponsorship an attractive approach and an appropriate starting point for such research, especially in secondary or expansion markets. A consortium in which Carleton College was already a member afforded an opportunity to explore these issues "after the fact" by analyzing the data from its perspective.

Carleton is a member of the Consortium on Financing Higher Education (COFHE), an organization that comprises thirty selective, high-priced, private institutions.[1] They are located through-

---

1. At the time this report was written, the members of COFHE were Amherst College, Barnard College, Brown University, Bryn Mawr College, Carleton College, Columbia University, Cornell University, Dartmouth College, Duke University, Harvard University, Johns Hopkins University, Massachusetts Institute of Technology, Mount Holyoke College, Northwestern University, Pomona College, Princeton University, Radcliffe College, Smith College, Stanford University, Swarthmore College, Trinity College, University of Chicago, University of Pennsylvania, University of Rochester, Vanderbilt University, Washington University, Wellesley College, Wesleyan University, Williams College, and Yale University.

out the United States and are both universities and colleges (coed and single-sex). For its members, COFHE conducts a series of market research projects (among other things), most of which draw heavily on the data made available through the Admissions Testing Program of the College Board. These reports had demonstrated that there are a number of states where COFHE institutions have collectively almost saturated the high-ability market and a number of other states where the collective share of the consortium is very low. In 1980 questions were raised among the COFHE members about why their collective share of certain markets was so low and what might be done to attract more students from at least some of them. Carleton offered the data from its Six-Market Study for an initial investigation. The results also serve our purpose in this chapter of showing how a consortial approach can help further to sort out attractive markets for either consortial or institutional attention.

Three markets were chosen for study in this COFHE project: the Baltimore/D.C. market is a traditional stronghold of COFHE institutions and could serve as a benchmark because it was well known to consortium admissions personnel; Dallas/Ft. Worth and Denver/Boulder are markets with relatively low current COFHE shares, which appeared as promising areas for expansion (primarily because of their demographics).[2] The highly selective Six-Market sample was somewhat further restricted for this analysis because of the very high selectivity of some of the COFHE institutions; students were included only if they had verbal PSAT/NMSQT scores of 49 or greater.[3] The following analysis from the consortial perspec-

---

2. Consortial and institutional perspectives are not always coterminous, and some adjustments or compromises may be in order in such efforts. The Baltimore/D.C. market is essentially a primary market from the COFHE perspective, although it is a secondary (and perhaps a potential expansion) market for the non-Eastern members. The other two markets were the only ones in the study that were not a primary market for any of the COFHE members and thus were of equal interest (or equally unthreatening) to all the membership. Although Dallas/Ft. Worth scored low from the Carleton perspective in Chapter 5, its examination from the consortial point of view afforded some important marketing insights — even for Carleton.

3. Students with SAT-verbal scores of 500 to 550 had a 50 percent chance of admission to a COFHE institution in 1979 if an application was made. (Of course, the admission rate for this score interval varies considerably among COFHE institutions; this threshold is far below the average SAT level of the total matriculating group at COFHE institutions and also far below the 50 percent admissions probability point for a number of them.) An average gain of 16 points is made between junior year PSAT/NMSQTs and SAT tests taken in the senior year. We have examined some data for the group of students with scores of 63 or greater, although such analysis is difficult because of the small number of students in each city.

tive is abstracted from a report prepared for COFHE from Carleton's Six-Market data (Litten, Finney, and Welsh 1981).[4]

BALTIMORE/D.C.

This is COFHE country. Private institutions dominate this Eastern market (hereinafter called the Washington area), and COFHE institutions stand head and shoulders above their fellow independents. When students were asked to name up to four colleges or universities that were the *best* schools for students with high academic potential, two-thirds of the responses were COFHE members (Question 7). Slightly over one-third of the students listed *only* COFHE institutions, and 58 percent listed a set that was more than half COFHE (only 9 percent did not name a, single COFHE school). The institutions most frequently named were all COFHE members.[5]

Table 7-1. COFHE Applications in Washington Area Market

	Applied to at Least One COFHE	COFHE First Choice	Applied to All COFHE
All PSAT/NMSQT-verbal 49+ ($N=216$) . .	52%	39%	15%
Students with 100% COFHE on "best" list ($N=72$)	78%	76%	28%

Applications are somewhat more difficult to come by than esteem in the Washington area. The COFHE applications represented 37 percent of all the applications listed by Washington area students, and 39 percent of the first-choice applications (Question 13). Table 7-1 shows COFHE application rates for all the students included in this report and for students who listed only COFHE institutions as the best schools.

The individual institutions that garner the greatest share of applications are also largely COFHE, although a public institution (University of Maryland) is most frequently cited as the first choice.

---

4. The COFHE report also involved some interviews with students from the two low-share markets who were enrolled at some COFHE institutions; in this chapter we restrict our attention to the Six-Market survey data.

5. When market-share analysis is performed on behalf of a consortium, it is important that the members share common characteristics. In COFHE's case the members are all private, well-endowed, high-tuition institutions that attract high-ability students.

(Also noteworthy is that the COFHE application rate in the District of Columbia is almost twice the rate in Baltimore.)[6]

This is a highly competitive market. Forty percent of the students listed four applications on their surveys (the maximum allowed in the question), and 58 percent listed at least three.

Student Attitudes and Preferences. Washington area students re-act well to phrases that relate to COFHE's type of institutions and show little positive feeling toward public universities. Table 7-2 shows strong positive responses to private colleges, private univer-sities, liberal arts, and the pursuit of excellence (Question 1).

Students from this Eastern market also display an attraction to the characteristics of COFHE members — private, selective, studious — when asked to choose (Question 10) between contrasting types of institutions (Table 7-3).

On the other hand, a sizable group of Washington area students express attitudes regarding educational costs that are not highly favorable to COFHE schools. Only 27 percent say they prefer or are indifferent to a high-priced school (contrasted with a moderately

Table 7-2. Washington Area Students' Reactions to College-Related Phrases

	Somewhat Positive	Very Positive	Total Positive
Private college	44%	26%	70%
Private university	45	29	74
Liberal arts	32	35	67
Racial diversity.	31	21	52
Pursuit of excellence	31	51	82
Public university	21	7	28

Table 7-3. Washington Area Students' Preferences in Paired Attributes

	Slightly Prefer	Greatly Prefer	Total Prefer
Private (vs. public)	30%	30%	60%
Academically select students (vs. students of varied academic ability).	38	29	67
Studious atmosphere (vs. social atmosphere).	37	14	51
Sizable minority representation (vs. mostly Caucasian)	20	18	38

---

6. This report for COFHE was produced before Georgetown became a member of the consortium; only Johns Hopkins was a local institution at this point.

priced alternative); 32 percent indicate that they *prefer* a low-priced school over a moderately priced institution. (Baltimore students show a higher incidence of concern about price than District of Columbia students do.)

Although students in the Washington area were, in general, positively disposed toward characteristics that pertain to COFHE institutions, they reported both positive and negative images when pushed to do so for a selected set of these attributes (Question 2). Four-fifths of the students listed a specific positive image (or several positive images), and almost three-fourths listed at least one negative image when asked about the term "private college."[7] Coded into broad categories of responses, the principal *positive* images were the following:

High-quality education, challenging	37%
Small classes, low student-to-faculty ratio, good student-faculty relations	20
Smaller campus, fewer students	17
Selective, elite, exclusive	18

The *negative* images associated with private colleges included:

Expensive	46%
Snobbish, upper-class, exclusive	22
Homogeneity, lack of diversity	12
Small	11

The term "liberal arts" evoked substantial numbers of positive images (80 percent gave at least one positive image), with considerably fewer negative images (only 42 percent of the sample listed one or more). The coding of these relatively amorphous responses is more arbitrary and elusive than for more concrete terms. The principal responses given by respondents who listed *positive* images were the following:

Broad opportunities, choices	42%
Basic foundation, preparation for life, general education	26
Breadth, rounding, whole person, balance	22
Explorational, experimental	14
Exciting, stimulating	12

Among the students who listed *negative* images, the following were most frequently listed:

Too broad, unspecialized	28%
Impractical, no career preparation	27
Poor science training, lack of technical focus	16

---

7. The questionnaire did not ask for specific images associated with "private university."

Students were also asked for their specific images relating to the term "public university." Positive images were listed by four-fifths of the students; negative images were given by an equal number. The predominant *positive* images were:

Inexpensive	32%
Diversity	31
Curricular breadth	20
Good facilities	12

Among the most frequently listed *negative* images were:

Large, crowded	55%
Impersonal, alienating, computerized	35
Low-quality teaching, faculty	19
Less selective	12

Washington Area Parents. A generation gap exists in the Washington area that is more extreme in some respects than in other markets. Parents and students had generally similar response patterns in the others. Parents are markedly more COFHE-oriented than the students are in the Washington market. Indeed, the students gave responses similar to those of students or parents in other markets; the Washington area parents stand out in the sample as a distinctive crowd. Selected items from the questionnaire are shown in Table 7-4 to illustrate these differences; included are data on reactions to college-related phrases (Question 1), aspects of colleges rated very important (Question 4), and preferences between contrasting types of colleges (Question 10).

Who Applies to a COFHE School in the Washington Area? We sought evidence regarding the attitudes or personal background conditions that contribute to, or hinder, a COFHE application. Multiple regression was used to see what would best predict whether a student applied to a COFHE institution. In the Washington area a five-variable regression model did a fairly good job of identifying phenomena that contribute to a COFHE application.[8] In our model we included personal background information, ratings of importance

---

8. The complete set of predictors used in these analyses were background — verbal PSAT/NMSQT score, father's education, mother's education, professional father (versus all other occupations), professional mother, number of professionals in family; important attributes — price, careers to which college might lead, graduate/professional school acceptance rate; preferences — public/private, church-related/non- or interdenominational, close to home/moderate distance, studious atmosphere/social atmosphere, students with select academic backgrounds/academically diverse students.

Table 7-4. Intergenerational Comparisons of Washington Area Ratings

	Students	Parents	Differences (Parents minus Students)
Reactions to college-related phrases ("very positive")			
Private college	26%	49%	+23%
Private university	29	45	+16
Small college	17	33	+16
Pursuit of excellence	51	71	+20
Important Attributes ("very important")			
Teaching reputation of faculty	66%	89%	+23%
Scholarly reputation of faculty	43	56	+13
% of faculty with doctorates.	13	34	+21
Graduate/professional school acceptance rate.	44	67	+23
Preferences between paired character- istics* ("greatly prefer")			
Private.	30%	54%	+24%
Studious atmosphere	14	58	+44
Academically selective	28	46	+18

* See Table 7-3 for other member of pairs.

given to various college attributes (Question 4), and measures of preferences for types of institutions (Question 10).

The degree to which a student was concerned about price (tuition, fees, room and board, without consideration of financial aid)[9] was the strongest predictor of an application to a COFHE institution (Question 4). The more important price was rated, the less likely the student was to apply to a COFHE institution. The father's educational level was the next most powerful predictor. Other predictors of consequence were a preference for private institutions over public (when asked to state a simple public or private preference), a preference for institutions moderately far from home over those close to home, and an interest in graduate or professional school acceptance rates (negatively associated, but very slightly). Thirty-

---

9. Students were asked to rate the importance of 25 institutional attributes when selecting a college. We interpret this particular concern about price as an indicator of price sensitivity, particularly when correlated with relevant behavior in the application process. A COFHE application was more highly correlated with interest in this gross price measure than with interest in financial aid or net cost, although the differences between the measures were not great.

nine percent of the variance in applications to COFHE institutions was accounted for by this five-variable model.[10]

Some relationships between these phenomena and COFHE-application rates are shown in percentage form in Table 7-5.[11] These data show the profound effects of the concern about price and of the father's education. Only 29 percent of the students who indicated that the gross price of a college was very important applied to a COFHE institution; almost all the students (96 percent) who rated price "not important" submitted an application. This constitutes a difference of 67 percentage points. While none of the students applied whose fathers had no more than a high school education, three-quarters of the children whose fathers had doctorates applied.

Among the students who listed only COFHE members on their best institutions list, an even better job of predicting COFHE applications can be achieved. The principal predictive variables were concern about price, preference for moderate distance over close to home, professional father, interest in graduate or professional school acceptance rates (negative), and verbal PSAT/NMSQT score. Forty-four percent of the variance in COFHE application probabilities was accounted for by this five-variable model.

When asked directly whether there were colleges they would like to consider but would probably not consider because of costs, over one-quarter of the Washington area students said yes (Question 16). Of the specific institutions listed in response to this question, approximately two in five were COFHE members.[12]

Washington Area Summary. The Baltimore/D.C. market is the strongest of the three COFHE markets we are examining, both because of its proximity to COFHE institutions and because of the educational values of the people in the region. Only the lowest-ability group (in our relatively high-ability sample) failed to submit applications to COFHE institutions at a high rate; this is prob-

---

10. As a benchmark, Spies accounted for 25 percent of the variance in his effort to predict application to a high-cost/high-selectivity institution in the Middle Atlantic region with 1976 data.

11. This table does not reveal the independent effects of each variable on a COFHE application (some of these variables are associated—e.g., father's education and "professionals in family"); regression analysis *does* show the independent effects.

12. We tend to trust behavioral correlations (e.g., applications) with indirect indicators of the effects of price (such as the degree to which price is considered important) more than we trust the direct question as evidence of price sensitivity; when people are asked directly about reasons for college selection, "cost" is too socially acceptable as an excuse for other reasons.

Table 7-5. Washington Area COFHE Application Rates for Various Types of Students

	Applying to a COFHE *School*	*N*	*Maximum Difference**
Importance of price			
Not at all important.	96%	28	
Slightly.	80	30	
Moderately	43	61	67%
Very	29	96	
Father's education			
High school or less	0%	19	
Some college	27	26	
Bachelor's degree.	51	57	47% (74%)†
Master's	57	54	
Doctorate.	74	43	
Student's religion			
Protestant	49%	65	
Catholic	33	64	42%
Jewish	75	24	
None	51	35	
Professionals in family			
None	28%	85	
One parent	58	107	51%
Two parents	79	24	
PSAT/NMSQT-verbal			
Less than 53	26%	50	
53–57	47	58	42%
58–63	51	51	
Greater than 63	68	57	
Preferences			
Public/Private			
Greatly prefer public	14%	7	
Slightly prefer public	21	33	
Indifferent	36	44	44%
Slightly prefer private	65	63	
Greatly prefer private	65	62	
Close/Moderate Distance			
Greatly prefer close.	13%	15	
Slightly prefer close.	16	19	
Indifferent	62	21	20%
Slightly prefer moderate	44	57	
Greatly prefer moderate	64	96	

* This is the greatest difference between groups in application rates (e.g., between Catholics and Jews); groups with fewer than 20 persons have been excluded from the calculation of the maximum difference.
† No one whose father had not been to college applied to a COFHE institution; the size of the group falls just shy of our threshold for minimum size.

ably based on realistic appraisals of admissions probabilities. Parents are particularly prone to display a favorable orientation toward a COFHE type of institution.

Nevertheless, it should be noted that a sizable number of relatively high-ability students do not apply to COFHE institutions in this market and that major obstacles appear to be the perceived price of attendance and the low levels of education among fathers. Efforts to overcome these obstacles might improve the COFHE share of this market, but the relatively high current share indicates that expansion might be difficult.

DALLAS/FT. WORTH

The COFHE position in the Dallas/Ft. Worth (hereinafter called Dallas) market is not strong. When asked to name the best schools for high-ability students, the respondents most frequently named Harvard, Stanford, MIT, Princeton, Yale, and five Texas institutions. In all, 40 percent of the schools listed by these Texans were COFHE members. Over one-third of the students did not name even one COFHE school.

Even fewer apply. Seventy-eight percent of the students in Dallas said they were *not* applying to any COFHE schools, and fewer than one in ten sent more than half their applications to COFHE schools. (See Table 7-6.)

Twenty-two percent of the Dallas students applied to four or more colleges; 39 percent applied to at least three. By these measures, this is the least competitive of the three markets.

Student Attitudes and Preferences. The college-selection behavior of Dallas students is grounded in some basic attitudes and preferences. Dallas students preferred many of the same characteristics in colleges as did students from other cities, but in varying degrees. They preferred an academically select student body over one of varied academic ability about 2 to 1. They preferred liberal arts over technical and vocational, but to a lesser degree than did stu-

Table 7-6. COFHE Applications in Dallas/Ft. Worth Market

	Applied to at Least One COFHE	COFHE *First* Choice	*Applied to* All COFHE
All PSAT/NMSQT-verbal 49+ (N = 170) . .	22%	14%	5%
Students with 100% COFHE on "best" list (N = 28)	64%	57%	29%

dents in other cities. They definitely preferred medium-sized over small or large institutions. They strongly preferred a moderately priced institution over a high-priced one, and a moderately priced institution over a low-priced one. They almost unanimously preferred coed schools over single-sex.

Dallas students preferred private over public (5 to 4), but fewer than 50 percent said they preferred the former. The main negative image associated with private colleges, given by 70 percent of the respondents to this question, was that they are expensive. The main positive image, high-quality education, was mentioned by only 28 percent. Universities were widely preferred over colleges (9 to 1). Public universities were seen as inexpensive and offering diverse programs, but also as large, crowded, and impersonal.

Dallas students expressed a preference for a studious atmosphere over a social atmosphere (2 to 1) slightly less often than did Denver students and somewhat more often than Washington students. The Texans preferred students from varied social backgrounds, but less strongly than did students in the East and much less than students in Denver.

Dallas students differ greatly from their peers in other cities in their preferences for racial diversity. Two-fifths of the students preferred a mostly Caucasian student body versus about a quarter in the survey group as a whole. Only 20 percent expressed slight or great preferences for a sizable minority representation, compared with 30 to 45 percent in the other markets.

These Texans preferred institutions at a moderate distance over those close to home, but not by as large a margin as in other cities, and there was little preference for a school far from home. An urban location was preferred 2 to 1 over a rural setting.

Texans gave the least positive ratings among our three markets to the following geographic terms: California, New England, and the upper Midwest (locations of COFHE institutions).

Who Applies to a COFHE School in Dallas? In our total Dallas group, the best predictors of whether a student applies to a COFHE school are preference for a private institution over a public, PSAT/NMSQT-verbal score, low level of concern about price, and preference for a college moderately far away over close to home (listed in descending order of predictive power).[13] The best predictors for the small group of students who list only COFHE schools as "best" were relatively low levels of concern about price, preference for private over public, and PSAT/NMSQT-verbal score.

---

13. These variables accounted for 41 percent of the variance in COFHE applications.

Table 7-7. Dallas Area COFHE Application Rates
for Various Types of Students

	Applying to a COFHE *School*	N	*Maximum Difference**
Importance of price			
Not at all important.	55%	11	
Slightly.	26	27	
Moderately	33	60	26%
Very	7	83	
Father's education			
High school or less	0%	18	
Some college	15	26	
Bachelor's degree.	19	54	20%
Master's	28	40	
Doctorate.	35	23	
Student's religion			
Protestant	21%	116	
Catholic	9	23	12%
Jewish	80	5	
None	18	17	
Professionals in family			
None	12%	81	
One parent	27	93	15%
Two parents	25	8	
PSAT/NMSQT-verbal			
Less than 53	9%	45	
53–57	12	58	53%
58–63	19	26	
Greater than 63.	62	26	

* This is the greatest difference between groups in application rates (e.g., between Catholics and Jews); groups with fewer than 20 persons have been excluded from the calculation of the maximum difference.

Table 7-7 shows how the application rates to COFHE institutions vary among different groups in this market. Particularly noteworthy is the high application rate in the very highest PSAT/NMSQT-verbal group.

Although concern about price was not statistically as strong a predictor of COFHE applications in Texas as it was in the other markets, when respondents were asked directly whether costs were keeping students from considering desired colleges, 43 percent replied affirmatively. Even though this number is larger than the Washington area percentage, the list of specific colleges is not as strongly a COFHE list; slightly fewer than one-third of the institutions named were COFHE members.

The Competition. The major competition in Dallas is from Texas institutions. The four most frequently given as first choice are Texas A&M University, University of Texas at Austin, University of Texas at Arlington, and North Texas State University. *The College Handbook* indicates that all these schools accept at least 70 percent of their applicants. Their sizes range from 12,000 to 34,500 undergraduates. Tuition ranges from $120 to $520 per year. Their minority student representation is generally comparable with, or greater than, that of COFHE schools.

The three next most popular first choices — Rice University, Baylor University, and Trinity University — are somewhat smaller (2,500 to 4,500) and are private schools with higher tuitions ($2,900 to $3,200 per year). They are still considerably less expensive than COFHE schools, and two of them are much less selective. Rice has a substantially lower acceptance rate than the others (32 percent), but preference is given to state residents.

Dallas Area Parents. Except for a somewhat greater parental interest in faculty teaching reputation, graduate school acceptance rates, and studious atmosphere, the preferences, important attributes, and ratings of college-related phrases among Dallas parents were similar to those of the students. (All the differences listed in Table 7-4 between Washington area students and parents were 10 percentage points or less in Dallas.)

Dallas/Ft. Worth Summary. This Texas market has not been a strong one for COFHE institutions, and, in general, attitudes toward COFHE characteristics do not present a very promising prospect. Although a few COFHE members figure prominently among the institutions recognized as the best opportunities for high-ability students, local public *and private* institutions make strong showings. The public institutions dominate applications. True to stereotype, Texans think big; this is university country. There is very little room for single-sex institutions.

Although price concerns are important in this market, other factors appear to set the stage when favorable attitudes do exist toward COFHE institutions. A stated preference for private colleges is important, and a student must be in the group with the very highest ability before COFHE applications are forthcoming; in the highest-ability group, the application rate matches the level achieved in the Washington area. The Dallas market also exhibited an unusually high rate of COFHE applications among the students who primarily identified these institutions as the best. A preference for an institution with a religious affiliation worked against COFHE in this market (it was not of consequence in the East).

DENVER/BOULDER

In the Denver/Boulder market (hereinafter called Denver), the same COFHE schools that appear in Dallas are on the "best" list, although Harvard and Stanford command even more respect in Colorado. Overall, COFHE institutions constituted 48 percent of the entries listed in response to this question, and they outranked local institutions to a greater degree than in Texas.

The gap between the institutions listed as the best and the institutions to which students actually applied was considerable (see Table 7-8).

Although esteem for COFHE institutions runs relatively high in Denver, local institutions dominate as in neither of our other two markets. Even among students who named only COFHE schools on their lists of best institutions, fewer than half applied to COFHE members.

Student Attitudes and Preferences. The institutional characteristics that Denver high-ability students find desirable and that pertain to COFHE institutions are sufficiently general to be of little assistance in developing a broader attraction in Denver. These include a preference for coeducational versus single-sex (91 percent to 4 percent); liberal arts versus vocational or technical (72 percent to 4 percent); residential versus commuter (83 percent to 3 percent); students of a varied social background versus a homogeneous student body (79 percent to 5 percent); and academically selective versus academically diverse (62 percent to 27 percent).

Denver respondents supported a pattern found across the country of an increasingly positive reaction to public universities as one moves from east to west. Equal numbers of students indicated preferences for private and for public institutions. The percentage of very positive ratings given the phrase public university by Denver

Table 7-8. COFHE Applications in Denver/Boulder Market

	Applied to at Least One COFHE	COFHE First Choice	Applied to All COFHE
All PSAT/NMSQT-verbal 49+ (N=207) . .	21%	15%	3%
Students with 100% COFHE on "best" list (N=39)	44%	36%	10%

students was nearly twice the percentage among students from the Washington area. Public institutions enjoy a strong reputation among Denver students as both inexpensive and offering diverse academic programs. The major negative image of private colleges among Denver students is "expensive," and — more than in any other market of the six surveyed — Denver students cited "snobbish" as a negative attribute of private colleges.

Who Applies to a COFHE School in Denver/Boulder? This market appears to be highly price-sensitive (although Boulder may be less so than the rest of the area). A regression analysis of variables that predict students' decisions to apply to COFHE institutions showed concern about price (tuition, fees, room and board) to be the most important factor — the lower the concern, the higher the application rate. Price concerns were followed by preference for moderate distance over close, preference for private over public, preference for non- or interdenominational atmosphere over denominational, interest in the college's graduate school acceptance rate, and mother's educational level.[14] Although PSAT/NMSQT-verbal scores showed a striking pattern in relation to COFHE applications, they did not appear prominently in the regression analysis because their effects were captured by other phenomena with which they are associated.

Forty-five percent of the students indicated there were colleges they had not considered because of costs, and 40 percent of the colleges listed in response to this question were COFHE institutions.

Denver/Boulder Parents. As in the Texas market, the patterns of important attributes, preferences, and ratings of college-related phrases were similar for parents and students. The three exceptions were the same as in Texas: greater parental interest in faculty teaching reputation, graduate school acceptance, and studious atmosphere.

Denver/Boulder Summary. The COFHE institutions and the COFHE characteristics are highly regarded in Denver, but COFHE members draw only modest numbers of applications. Denver/Boulder students show a greater incidence of positive sentiment toward private institutions, a greater willingness to travel, and a greater receptivity toward other regions of the country than do students in Dallas. Despite these favorable aspects, however, fewer than half of even the highest-ability group apply to COFHE institutions.

---

14. These variables accounted for 41 percent of the variance in COFHE applications.

Colleges (as opposed to universities) are more highly rated and also appear with greater frequency among the top application recipients in Denver than in Dallas.

Low levels of concern about price and a willingness to leave the immediate area are the strongest predictors of COFHE applications in this market.

COMPARISON OF THE THREE MARKETS FROM THE COFHE PERSPECTIVE

Common traits in the "cultures" of these three markets are noted in Table 7-9. (None of these markets showed a concern regarding price to the degree of its importance in Chicago or the Twin Cities.) Noteworthy differences among the markets, which affect COFHE institutions in general, are noted in Table 7-10.

The Washington area not only exhibits *behavior patterns* that are more oriented toward COFHE institutions than are those of the low-share markets, the latter exhibit some *attitudes* that are less favorable to COFHE as well. Public institutions have a more positive image in both of the low-share markets than they do in the East.

Table 7-9. Phenomena Common to All Three Markets*

Public/Private
At least 50% positive response to private college, private university; not as high for public university.

Price
Rating of importance of price predicts COFHE application slightly better than does importance of financial aid or net cost.
≈ 1/4 at least indifferent to high price versus moderate price.†

Qualitative Issues
At least 60% prefer academically selective over academically diverse student body.
At least 50% prefer studious over social atmosphere.
At least 50% give positive response to liberal arts, independent studies, international programs.
At least 75% give positive response to pursuit of excellence.

Important Attributes
At least 50% report following attributes very important: teaching reputation, fields of study, career outcomes.

Background Variables
Parental education: important contribution to COFHE applications in each market.

* Data from student responses.
† Two choices were requested: high versus moderate price and low versus moderate price.

Table 7-10. Principal Differences among Markets*

Baltimore/D.C.	*Dallas/Ft. Worth*	*Denver/Boulder*
Public/Private		
Prefer private 3:1	Slight edge for private	Equal public/private
Less than 1/3 positive rating for public university	Slightly less than 1/2 positive for public university	Over 1/2 positive for public university
Distance		
Prefer moderate over close 4:1	Prefer moderate over close only 1.7:1	Prefer moderate over close 2.3:1
≈ 1/3 at least indifferent to great distance from home	Same as Washington area	45% at least indifferent to great distance
Price		
Concern about price best predictor of COFHE application	Price third best predictor	Same as Washington area
Qualitative Issues		
6% negative reaction to liberal arts	19% negative to liberal arts	12% negative to liberal arts
≈ Equal preference between mostly Caucasian and sizable number of minorities	Prefer mostly Caucasian 2:1	Prefer sizable minority 2:1
12% negative reaction to racial diversity; 50% positive	20% negative; 32% positive	10% negative; 52% positive
Important Attributes		
10% social atmosphere very important	25% very important	33% very important
10% religious atmosphere very important	20% very important	16% very important
Ability		
PSAT/NMSQT-verbal not shown in application prediction model	PSAT/NMSQT-verbal second-best predictor of COFHE application	Same as Washington area
Increasing application rate with increasing scores; only lowest quartile has low rate; 2/3 of top quartile apply	Only highest quartile students apply at greater than 25% rate; ≈ 2/3 of top quartile apply	Steady increase in applications with higher score levels

* Data from student responses.

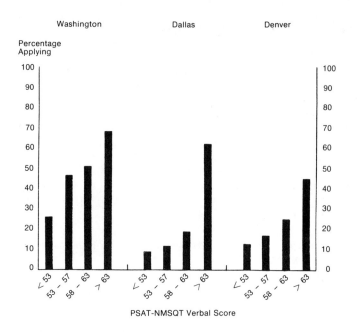

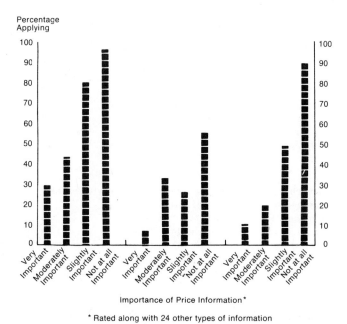

Figure 7-1. Percentage of Students Applying to a COFHE School by Verbal Score and Concern about Price

There are some differences between these less familiar markets, however, that should be noted. Although Dallas's students appear more likely to be favorably oriented toward private institutions than Denver's, its students also appear less likely than Denver's to be willing to travel beyond the local area, less favorable toward the liberal arts, and not very positively disposed toward multiracial environments. Dallas also has the largest minority in the three markets with strong concerns about an institution's religious atmosphere.

The ability threshold for applying to a COFHE school is much higher in Dallas than in the other two markets; once this threshold is crossed, however, the highest-ability group in the Texas market exhibits behavior similar to the Washington area patterns. Figure 7-1 shows these relationships in graphic form. In the Dallas market the most effective strategy would appear to be cultivation of the group just below the highest-ability levels (verbal PSAT-NMSQTs 58–63), since almost two-thirds of the highest-ability group already submit applications to COFHE schools; this second-level group is still highly admissible (to the limited degree that test scores reflect admissibility). In Denver, on the other hand, application rates are more directly tied to verbal score levels across the entire spectrum; but even in the top group, fewer than 50 percent submit applications. The top-ability group in Denver appears to offer opportunity for expanded recruitment.

Figure 7-1 also shows the inhibiting effects of concern about price in each market. The effects are strongest in Colorado and weakest (or most inconsistent) in Texas.

LOW-SHARE MARKETS AND SPECIFIC TYPES OF COFHE INSTITUTIONS

In this section we dig for as much evidence as we can regarding the relative advantages that different types of COFHE institutions may have among students in each of the two low-share markets.[15]

Universities. Dallas students slightly prefer universities over colleges (45 percent to 36 percent), but the proportion who prefer universities in Denver is almost equal to the Dallas proportion

---

15. This cannot be an exhaustive treatment of COFHE issues because the research was not designed specifically to answer these questions for the COFHE membership. Unless otherwise noted, "preference" combines both "strongly prefer" and "moderately prefer."

(43 percent). A slightly larger proportion in Dallas than in Denver are indifferent to this distinction. Dallas students are slightly more likely to rate the phrase private university very positively (31 percent) than they are to give very positive ratings to the phrase private college (24 percent); Denver students rate the two types of private institutions almost equally.

Colleges. A very slight advantage exists for colleges in Colorado (especially outside the city of Denver), compared with Dallas. In Denver the number who prefer colleges equals the number who prefer universities, whereas fewer students in Dallas favor colleges than the number who prefer universities.

Single-sex institutions. Preferred by a very small number in either market, single-sex colleges enjoy a considerably stronger attraction in Denver than in Dallas (2.4 percent strongly prefer single-sex colleges in Denver, an additional 1.44 percent slightly prefer; no one strongly prefers single-sex colleges in Dallas, 1.14 percent slightly prefer).

Urban institutions. Preferred over rural institutions in both markets, but more strongly in Dallas (54 percent, or 2.2 times the preference rate for rural in Dallas; 43 percent, or 1.2 times the rural preference rate in Denver).

Rural institutions. Stronger attraction in Denver than in Dallas (35 percent prefer them in Denver, where 43 percent prefer urban institutions; only 24 percent prefer them in Dallas).

California institutions. More positively regarded in Denver than in Dallas (68 percent positive rating for California in Denver; 41 percent in Dallas).

New England schools. More positively regarded in Denver than in Dallas (56 percent positive and 14 percent negative in Denver; 34 percent positive and 28 percent negative rating for New England in Dallas).

Upper Midwestern schools. Slightly better regarded in Denver than in Dallas (25 percent positive and 30 percent negative rating for upper Midwest in Denver; 10 percent positive and 29 percent negative rating in Dallas).

MARKETING IMPLICATIONS

The Consortial Perspective

At this point we leave the COFHE report per se. Many marketing implications for COFHE institutions were explored in the report, based both on the Six-Market data and on interviews held with

COFHE students from the low-share cities and with admissions officers who knew these markets directly. We will not dwell in detail on these recommendations here, but simply report their major thrusts. The "saturation" of the Baltimore/D.C. market and of the very top group in Texas were noted; in the latter market, the possibility of expanding into the second-level ability group was discussed. In the Colorado market, the top-level ability group was identified as a prime target. The effects of price sensitivity in all three markets were observed, and the need to promote the distinctive benefits offered by these institutions (particularly their national student bodies and national socioeconomic roles) was stressed.

The Institutional Perspective

We have advocated consortially sponsored market research as a mechanism for producing collective marketing insights and generating initiatives that can benefit a group of similar institutions. It has also been held up as a cost-effective means of obtaining expensive, but valuable, inputs into institutional planning. (Given the politics of cooperative direct action, the latter may be the most viable benefit of collectively sponsored research.) Because this report is essentially an institutional case study, we continue along this path by examining the marketing implications of this consortial analysis for Carleton College.

Baltimore/D.C. Although recognition of Carleton is relatively low in the Washington area market (28 percent had heard of Carleton), the attraction of the kind of institution Carleton represents is very strong. The marketing challenge for Carleton is to achieve identification with the set of schools that is so highly esteemed in this market and that commands a strong share of the applications, and then to differentiate itself in important ways. (It should also be noted that name recognition among parents occurs at over one-and-a-half times the rate that it does among students; 45 percent of the parents had heard of Carleton.) By most objective indicators, Carleton does compare favorably with the institutions that are highly regarded in this market. Furthermore, Carleton can compete favorably on the basis of cost; it is among the least expensive institutions in the COFHE set. It also has an opportunity to exploit the fact that it is in a region of the country different from that of most of the institutions that dominate the Washington market. Carleton can appeal to students from these Eastern markets who have a sense of adventure and want to experience the Minnesota culture (shared by Carleton), which is characterized by openness, lack of pretentiousness, and appreciation of hard work.

The general orientation of students in this market toward Minnesota, however, means that Carleton has its work cut out for it. Figure 7-2 shows that approximately one-third of the students gave a negative rating to Minnesota in Question 1; fewer than 1 in 10 gave it a positive rating.[16] When respondents were asked to give positive or negative images they associated with Minnesota, 29 percent gave positive images (30 percent of these students mentioned something relating to scenic beauty; 15 percent mentioned winter and winter sports), whereas 63 percent listed a specific negative image. The cold winters dominate the negative images (54 percent mentioned them), followed by comments relating to the state's isolation, parochialism, dull or mediocre culture (21 percent).

The unenthusiastic response that students have to Minnesota is compounded by the positive regard in which they hold New England. Fewer than one-tenth of the students gave negative ratings to the phrase New England, with over two-thirds rating it positively. Eighty percent of these students gave a specific positive image for New England; slightly over one-half gave a negative image. The negative image most frequently associated with this region is cold and snow (52 percent), followed by something relating to snobbishness, stuffiness, or class rigidity (15 percent). California also has a more positive position among students in this market than Minnesota enjoys, but not by as much of a margin as New England.

Among parents in the Washington area market, however, the picture is not so bleak. The percentage of parents who had a positive reaction to Minnesota was over twice that of students. Although parents were as equally well disposed toward New England as were students, they were not so positive about California.

Carleton may well have an opportunity to market against the perceived snobbishness of New England by setting the openness of Minnesota's culture against this particular negative association with the region of many of its most formidable competitors in the Baltimore/D.C. market. Working to Carleton's advantage is the emergence as a national hit of a public radio program from Minnesota ("A Prairie Home Companion") and a book by the show's host (*Happy to Be Here*), which aggressively extol the very Minnesota

---

16. Data from the entire sample (not just the more selected sample used in the COFHE report) are used in the following analysis of geographic perceptions.

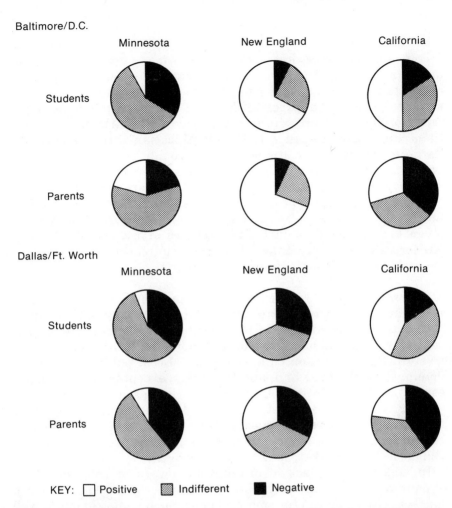

Baltimore/D.C.

	Minnesota	New England	California
Students			
Parents			

Dallas/Ft. Worth

	Minnesota	New England	California
Students			
Parents			

KEY: ☐ Positive ▨ Indifferent ■ Negative

Figure 7-2. Ratings of Other Geographic Areas by Students and Parents in Washington and Dallas Markets

cultural values noted above. These cultural expositions may even help glamorize the specific negative images of the state cited by respondents and turn them into assets. (On the other hand, it will be difficult to pit the climate of Minnesota against the other major negative image of New England—cold weather—and come out ahead; the major challenge here is to disassociate the Twin Cities region from the climatic notoriety of International Falls.)[17]

17. George Dehne used to say that one of his most important challenges was to help people from beyond the Midwest who listen to weather reports of the coldest temperatures in the nation realize that International Falls is almost as far from Northfield as the northern tip of Maine is from Boston.

Principal resources that Carleton may wish to use in this market are its alumni and the parents of current students. They can help carry its message to other parents, who are more likely than students to know and appreciate Carleton and less likely to be negatively oriented toward Minnesota. In addition, Carleton's publications can be used to cultivate the identification of the college with its better-known institutional peers through objective indicators (such as showing where Carleton stands among institutions with regard to endowment per student, merit scholars per 100 students, average SAT scores). These publications can also show, by picture and anecdote, Carleton's association with the culture of Minnesota (even to the extent of including pictures of radio host Garrison Kiellor's appearances on the Carleton campus, or college-sponsored excursions to "A Prairie Home Companion").

Dallas/Ft. Worth. This Texas market presents one of the most formidable prospects among our six sites. Not only is there little recognition of Carleton (only 14 percent of the students and 26 percent of the parents had heard of it), kindred institutions have relatively little recognition or appreciation. Local public institutions dominate much of the high-ability market, except in the very highest ranks. In this latter, elite group, Carleton's strategy might be similar to the one suggested for the Washington area. (A major further burden here, however, is that there is even less positive regard for Minnesota among both students and parents than in the Baltimore/D.C. market; see Figure 7-2 above.)

In addition to a lack of orientation toward private, selective, expensive institutions of higher education, the Dallas/Ft. Worth market is infertile soil for small colleges. Such a market might well be written off as a loss. Its demographic and economic projections make it difficult to dismiss so easily, however. And an institution that seeks a national constituency is reluctant to ignore any part of the country. Therefore, some basic work is required. If this market is to be cultivated by an institution like Carleton, it would be advisable first to sow an appreciation for the type of institution Carleton is. This is a prime candidate for the consortial marketing effort to which we have been alluding. Such long-term, relatively high-risk investments can best be undertaken by spreading the costs of the basic development work over several similar small institutions. Joint recruiting efforts by like institutions would be in order, with both the costs shared and the burden on institutional personnel rotated. Public relations efforts with local media, which feed stories about students at small, private institutions, might also be jointly sponsored. If the cooperating institutions offered a variety of locational benefits (different parts of the country, different rural and urban locations), some variation in specific programs of study, and perhaps different religious affiliations (including none at all), they would be able to maximize the likelihood of benefit to each participant with a minimum of cannibalization of each other's interests. It would be desirable to have a basic comparability of institutional quality and cost, however, so that any classification of institutions by students (or potential for ranking) would be tied to the kinds of benefits just cited; this makes it easier from the recruiters' points of view and easier to legitimate the effort back on campus.

Denver/Boulder. Both in Chapter 5 and in this more detailed analysis from the perspective of some generally similar institutions, the Denver market has emerged as a relatively attractive expansion market for a national college like Carleton. Therefore, we examine this market in greater depth in Chapter 8.

8.

Further Exploration of a Potential Expansion Market (the Denver/Boulder Market)

Denver is a metropolitan area with very promising demographic and economic projections; indeed, it can be considered the "capital" of the region that Joel Garreau (1981) calls the Empty Quarter, the most richly endowed of the "nine nations of North America." He asserts, "If our short-term futures will be shaped by new limits, then the Empty Quarter is on the potter's wheel of history" (310). A sizable portion of the Denver/Boulder student population is oriented toward Carleton's type of institution. And Carleton itself has a modest degree of name recognition in Denver. Of the six markets in this project, Denver emerged as the most attractive target for expansion of the Carleton marketing effort.[1]

---

1. Chicago was an attractive market for analysis as a secondary market. It scored second only to the Twin Cities in our mechanistic Market Attractiveness Index (Chapter 5). To a large extent, however, this was because of its proximity to Carleton and the absolute size of the market. Analytically, Chicago was also attractive. It is the market for which we had the largest number of institutions with significant shares that were included in our Question 20, where we obtained institutional ratings and images (Northwestern, Oberlin, Wisconsin, and, to a lesser extent, Carleton and St. Olaf); this permits an even more comprehensive analysis of the kind performed in the Twin Cities for Carleton and St. Olaf. But Chicago is not a growing market and it is a crowded market, and even though we believe in sharing the fruits of this kind of inquiry, we believed it wasn't necessary to reveal our entire hand in one round. Finally, for our purposes here, Denver offered a better opportunity to illustrate how an institution might use data such as ours to analyze the marketing opportunities and strategies in an attractive but very low share market.

An ironic development occurred with respect to Chicago, however. Just as the final chapter of this book was being completed, one of the authors learned of the existence of an unpublished report in which the college-selection processes of Chicago-area students were discussed. The data were collected in the late 1950s. The images and ratings of six institutions were reported, and Carleton College was used as a specific example for detailed analysis. The irony was compounded by the fact that the report was in the library of the National Opinion Research Center

The analysis of this market begins with a look at basic preference patterns and geographic ratings, followed by data on the structure of the competition (both in esteem and in applications). The preferences, concerns, and personal or family characteristics that correlate with ratings of Carleton are then examined. We look in some detail at two groups: (1) students who rate Carleton high but are applying elsewhere and (2) students who indicate that they prefer an institution such as Carleton but report that Carleton is unknown to them. Finally, we investigate distinctive attitudes, preferences, and application behaviors among geographic areas within the Denver/Boulder market.

GENERAL ACADEMIC ATTITUDES AND PREFERENCES

The preference patterns for institutional characteristics among Denver/Boulder students parallel the patterns found in the total sample, with two exceptions. A stated preference for a public institution is more pronounced in this market than in any of the others; in the total sample the proportion who preferred private institutions was about one-third larger than the group that preferred to go public, but in Denver the two groups were equal in size. Denver students are also less likely than students in any other market except San Francisco to report a preference for a college that is a moderate distance from home over one that is far away; they are only about two-thirds as likely as their peers in the Twin Cities (the most parochial market) to exhibit such disinclinations toward distance. Their preferences for public institutions work against Carleton, but their relative willingness to travel works in its favor.

We also examined the attitudes of students and parents in this market toward other geographic regions. Figure 8-1 shows that Minnesota fares more poorly than either New England or California (the locations of major nonlocal competitors for esteem and,

---

(where the author who discovered it once worked 10 years ago); it had been written by a former director of NORC. The irony was further compounded by the fact that it was produced for the College Board. Information does indeed get lost!

The San Francisco Bay Area market also scored high, as did the Baltimore/D.C. market, on our Market Attractiveness Index. They both achieved their scores by being first on one component, even though they scored relatively poorly on the other components. Denver presents some marketing advantages over these two markets, however, which were not fully captured by the scoring methods in our index— proximity, relatively strong orientations toward Carleton-type institutions and toward Minnesota, and an exceptional set of demographic and economic prospects.

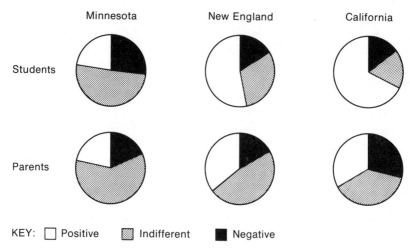

Figure 8-1. Ratings of Other Geographic Areas by Denver/Boulder Students and Parents

to a lesser extent, for applications). Minnesota is more likely to be viewed negatively by students than by parents, but it is less likely to be viewed negatively by students in this market than in most of the others, with the exception of Chicago and, of course, the Twin Cities. California is more attractive to students than New England, but a substantial group of parents react negatively to the Golden State. Indeed, more parents rate California negatively than rate Minnesota poorly—indifference to Minnesota reigns among Denver/Boulder parents. In most of the six markets, parents and students are about equally likely to rate New England negatively, but parents are more likely to be indifferent. On the other hand, in most markets parents are much more likely to rate California negatively than the students are. In their ratings of Minnesota, parents are generally less likely than students to be negative. In Denver/Boulder, Carleton will have to fight the geographic appeal of other locations; it may be able, however, to enlist parents to some degree in these battles.

THE COMPETITION

To understand the structure of competition in this market, we turn again to a multidimensional scaling analysis of the institutions considered by Denver/Boulder students to "present the best opportunities for students with high academic potential" and the institutions to which they are submitting applications. Private uni-

Table 8-1. Institutions Named "Best" by Denver/Boulder Students

Code*	Institution	Times Named
H	Harvard University	117
S	Stanford University	83
Y	Yale University	59
UC	University of Colorado	56
MIT	Massachusetts Institute of Technology	52
P	Princeton University	40
CS	Colorado State University	34
CSM	Colorado School of Mines	27
UD	University of Denver	26
CC	Colorado College	25
LA	University of California at Los Angeles	15
B	University of California at Berkeley	15
CU	Cornell University	14
UNC	University of Northern Colorado	13
N	Northwestern University	11
BU	Boston University	10
D	Dartmouth College	10
CT	California Institute of Technology	9
C	Columbia University	9
USC	University of Southern California	8
ND	University of Notre Dame	8
W	Williams College	8

* Codes used in Figure 8-2.

versities dominate the list of "best" institutions, with Harvard leading the pack by a comfortable margin (Table 8-1). (In Minnesota the top of the list was much more diffused across institutional types — private universities, private colleges, and a public university.) The University of Colorado is the top-ranked local institution, followed by Colorado State with a little more than one-half the citations of the former. Only two small colleges appear on the list — Colorado College (with about as many citations as the University of Denver and the Colorado School of Mines) and Williams College (which barely appears at the lower threshold of the list).

The topography of the higher education market is dramatic in this land of towering mountains. Figure 8-2 shows the two-dimensional plots and the hill diagrams for the institutions named "best" by the Denver/Boulder area students (see Chapter 6 for an explanation of the methods and components of these diagrams). The grouped hills vividly reveal three principal clusters of esteemed institutions. Dominating the picture is a ridge of the most prestigious private universities in the country. To the west, in our diagram as well as in geography, is a cluster of Colorado universities. (This pattern led one of the authors to note at a College Board meeting

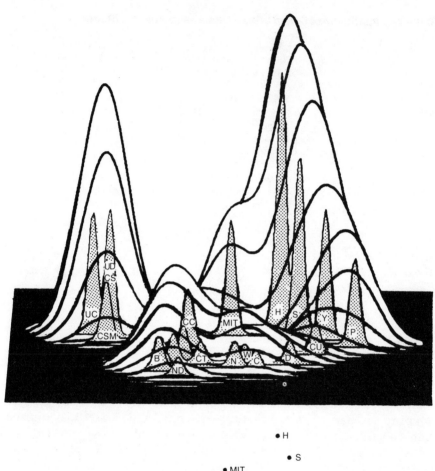

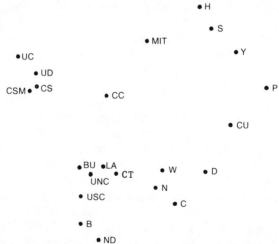

Figure 8-2. Structure of Esteem for Colleges among Denver Students (Best Institutions)

Table 8-2. Applications Submitted by Denver/Boulder Students

Code*	Institution	Times Named
UC.	University of Colorado	107
CS.	Colorado State University	79
UNC.	University of Northern Colorado	20
UD.	University of Denver	18
CC.	Colorado College	17
CSM.	Colorado School of Mines	16
S.	Stanford University	15
H	Harvard University	10
LC.	Lewis-Clark State College	10
CCC	Colorado Community Colleges	9
Y	Yale University	8
G	Grinnell College	7
N	Northwestern University	7
P.	Princeton University	7
W	Williams College	7
M	Metropolitan State College	7
B	Bowdoin College	6
BU.	Boston University	6
A	Amherst College	6
SO	St. Olaf College	6

* Codes used in Figure 8-3.

that we were going to reveal startling evidence that the Berkshires are indeed higher than the Rockies.) In the foreground is a much smaller cluster of geographically dispersed universities and colleges, largely private. Colorado College occupies a position much like St. Olaf's in Minnesota (see Chapter 6) – squarely in the middle of the picture.

When applications are considered, the picture shifts markedly, just as it did in the Twin Cities. Local public universities dominate the list in Table 8-2. The relative ordering of the University of Colorado and Colorado State is maintained, but the University of Colorado's advantage is widened. The local private university, the University of Denver, suffers a substantial relative disadvantage when it comes to applications. Stanford gains over Harvard at application time, and a number of private colleges enter this list. (Although the number of citations at the lower limit is fewer than the number on the "best" list, there were also more institutions on the best list.) Two midwestern colleges appear, including Carleton's hometown competitor, St. Olaf.

Figure 8-3 shows the dominance of local institutions in striking and intriguing patterns. Although the Colorado universities are clustered in the northwest corner of the two-dimensional matrix,

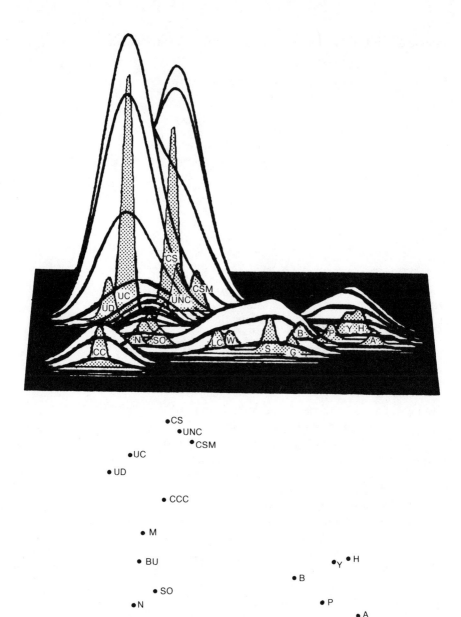

Figure 8-3. Structure of College Choice among Denver Students (Applications)

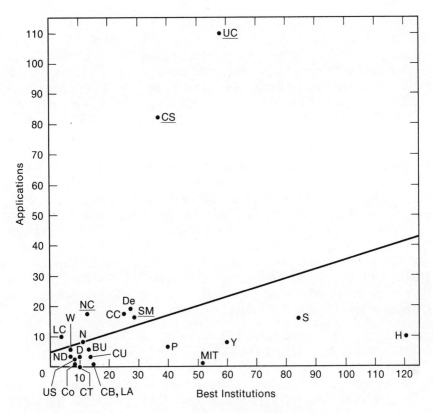

Key to Denver/Boulder Codes

BU – Boston University
CB – University of California at Berkeley
CC – Colorado College
Co – Columbia University
CS – Colorado State University
CT – California Institute of Technology
CU – Cornell University
D – Dartmouth College
De – University of Denver
H – Harvard University
LA – University of California at Los Angeles

LC – Lewis and Clark College
MIT – Massachusetts Institute of Technology
N – Northwestern University
NC – University of Northern Colorado
ND – University of Notre Dame
P – Princeton University
S – Stanford University
SM – Colorado School of Mines
UC – University of Colorado
US – University of Southern California
W – Williams College
Y – Yale University

Note: Plot is limited to institutions with eight or more citations on at least one dimension. Public institutions are underlined.

Figure 8-4. Institutions Named Best and Institutions Receiving Applications among Denver/Boulder Students

the hill diagram assigned separate hills to the University of Colo-rado–University of Denver group and to the Colorado State Uni-versity–University of Northern Colorado–Colorado School of Mines cluster. The world becomes much more highly differentiated when it comes to putting applications on the line. There is an Ivy-Eastern college hill in the east, and Colorado College occupies its own small hill in the left foreground. There appear to be several positioning possibilities for Carleton, with the most promising in or near the central set that includes Northwestern and St. Olaf, or the grouping that includes Stanford, Grinnell, Williams, and Lewis and Clark.

The relationships between citation as one of the best institutions and the institutions to which students are applying are shown in Figure 8-4. Some of the Ivy League institutions are very high in esteem and very low in market share of applications, just as in the Twin Cities. Also as in the Twin Cities, local institutions do better in recruitment than their prestige would predict. Unlike the Twin Cities, *two* public universities dominate the market, making posi-tioning a private institution that much more difficult.

ORIENTATIONS TOWARD CARLETON

Using the ratings of specific institutions from Question 20 in the survey, we examined background and ability variables, importance of college attributes, and preferences for institutional character-istics in relation to students' ratings of Carleton. This analysis was performed from two perspectives: (1) Students who did not know Carleton were assigned a Carleton rating of 0. (2) The rating of Carleton and the other variables were correlated only for stu-dents who rated Carleton on our 1 to 8 scale. The results are shown in Table 8-3.

In the total sample the rating of Carleton (0–8) is a combination of desirability and familiarity, with a weighting toward the famili-arity element because 54 percent of the Denver students who answered this question were not able to rate Carleton. Tested abil-ity showed the strongest, albeit modest, correlation with desirabil-ity and familiarity, followed by preference for a private institution, preference for an institution that is moderately far away as op-posed to close to home, parents' levels of education, preference for a high over a moderate price, and relative lack of interest in the career outcomes of college. A multiple regression analysis of the rating of Carleton accounted for 20 percent of the variance in the

**Table 8-3. Variables That Correlate with Students' Ratings
of Carleton in Denver/Boulder***

	Total Sample†	Students Who Know Carleton
Combined PSAT/NMSQT score	.30	
Prefer private over public	.28	
Prefer moderate distance over close	.24	
Parents' educational levels.	.23	.23
Prefer high over moderate price	.23	
Importance of career outcomes.	−.22	
Prefer college over university	.19	
Prefer far over moderate distance	.19	
Prefer no fraternities or sororities	.15	
Prefer sizable minority representation	.15	
	N = 179	83

* Only correlations with statistical significance of .05 or less are reported.
† Carleton was rated 0 for students who had not heard of it.

rating with four variables. In order of independent explanatory
power these variables were the following: combined PSAT/NMSQT
scores, preference for a private institution, preference for a nondenominational institution, and preference for a college (over a
university). Among only the students who rated Carleton, most of
the statistically significant correlations disappeared, largely because of the reduced size of the sample — smaller sample sizes mean
that observed correlations are more likely to be due to chance — but
partly because of the greater homogeneity of the remaining students. Only parental educational levels correlated significantly
with the ratings of Carleton in this group, and the correlation is
relatively small. These data suggest that if Carleton is to search for
students in the Denver market, it may be well advised to start its
quest among relatively high-ability students in families where educational levels are high.[2]

Well-Disposed Nonapplicants

Let us turn to an analysis of the 41 students who rate Carleton a
highly desirable institution (rated 6 or greater) but are not applying. As in the Twin Cities analysis, we call these students the well-

---

2. Among students who rated Carleton, the following correlations with other institutions' ratings were observed (nonraters of the other institutions were scored 0
on the ratings of each institution) — Stanford (.45), Harvard (.40), Oberlin (.35), and
St. Olaf (.25).

disposed nonapplicants. First we need to understand the specific images these students have of Carleton. Several simply wrote "liberal arts" when asked for a specific image. Others wrote "good education," "excellent school," or something in that vein. One student wrote "radical, liberal students."[3] These are generally positive, if not very telling, images.

Where are the well-disposed nonapplicants going and what kinds of academic preferences and concerns do they exhibit? Seventy-five percent of the first-choice applications of this group went to private institutions, and 69 percent of all their applications went to the private sector. Only 23 percent of the first-choice applications, however, went to institutions like Carleton (small, rural, private, coed colleges). The most frequently named first-choice institution in this group was Colorado College, with 15 percent of the entries; for this college, however, it is almost a first-choice-or-nothing situation—only an additional 2 percent of the students submitted a lower-ranked application. Apart from Colorado College, Grinnell College in Iowa was the closest competitor of a type similar to Carleton (it received applications from 13 percent of these students).

The second-largest number of first-choice applications from this group went to Colorado State; it suffers a situation similar to Colorado College's—10 percent of the students submitted a first-choice application and 17 percent submitted an application among their first four choices. The University of Colorado, on the other hand, enjoys a wide share of applications, but most of them are backups to other institutions—8 percent of the students who rated Carleton high submitted a first-choice application to Colorado, but a substantial 37 percent reported that they had applied to the University of Colorado (first through fourth choices). Collectively the Ivy League institutions received first-choice applications from 15 percent of these students. Although there is a higher correlation between Carleton's ratings and the ratings given to Stanford, Harvard receives five applications from this group to Stanford's three. (Further research in this market would seek detailed image information regarding Colorado College, Grinnell, the Ivy League, the University of Colorado, and—previously unknown to us as a major competitor—Colorado State; certainly our eyes will be open

---

3. These images are a little more on target than some held by students who thought they knew Carleton, but who rated it below a 6. One student gave it a 5 and associated the phrase "medical program" with it (if this meant "premed," it wasn't so far off, but if it meant medical school, it was a gross misperception).

and our ears tuned in regarding these institutions until more formal research is undertaken.)

The well-disposed nonapplicants in the Denver/Boulder market exhibit patterns of concern about college attributes, important characteristics, and important information that are very similar to those of their peers in the Twin Cities. They are somewhat more likely, however, to rate international programs very positively (48 percent versus 36 percent in Minnesota). Indeed, among the Question 1 phrases concern for the whole person, character building, independent study, and international programs, the last received the most "very positive" ratings in the Denver/Boulder market, whereas it was second to concern for the whole person among well-disposed nonapplicants in the Twin Cities. The further development or promotion of Carleton's international programs might be marketing steps with a payoff among these students, although how responsive they would be to specific developments in this area remains to be ascertained.

The specific positive and negative images these students associated with phrases such as small college, private college, public university, and liberal arts were very similar to those discovered among their fellow travelers in the Twin Cities. We also explored images associated with geographic regions. The principal negative image of Minnesota is its winters; 52 percent of these students mentioned them. Its scenery was its principal positive image, but only 14 percent mentioned it. To market against New England, Carleton might work to exploit the image of Midwestern openness and friendliness; 25 percent of these respondents associated "snobbishness and cliquishness" with New England.

Carleton-Blind Students

A marketer can always hope to discover a pool of students who seek the characteristics of his or her college, but who simply do not know it exists. We found 19 students in the Denver market who indicated a preference for five of the characteristics that define Carleton, *but who had never heard of Carleton*. For convenience we'll call these students the Carleton-blind. The Carleton characteristics were non- or interdenominational, rural, studious atmosphere, medium size (as opposed to large), and moderate price (as opposed to low); the latter two variables were included to avoid students who preferred a radically different type of institution. The application behavior of these students differs markedly from that of the well-disposed nonapplicant. The Carleton-blind group submitted first-choice applications primarily to local public institutions, with Colorado State in a dominant position (33 percent of the first-choice applications and an application ranked among the first four preferences from 56 percent). Whereas the Carleton-blind students submitted 66 percent of their first-choice applications to public institutions, only 25 percent of the first-choice applications of the well-disposed nonapplicants went to public institutions. (Note that the problem of very small numbers afflicts us again here; the comments that follow are highly tentative.)

Financial considerations appear to play an important role in the decisions of the Carleton-blind students. Not only do they apply in relatively large numbers to local public institutions, they are somewhat more likely than the well-disposed nonapplicant from this market to indicate that price is very important (53 percent versus 41 percent) and much more likely to report that net cost is very important (63 percent versus 36 percent). Thirty-two percent of the Carleton-blind students indicated that moderate cost was among the four most important characteristics in the college they would choose—versus 17 percent of the well-disposed nonapplicants. On a related dimension, Carleton-blind students are much more likely than the well-disposed nonapplicant to associate expensive with private college as a negative image (84 percent versus 48 percent); interestingly, they are also more likely to associate quality education with private colleges (50 percent versus 29 percent). To reach this group, it seems likely that the benefits associated with the costs of a private education would have to be marketed, as well as the financial aid arrangements that can facilitate financing such an education.

Several benefits or promotional themes might have relatively greater promise in reaching the Carleton-blind student than in pursuing the well-disposed nonapplicant. The former are relatively more concerned about career outcomes (79 percent versus 58 percent "very important"), graduate and professional school acceptance rates (63 percent versus 46 percent "very important"), and social atmosphere (58 percent versus 41 percent "very important"). The Carleton-blind students are relatively less well disposed toward the idea of independent study (10 percent versus 29 percent "very positive"), but much more positively oriented toward the concept of concern for the whole person (84 percent versus 45 percent "very positive").

The Carleton-blind students do not appear to be simply waiting to find out that Carleton exists so that they can fulfill their desires; they probably would have applied to Colorado College in greater

numbers had this been so (only 2 of the 19 did). Although they prefer some of Carleton's characteristics, selling of its other basic
features would be necessary with this group in addition to bringing
Carleton to their attention. For example, they are not nearly so
positive about the liberal arts as are the well-disposed nonapplicants (26 percent versus 46 percent "very positive"). Only 11 percent of the Carleton-blind students listed liberal arts as one of the
four most important characteristics of the college they select, and
it was listed fourth by these two students. Among the well-disposed
nonapplicants, one-third of them listed liberal arts as one of the
four most important characteristics, with over one-third of these
students listing it first. More specifically, the well-disposed nonapplicant is much more likely than the Carleton-blind student to
associate breadth of opportunity, choices, and so forth, with the
liberal arts as a positive image (36 percent versus 14 percent).

In the balance, the Carleton-blind student appears to be a somewhat more pragmatic, less intellectual, more cost-conscious individual than is the well-disposed nonapplicant. It will probably be
easier to position Carleton with some singular benefits among the
schools considered seriously by the well-disposed nonapplicant than
to do so for the student who prefers some of its basic characteristics but has never heard of Carleton.

Carleton would search for well-disposed nonapplicants among
types of students different from the groups where Carleton-blind
students are to be found. The former come disproportionately
from well-educated families and are more likely to be students
with very high ability. They are more likely than the Carleton-
blind students to have mothers with graduate-level education (25
percent versus none) and fathers with doctorates (31 percent versus
11 percent). The well-disposed nonapplicant is more likely than the
Carleton-blind student to have average PSAT/NMSQT scores of 59 or
greater (44 percent versus 5 percent).

Three Competing Institutions

In all the analysis to this point, three institutions have stood out
as powerful competitors in the Denver/Boulder market—Colorado
College, the University of Colorado, and Colorado State University.
To understand this market fully and to plot specific strategies and
tactics that take these major competitors into account, an institution would need to know how these three are perceived, their relative strengths, and their weaknesses; in other words, we would
want the kinds of institution-specific ratings and images we had in

the Twin Cities market for St. Olaf and that we indicated a desire to have for the University of Minnesota. A major step in this direction could be taken with the data in this study by means of the analysis of strengths and vulnerabilities that was performed in the Twin Cities for St. Olaf and Minnesota via their applicants or their nominations as "best" institutions. In the Denver/Boulder market this task would be even easier because of the relatively larger number of applicants to each of these three institutions and their high levels of esteem. Since we have already demonstrated this type of analysis, however, we move on in the remainder of this chapter to explore another set of considerations — differences among geographic areas within a metropolitan market.

GEOGRAPHIC DISAGGREGATIONS

To facilitate analysis by submarket, we divided this metropolitan market into its component three-digit zip codes. The areas' names (and zip codes) and the number of cases for each are as follows: Arvada (800), $N = 34$; Littleton (801), $N = 67$; Denver (802), $N = 80$; Boulder (803), $N = 34$; Golden (804), $N = 20$; Ft. Collins (805), $N = 26$; and Brighton (807), $N = 8$. Denver, the central population and business concentration of this area, includes the University of Denver (which does not figure strongly among the groups we were examining). Boulder is the site of the University of Colorado, and Colorado State University is located in Ft. Collins. We have deleted the Brighton area from further analyses because of the extremely small number. The small numbers in some of the other areas should also be kept in mind.

Table 8-4 shows one item from the limited demographic data obtained via the survey — parental educational levels as recorded by the students. Boulder stands out as an area with very high levels of parental education; both mothers and fathers show the highest levels among the six areas. Ft. Collins has relatively high levels of paternal education, but fewer than half the mothers had college educations, and the Ft. Collins area mothers were the least likely to have graduate-level education. Littleton was the third area with high levels of education among fathers, but its mothers were not distinctive on this measure. On another dimension, Boulder students were the most likely to declare "no religious affiliation" by a wide margin (45 percent), and Ft. Collins students were the least likely (9 percent); the four other markets ranged from 21 percent to 25 percent. The PSAT/NMSQT distributions were very similar among the six areas.

Table 8-4. Parental Education in the Denver Market (by Geographic Area)

	Arvada	Littleton	Denver	Boulder	Golden	Ft. Collins
Mother's education						
College plus	53%	50%	44%	71%	42%	46%
Graduate level	16	11	13	21	11	4
Father's education						
College plus	55%	79%	67%	85%	60%	79%
Doctorate	10	16	24	39	15	29
N =	34	67	80	34	20	26

Table 8-5. Important Attributes and Types of Institutions Preferred by Denver Market Students (by Geographic Area)

	Arvada	Littleton	Denver	Boulder	Golden	Ft. Collins
Attributes (very important)						
Career outcomes	76%	76%	76%	56%	65%	69%
Price	59	43	46	38	50	62
Net cost	59	31	49	41	55	69
Faculty scholarship	35	37	44	53	50	62
Setting (neighborhood, etc.)	41	40	45	47	45	31
Preferences						
Private	44%	35%	40%	51%	50%	46%
Rural	30	37	34	30	50	50
College	12	14	19	24	15	21
Nondenominational	60	71	67	73	65	55
Church-related	21	5	20	18	15	16
Selective	70	65	55	67	65	66
Studious	53	47	57	64	55	62
Social atmosphere	21	32	21	18	20	17
Sizable minority group	41	27	30	39	45	30
Small	27	26	23	32	20	39
Far	12	24	22	25	25	26
High price*	15	25	23	48	15	12
	N = 34	67	80	34	20	26

* Prefer or indifferent.

The attributes that students in each of these areas consider to be very important and their preferences between opposite types of institutions are shown in Table 8-5. Three areas show the most distinctive patterns — Littleton, Boulder, and Ft. Collins. The last two reveal their academic ties, but in different ways. Boulder is the academician's dream. Its students are the least likely to be concerned about price and career outcomes and are the most desirous of a studious atmosphere. From Carleton's perspective there are even more attractive aspects to students in the Boulder area. A majority (barely) prefer private institutions, and this is the set of students most likely to prefer a college over a university (here in the home of the University of Colorado, the state's largest and most prestigious public university). The Boulder student is most likely among students in the six areas to prefer a nondenominational institution. These students are also the most likely to prefer, or at least to be indifferent to, high price in a college, by almost twice the rate of any other area. The principal shortcoming in the Boulder area, from Carleton's perspective, is the relatively low level of preference for a rural institution.

Ft. Collins, the site of Colorado State University, the other large and prestigious public institution in the state, presents a much more mixed picture, especially from Carleton's perspective. Students in this area show a very high incidence of preference for a studious atmosphere, relatively high levels of preference for colleges over universities, for rural institutions, and for private institutions. They report the highest level of interest in faculty scholarly reputation among the six areas. Although they report relatively low levels of preference for nondenominational colleges, there is compensation (from Carleton's perspective) by a very high incidence of indifference on this dimension. Two-fifths of these students prefer a small institution. On the less positive side, from Carleton's perspective, these Ft. Collins students exhibit relatively high levels of price sensitivity and relatively low incidence of preference for racial heterogeneity.

Students from Littleton are a more enigmatic group. They show the lowest incidence of concern about net cost, but are the least likely to report a preference for a private institution. There is virtually no demand for church-related institutions in this area, although these students report personal religious preferences similar to those in the majority of the other areas. The students from Littleton are the least likely to prefer a studious atmosphere by a small margin, and the most likely to prefer a social atmosphere by a more substantial margin.

Table 8-6. Denver Market Students' Orientations toward Carleton and Application Behavior (by Geographic Area)

	Arvada	Littleton	Denver	Boulder	Golden	Ft. Collins
Know Carleton	22%	34%	26%	50%	20%	23%
Carleton-blind	9	4	11	3	10	4
Open, know Carleton	+6	+3	+0	+9	+0	+4
	15%	7%	11%	12%	10%	8%
Well-disposed nonapplicants	9%	19%	9%	32%	15%	8%
Private first choice	37	45	39	58	59	43
Very selective first choice	13	25	20	26	18	10
N =	34	67	80	34	20	26

Students in these six areas also differ considerably in their awareness of Carleton, their ratings of the institution, and their application behaviors. Table 8-6 shows that one-half of the students in Boulder knew of Carleton and one-third gave it a rating of 6 or greater (Question 20). They show the highest incidence of preference for the five characteristics used in identifying the Carleton-blind students, but 75 percent of these students who prefer such characteristics are *not* blind to Carleton. On the other hand, Ft. Collins students show relatively little awareness of Carleton, and there are very few well-disposed nonapplicants. Among the students who prefer the five Carleton characteristics, half did not know Carleton. In the Littleton area, one-third of the students knew of Carleton, and one-fifth are well-disposed nonapplicants. Slightly more of the students who prefer the five Carleton characteristics did not know of Carleton than the number who were familiar with it. It is worth noting, in addition, that there are two areas—Denver and Golden—where substantial proportions of students prefer the five characteristics ("substantial" in a relative sense) and in which not a single student with these preferences knew of Carleton. The absolute number of Carleton-blind students is considerably greater in Denver than in Golden, however.

Over one-half of the students in the Boulder area and in the Golden area applied to private institutions as their first choice. A higher percentage of the first-choice applications in Boulder went to very selective institutions than in Golden. Ft. Collins students showed a modest orientation toward private first-choice institutions and a very low incidence of first-choice applications to very selective institutions (even though their incidence of stated preference for selective institutions was similar to the levels in the majority of the other areas). Littleton students were moderately inclined toward first-choice private institutions, but over one-half of those applications went to very selective institutions. There appears to be a solid core of students in Littleton who are oriented toward selective, studious institutions in an environment that has a substantial element of less serious students.

TOWARD A DENVER STRATEGY

There do not appear to be substantial numbers of students in this market who are looking for an institution like Carleton and just waiting to find out that Carleton exists. There are two subareas, however, where Carleton does not appear to be known among students who seek at least some of its characteristics—Denver and Golden. In the entire sample the students who prefer Carleton's characteristics, but who do not know about it, may have other characteristics that reduce the probabilities that Carleton would appeal to them (especially their price sensitivity, career orientation, and relatively low regard for the liberal arts). If Carleton were to pursue these students, not only would it need to make itself visible, it would have to promote its financial aid programs and some of the practical benefits of its programs.

The well-disposed nonapplicant appears to be a more promising target for increased recruitment by Carleton. Local institutions constitute major competition for these students, although a widely dispersed set of private institutions also figures strongly in the overall picture. To plot a strategy effectively for this group, considerable further research is necessary. Some of it can be based on the data in the Six-Market Study (a la the Twin Cities analysis reported in Chapter 6). Much more specific information on the images of these competitors is also necessary, however. Now that they have been identified from this research, these matters can be pursued through conversations with friends of the college who know the market, through additional formal research directed specifically at this market, or both.

Carleton might position itself to take some first-choice applications from Colorado College by emphasizing the educational and developmental advantages for students of distance from home and Carleton's wider visibility or recognition. It might seek to displace some first-choice applications to Ivy League institutions—or to other distant and expensive small, selective colleges—by stressing comparable quality at lower cost, with easier access, in a congenial culture; it might seek, on the other hand, to become a strong second-choice candidate for these very highly selective institutions (which reject over half their highly qualified applicants). There may also be an opening for a University of Colorado–oriented or a Colorado State–oriented strategy similar to the University of Minnesota strategy suggested for the Twin Cities. In each case we would need to know more detailed information on the strengths and weaknesses of these specific competitors; the position of Colorado State appears to warrant particular attention.

Students who are most susceptible to cultivation by Carleton in the Denver market appear likely to be found among the higher-ability groups and among families with high levels of education. Boulder is a particularly attractive market; the principal strategy would be to establish Carleton's identity as a member of the set that includes the nation's most prestigious institutions (name recognition is not a problem) and then to differentiate its benefits (relative proximity, costs, compatible students). Ft. Collins also appears to be an area where Carleton might make some headway, although it is a relatively small market and the cost issues would have to be handled differently than in Boulder (aid and cost-benefit issues would be relatively more important in Ft. Collins).

The analysis of Denver/Boulder as a potential expansion market has not come together quite as neatly as the analysis of Minneapolis/St. Paul as a primary market. Two limitations contributed to this result—Carleton had considerably less visibility and image, and there were virtually no applicants to analyze. We did not know this market well enough to specify a priori the institutions that should be examined as competitors, and we were limited in our capacity to include such coverage when designing a single survey for six markets. Nevertheless, this research has led to a much clearer picture of the relevant competition and has suggested some major components in developing a strategy for targeted advancement of Carleton's recruiting program in this market. Finally, it has suggested key foci for further observation and inquiry, formal and otherwise.

9.

Developing and Implementing a Market Research Agenda

Carleton's market research program seemed just to evolve. There is considerable merit in moving from question to question, problem to problem, research opportunity to research opportunity; such a process has a kind of organic integrity and maximizes the linkages between the research and the institution. On the other hand, working through our various projects and reflecting on the process, we have also seen ways in which it might have been more efficient, more thorough, and more effective. This chapter discusses considerations that contribute to the efficacy of a market research effort and outlines the steps in one approach to a thorough, but affordable and manageable, program. We are not proposing a *model* research program. Institutions of higher education are too complex and too various to impose any such model. The most effective starting point in an institutional market research program is frequently a function of the particular office that is motivated to get started and the issues of interest to its personnel. We propose merely to outline several research activities and to discuss considerations that relate to their execution.[1] We should repeat that our concern is focused on the traditional college-bound student; other considerations may be relevant to older adults or nontraditional markets.

In developing a market research agenda for a particular college, it is advisable to build from the simple to the more complex; from the information close at hand to less accessible data. The market research process should be a dual effort that is both ongoing and evolutionary, on the one hand, and focused on particular problems at any given moment. The major piece of research reported in this volume represents a fairly advanced stage in a multiple-project, multiyear process. In this chapter steps are suggested that could profitably precede such research.

---

1. We also suggest an organizational model for such efforts (the marketing team); see Green, Kemerer, and Baldridge (in press) for a discussion of several other organizational models for enrollment management, another term for marketing.

Several firms are offering to colleges research packages that include surveys of multiple audiences, usually along with a proposal to develop a marketing or publications strategy. We believe the costs of such efforts often exceed their value and that they have some characteristics that severely limit their utility (especially when compared with the general strategy we are recommending). These massive, one-shot, externally produced efforts carry several major risks:

- The research process is not institutionalized so that it becomes an integral part of the institution's thinking and behavior—that is, research fails to become an attitude as well as an activity.

- The process of successively refining the questions relating to the complex phenomena under study and the ongoing sensitizing process associated with an evolutionary approach are compromised —that is, individual and institutional learning processes are often pushed beyond an efficient limit.

- The capacity of the institution to absorb the changes that may be suggested by the research can often be strained beyond limit when too much is learned about too many things at once; therefore, these reports often get shelved before they are sufficiently exploited.

- There is a risk that someone else's questions (or a standard set of questions) will be asked on the institution's behalf.

There are many times when external assistance or counsel are essential for the conduct of academic market research, but we firmly believe that the role of these resources is limited and should be used only as an adjunct to a homegrown effort.

A BASIC MARKETING ASSESSMENT PROJECT

A useful starting point for any well-grounded and well-developed market research program is a systematic examination of the assumptions that people in the college make about the institution and its markets, an exposition of the intuitive wisdom and experience of its marketing personnel (informal data), and a review of relevant formal operations or research data already in hand. No existing institution starts the market research and marketing process in a vacuum. A great deal of intelligent insight is present in any academic institution; it is often the product of extensive individual experiences in higher education and close contact with the institution's clientele. (Considerable bias and misinformation probably also exist; sorting the information from the error is one of the functions of formal research.) A staff retreat or an ongoing seminar that focuses on the marketing challenges of a college is a good vehicle for provoking the systematic and comprehensive review of these several phenomena; such an activity can be valuable even for institutions that have already conducted one or more of the specific formal market research activities reported in this book, or other research activities.

Let us describe such an undertaking, with suggestions of possible participants, foci, and formats; as in the rest of this volume, the focus is on the student market and related research.[2] The Basic Assessment Project can be either a retreat of approximately two days or a seminar spread over a number of weeks with meetings of one-and-a-half to two hours. Because of the travel schedules of most admissions personnel, the first format is probably preferable. Carleton, on the other hand, created a Marketing Task Force, which met on a regular basis to review research and to lay marketing plans.

In view of the production and marketing processes of an academic institution, many important participants in such an activity can be identified; in view of the differences across specific academic organizational structures and governance processes, however, there is bound to be variance across institutions. The diffused authority structure of an institution of higher education requires that there be commitment to the marketing and market research activity from the highest levels of the administration. Without such a commitment, the research findings are unlikely to be channeled to key personnel or to be translated into effective action of sufficient scope to make much of an impact. Indeed, there is a good chance that without such oversight and coordination of effort, different parts of the institution may well be working at cross-

---

2. Although we use the term "college" in this chapter to refer to both four-year colleges and the undergraduate units of universities, the marketing problems of the latter are relatively more complex than our "model" explicitly accommodates. Research and marketing planning in universities will generally have to keep the perspectives of both their constituent colleges and the total institution in view. The colleges will probably relate to somewhat different market segments, participate in different competitive structures, and have distinctive market positions, but the general image and position of the university will also affect these phenomena for each college; similarly, the position and the image of the university will have to be attended to in its own right. A multilayered research, planning, and marketing process will probably be required; we have addressed only a single layer in this chapter. Whether a process such as we suggest is simply repeated at the various levels, or a more complex, hybrid model is implemented, will depend on both the structure and the politics of a given university.

purposes. It is important, therefore, to have the chief administrative officer of the campus involved in this Basic Assessment Project. On many campuses this will have to be the president; on other campuses, where the president is principally a fund raiser or political representative, the provost (or the equivalent) may well be the appropriate officer. Most of the productivity of academic institutions is the responsibility of the faculty. In a college, the faculty are not only in charge of production; they also make the critical decisions regarding *what* is to be produced. Therefore it is critical that the dean of faculty (or the equivalent administrator) participate in these discussions and carry the insights of the faculty regarding both their disciplines and their students into these meetings; it will be equally important that the dean carry the insights derived from these meetings back to the faculty.

Pricing in an academic institution can be developed in a variety of ways, with several reference points (Zemsky 1981). Nevertheless, it is usually within the purview of the vice-president for finance that many of these decisions originate or end up. This person may well be an appropriate participant in this discussion. In higher education an elaborate system of net pricing exists, based both on considerations of social welfare and on institutional competition; it is called financial aid. The director of financial aid could be an important participant in this project. Certainly, the director of admissions will be a critical member of the group. The extracurricular life of a college is a major part of its portfolio; the dean of students should be involved in this project. Since much of what the public knows about an institution comes from its public relations activities, the director of public relations may be an important participant. Directors of institutional research, planners, and other officers may well be appropriate persons to include, where they exist. It may also be desirable to include some faculty members, other members of the admissions staff, or some students. Finally, a consultant with experience in academic market research, marketing, and strategic planning can contribute considerably to the direction and level of the activity, if an individual with sufficient expertise (e.g., a marketing professor) is not available on campus. It seems unlikely, however, that a group of more than 10 to 12 persons will be very productive, and 6 to 10 would probably be more desirable.

Working papers prepared by the participants – or by staff members in the admissions office, the institutional research office, or both – will greatly focus and advance the discussion. The purpose of the meeting is also to bring the intuitive and experiential wisdom of the participants into relief for examination and discussion. From the outset the participants should understand that statements about the institution, the market, or the recruitment process should be supported by evidence, anecdotal or otherwise. Each person has a responsibility to ask for evidence from other participants when they make an unsupported statement of "fact" or prescription. An external consultant can often be an effective mechanism for getting beyond statements of opinion to the evidence, or lack thereof, and challenging a given statement with other possibilities. From these statements, and the evidence or lack of evidence, will flow both the initial formulation of a marketing strategy and the market research strategy. Generally accepted facts will move into a marketing strategy; unsupported or conflicting opinions will move into market research questions.

Four broad topics can serve as foci for such a Basic Assessment Project. They are briefly outlined in the following sections; a more detailed market audit can be found in Kotler's text on marketing for nonprofit organizations (1975). A separate working paper on each topic would be an appropriate starting point for each discussion.

I. The Nature and Benefits of the College

Both the generic benefits of the college and its particular benefits should be specified—that is, the benefits it provides by virtue of being a college and those it provides by virtue of being the particular college that it is (type, location, distinctive features). Areas of both strength and weakness should be addressed. It is important to specify not only the academic and intellectual benefits but also the social and economic benefits (including the often ignored benefits of social and career contacts, credentialing, social status conferral, etc.). The costs of obtaining these benefits should also be acknowledged, in terms of dollars, time, and effort. The discussion has to move beyond the rhetoric of a college catalog to scrutinize the college as a social and economic institution that operates within a system of other institutions and as a marketplace where resources are exchanged. The discussion should move with dispatch beyond a focus simply on the institution itself to concern for the institution *and* its relationships with its market(s).

II. The Markets Served

The markets the institution serves should be specified, both by geography and by type of student. It may well be that different types of students are served in different geographic markets (e.g., a denominational college may serve both members and nonmembers in a local market, but only denominational members in a more distant market). The specific benefits from a college (see Chapter 4) that are desired by different market segments should be specified, along with particular needs they may have for services, financing, and so forth.

III. Market Position and Competition

Application and enrollment history should be reviewed in this session, along with some assessment of market share by market segment (or at least the relative position of the institution — e.g., is it dominant or marginal?). The specific institutions with which the college competes for applicants and for matriculants (among applicants admitted to both institutions) should be identified, along with the relative strengths and weaknesses of each competing institution in relation to the college. Since the competition is likely to differ for the various market segments that are served, it should be specified separately for each principal segment.

IV. Future Developments

Possible, or likely, developments in the market and the college should be sketched out, and their implications for the college's specific benefits and relative attractiveness should be explored. Attention should be given to demographic patterns (numbers of people and migration), occupational and economic conditions (and the demand for education at various levels and of various types), financing infrastructure (e.g., the availability of aid), developments by principal competitors (expansion, contraction, etc.), new competitors (e.g., corporate education programs), and any other phenomena that could affect a college's absolute or relative well-being. After a variety of considerations in these areas are developed, a follow-up session might be desirable to explore in detail a limited number of specific scenarios.

Another focus for a session in a Basic Assessment Project might be to test the findings in this book against the particular experiences of personnel in the college or against its own data.

The experiences and wisdom of institutional personnel will be a central resource in this effort. Other available data should not be overlooked, however. The Admissions Testing Program of the College Board is a major source of data, especially if the college has participated in Round II of its Summary Reporting Service. The analytic worksheets printed in the *College Guide to ATP Summary Reports*, which is published by this program, are invaluable aids in collecting and analyzing data on a college's applicant pool.

The comparative data of the Cooperative Institutional Research Program (American Council on Education/University of California at Los Angeles) can occasionally provide insights, although the questions are often of marginal relevance to marketing issues. Furthermore, the standard reports provide institutional "profiles," which have little power of discrimination among institutions, especially within major types, and which distract attention from the essential marketing focus on specific segments that may have distinctive needs, desires, behavior patterns, or problems.

State agencies often have valuable information that can be used in institutional market analysis. Minnesota has a testing program that includes research items about educational plans and specific colleges being considered. The New York State Department of Education has conducted extensive analyses of market structure and institutional position through state testing and financial aid program data; exemplary institutional marketing profiles are available from the department (see Rowse and Wing 1982).

As the marketing and market research program proceeds, a variant of the Basic Assessment Project can be repeated annually to good effect. New data become available through successive projects in the research program. Specific marketing activities need to be reviewed and evaluated. Conditions in the environment and the actions of competitors should be monitored. The experiences of marketing personnel need to be related to other data and appropriate adjustments made in the assessment of each. Occasional review of these concerns by outsiders can make an important contribution.

Although alumni are not an integral part of a college's marketing and market research team, periodic counsel from those with marketing expertise can be an invaluable resource for a college. It is also an excellent means of involving alumni with the institution through their particular expertise, giving them both an understanding of the college—its successes and its problems—and an opportunity to serve where they can often serve best. Although some members of the body academic may not trust nonacademic marketers, if an institution cannot trust its own alumni to give sensitive and responsible marketing counsel, it is in part an indictment of

the quality of the education initially provided by the institution.[3]
Alumni marketing counsel can be used in conjunction with specific
projects (such as the Six-Market Study) or every two or three
years as a general review of marketing activities, market research
projects and findings, and plans for future developments.

MOVING TOWARD THE FUTURE

Following a review like that suggested in the Basic Assessment
Project, a college should determine where it would like to be in the
short term and the midterm (what its character will be, what its
market position will be, etc.). This assessment should attend both to
the protection of the institution's current position against sources
of erosion and to an enhancement of the institution's position
through the exploitation of new opportunities. (These opportunities may emerge from analysis of unfulfilled desires in the market,
weaknesses observed in competitors, or, most important, proposals
that rise out of the creative forces on campus.)

Two steps will probably have to follow simultaneously the specification of institutional marketing and positioning goals. A tentative strategy for reaching these goals will need to be developed;
research should be specified to fill in the gaps in information on
which a more definitive strategy should be based.

The objectives of an institutional strategy are to identify opportunities for the enhancement (or solidification) of an institution's
position in the market and then to specify goals, tactics, and a time-
table for exploiting these opportunities. There are several interrelated starting points for developing such strategies – program
offerings, markets to be served, or competition to be outserved. For
example, an institution may start with a particular program that
it wants to develop, expand, or sustain and then identify the type
of student who is appropriate for the program or who might desire
it, along with the existing alternatives students have for obtaining
the benefits offered by the program (i.e., the competition). Alternatively, a particular type of student might be specified as a desirable
market, the competition identified, and a program-promotional-

---

3. At the same time it must be recognized that a four-year tenure in the role of an
undergraduate is hardly sufficient basis for full socialization to the professional
norms of higher education; even alumni marketers require further education regarding the essence of academe.

pricing strategy devised to attract those students to the college instead of sending them to the competition (either the principal or the most vulnerable competition).

Abstract concerns such as the "character of an institution ten years from now" can become real sinkholes in institutional planning efforts. Unless a highly placed institutional official is especially adept at formulating such a vision in concrete terms, and can generate broad institutional support for such a formulation, committee efforts can grind up hours of effort without much practical result. It may well be advisable to start the strategy planning in a narrow, focused effort: how will we position our institution in the competition for students of type A or against competitor B? This runs the risk of never seeing the forest for the trees, but one cannot cut a path through the forest without tackling a few trees – and academicians are exceptionally adept at retreating from, or avoiding, practical steps in favor of more abstract considerations.

Both the Basic Assessment Project and the efforts to formulate broad or narrow concrete marketing strategies and tactics will undoubtedly raise questions for which answers are not readily available. This will indicate the need for research. In the following section we discuss various means of collecting market research data.

Gathering New Information

There are many ways of gathering information about people, institutions, and markets. The most appropriate method in a given instance depends on what one seeks to know, from whom, and for what reason. It is important to have a clear idea of the questions to which answers are needed, and at least some of the ways in which the answers can be used to formulate actions or clarify issues, before implementing the design of the research and well before its execution. The Introduction to this book gives a general outline of the kinds of questions market research might answer; more detail is provided in our accounting of the questions asked at Carleton College.

When an institution moves on to collecting market research data via direct questioning of students, or prospective students, we believe strongly that current students constitute the primary starting point.

Interviews with Current Students. One major objective at this point in the market research program is to begin to understand the college-selection process and the perceptions of an institution from the students' perspectives—to be able to think like a student. Another objective is to nurture a critical, reflective attitude on the part of the institution's marketing personnel so that all contacts with students and those who influence them provide new information, or reinforce existing conclusions, about the market and the institution's place in it. One useful starting point for gathering new primary data is a series of informal interviews with current students, especially with freshmen. We have found it valuable to have two interviewers present with a group of four to five students. The interviewers can be students, faculty, or administrators (members of the marketing or market research team or an admissions committee, perhaps), and members of a given interview team should be from different constituencies. It may also be useful to have someone from outside the institution participate in some of the interviews (and, perhaps, to conduct a few interviews alone). Although each team member should have a clear idea of the questions to be answered or lines of inquiry to be pursued, a formal interview schedule may undesirably constrain this kind of activity. The two interviewers should discuss their observations after the session and be honest about differences in both their observations and their interpretations of things heard and observed. (It would also be desirable to have one *trained and experienced* interviewer as a member of as many teams as possible.)

The interviews can seek information about the college-selection processes of the students, including the following:

■ Colleges that were involved at several points in the process—institutions considered, investigated, applied to, and chosen among.

■ Sources of information and influence.

■ Benefits or attributes sought in a college.

■ Reasons for selecting specific institutions for consideration or application, for eliminating others, and, finally, for choosing the college attended.

■ Impressions formed about specific institutions and sources of these impressions (especially publications, persons, and experiences).

■ Reasons that friends who might have been admissible at a student's college chose not to apply or not to enroll (this secondhand information has to be treated with due caution, but it is an invaluable source of hypotheses for testing through other means of inquiry).

Periodic interviews with student tour guides can also generate valuable information; in addition, the guides can be asked to make notes following tours or interviews and to write up brief annual reports covering aspects of interest. Tour guides can provide information regarding the kinds of concerns students and their parents express, the kinds of questions they ask, the campus aspects that seem to be noticed (favorably and unfavorably). The tour guides are usually students who are very well disposed toward the college and have thought about what they most like (and perhaps dislike) about it; their own opinions and observations about the campus are also important data regarding what the college is doing right. (As noted in Chapter 2, it is also important to discover whether the tour guides represent specific segments in the student body, in order to understand both the nature and the possible limitations of their observations.)

Application-Form Analysis. A great deal of valuable market research information can be obtained from most application forms, and in successive years they can be modified to provide additional data. The major advantage of application-form information is that it comes without a specific request for research data and is available on all applicants as a natural result of the application process. On the other hand, such data are generally limited to items that are not strictly research items and that have direct significance for the admissions process per se (e.g., the relative ratings of institutions are hardly fair game on an application form). It should be recognized that students' answers to most questions posed on such forms are intended to maximize chances of admissions, sometimes at the cost of more balanced or accurate perspectives. It is usually possible to ask some optional basic information questions that are acknowledged on the application form as strictly research questions (e.g., race, religion, parental occupation or educational background); this "research section" may even be contained on a tear-off portion to stress its separation from admissions (this can be preferable from a research perspective to "optional" questions).

The principal use of application-form data is to ascertain which types of students are most likely to accept offers of admission; the data can also be used to study the correlates of persistence. As much data as possible should be obtained regarding ability, interests, socioeconomic background, level and type of parental education, and education and career goals. Upon reaching this point in a market research program, computer support is essential, especially the capacities for efficiently retrieving data from admissions files and flexible statistical analysis (usually via a computerized statistical package).[4] The Automatic Interaction Detection program mentioned in Chapter 4 is a powerful way of initiating the identification of groups with high, moderate, and low levels of matriculation following admission. Regression analysis, multiple discriminant analysis, or even cross-tabular analysis can also be used to determine whether some characteristics lead to a higher yield than do others. With the judicious use of several "interaction variables" (combinations of characteristics—e.g., home-state males, home-state females, other males, other females), specific groups can be identified that might benefit from targeted marketing efforts. (Of course, one has to move beyond simply documenting differential yield rates to an analysis of why behavior differs—by means of interviews, questionnaires, etc., which get at perceptions, evaluations, and attitudes regarding the institution and its competition.)

Admitted Applicants Surveys. The next escalation of the market research program following exploitation of application-form data may well be a survey of admitted applicants—both matriculants and those who go elsewhere. Models of questionnaire forms for such a survey are easy to come by; several variations are displayed in Appendix C. An early entry in the field was produced by William Elliot at Carnegie-Mellon University and has spawned a number of progeny at other institutions. Of recent questionnaires we have seen, those used by Boston College and by Boston University are especially noteworthy. Chapter 2 demonstrates analysis that can be applied to such questionnaire data; Boston College has also reported some exemplary analysis of their admitted applicant surveys (see various publications by Robert Lay and John Maguire).[5]

A major decision on a survey of admitted applicants is "when to do it?" Carleton has always incorporated its survey as part of its candidate's reply form, via which the admitted student indicates his or her intention to enroll (or not to enroll). This not only expedited the distribution of the questionnaire (only one mailing was necessary and it had to go out anyway, since it was the notification of admission); this mechanism also, it was believed, contributed to the relatively high questionnaire completion rates. On the other hand, some institutions have obtained similarly high return rates

4. Larger institutions, especially research-oriented universities, generally have appropriate computer support for such efforts; its existence is more problematic, but no less imperative, in smaller institutions.

5. It is essential to have the capacity for efficient data entry for computer-assisted analysis when survey research is undertaken; this can often be a problem in smaller institutions.

with questionnaires sent out early in the summer, although the overall picture for summer administrations of such a survey is mixed.

At one point Carleton's marketing advisory group suggested strongly that it was a serious mistake to contaminate the marketing activities of the college with the market research effort; in essence, they said that the good news of admission to Carleton College should not be diminished by the burden of a research request. They speculated that the survey might negatively affect yield. We conducted an experiment that year by attempting to divide the notices of admission randomly into two groups, with one group receiving the survey as part of the candidate's reply form and the other receiving it through a separate mailing one month later. Unfortunately, the two groups did not end up equal in size as random assignment would have made them (one was approximately 400 persons and the other 300). Although we do not know whether there was any systematic bias in the two groups, since they were unequal, the results suggested that the combination of the survey with the notification form did *not* harm the yield of admitted applicants. The simultaneous distribution group had a 3 percent higher yield than the delayed distribution group. The early, combined distribution greatly contributed to the return rate for the survey (77 percent versus 36 percent). The similarity of the yield rates of the groups lead us to believe that the 50-person discrepancy from a random assignment of individuals (350 in each treatment group) did not involve any systematic bias, although this problem was noted too late to permit further investigation, and the experiment has not been repeated. (Another institution has informed us that they delayed the distribution of their form one year with a dramatic reduction in the returns.)

There is always more information that is worth knowing than can be gathered reasonably or analyzed efficiently at any one time; questionnaires should be reasonably short. Certain types of information bear gathering every year: other institutions to which a college's applicants are applying and being admitted to, aid and packaging patterns at competing institutions. Other kinds of information can be gathered periodically, since it is unlikely that patterns will shift dramatically from year to year; it is good to have a set of questions that can be rotated into the questionnaire on a periodic (two- or three-year) basis. Some smaller institutions may well have to repeat a question for two or three years if sufficient numbers of cases are to be available for the analysis of smaller market segments (e.g., geographic areas, religious or ability groupings); the data from several years can then be combined for such analysis. If a new recruiting practice or a new admissions policy is to be evaluated, questions pertaining to that concern may well preempt other basic items in a given year.

One of the things that has not been tested, however, is how much research the market will bear. Carleton's response rates have dropped over the years. Although causal factors are difficult to specify, it is known that the incidence of admitted applicant surveys conducted by colleges and universities has increased over the years. Later in this chapter we discuss various areas that might gain from cooperative market research. The means could probably be devised for distributing a common survey on behalf of a number of institutions that share considerable overlap in applications, and for reporting each institution's own data back to it (with the student filling out only one form). This not only would reduce the burden placed on the student; it might increase the probability of student cooperation so that each institution's research efforts would be enhanced. (Where institutions are willing to share certain kinds of data—e.g., the COFHE institutions—a common form would also increase the value of the research through comparative data.)

Inquiry and Prospect Pool Surveys. Most colleges have many more students who indicate at least a passing interest in the college than the number who eventually apply. These are students with whom visibility is not a fundamental problem, although the degree of familiarity with the college can vary enormously. One of the best directions to expand a market research program beyond an institution's admitted applicants is to this inquiry pool; they at least recognize the college's name, and the college can identify *them* by name. An effective admissions system will record as much relevant information as possible about people who have test scores sent to the college, talk to admissions personnel, write for information about the college, or are called to the attention of college personnel by alumni, counselors, and others. This last source stretches the term "inquiry" to include "prospects"; prospects may not really know about the college, but they have the advantage over inquirers that someone has made a judgment that they may be appropriate for the college; a number of student-initiated inquiries are simply misdirected or naive.

Again, models are available for the conduct of inquiry and prospect pool research. Chapter 2 refers to such a project at Carleton; a paper produced jointly by Boston College and Boston University provides another interesting example of such research (Lay and Bradley 1981).

General Market Survey. Moving out beyond the inquiry and prospect pool is the only way to understand fully the environment in which an institution operates and to test potential expansion markets. It is also the most difficult and expensive kind of market research for a college to undertake.

The focus of such research is the first thing to be determined — what is to be learned about whom? A variety of foci are possible, and an institution will probably want to choose several but not all of them:

- The college's visibility and its specific image(s).
- Who the competition is at various points in the process.
- The basis for college-selection behavior — benefits sought, trade-offs made, knowledge possessed.
- Unmet student desires — programs, information, financing, access.
- Testing potential marketing actions — programs, information and images, pricing and financing, access and distribution. (This element should be a part of all market research to some degree, since information that does not reflect a strong concern for action is not market research.)
- Basic demographic measures — the means by which marketing efforts can be targeted to identifiable groups of individuals.

Certainly the institution will want to direct its research efforts efficiently to markets (groups of students) that it can reasonably hope to serve. "Market" is used here to refer to any grouping of individuals who share certain characteristics, whether it be geographic location, socioeconomic characteristics, or type of benefits sought (or needed). A market research effort should provide the means to refine the understanding of those markets that are the principal sources of current students, and those markets where some expansion of its market share might occur, or perhaps even where an initial foray might be made (although the last is a high-risk venture, both in identifying such a place and then in designing cost-effective marketing initiatives). Existing primary markets are important for several reasons: (1) An institution wants to understand these markets to protect itself against potential erosion. (2) Almost no institutions enjoy such dominant positions in any market that no expansion can take place. (3) The supporting resources — for example, students and alumni who carry goodwill into the market — are usually most available in these markets. Potential expansion markets are those in which the institution now has a marginal share and where similar institutions do not currently dominate the market. (Except for geographic markets, it is often difficult to identify a priori just what the competition is in a particular market segment.) An institution may also have a promising expansion market even where similar institutions enjoy a commanding collective share, if it can effectively differentiate itself on the basis of price, quality, benefits offered, or other marketing factors.

In choosing markets to be studied, however, the difficulties of institutional differentiation (positioning) in higher education should not be underestimated, particularly in geographically distant markets where the probability of firsthand knowledge of either the institution or its students and alumni is greatly reduced. Persuasively demonstrating qualitative differences in higher education is difficult, and the demonstration of other attributes such as ambience and life-style can be even more difficult. Pricing differentiation is easier, but the nexus between price and perceptions of quality is not well understood. Distinctive programs are relatively easily demonstrated to prospective students (especially if the distinction is one of substance or form and not just "quality"), but programs are usually costly to introduce in higher education, at least in relation to the potential scale of demand for specific programs. And the degree to which the consumer of educational services is responsive to innovation, at least in the current socioeconomic climate, is problematic.

Once the topics and the markets to be studied are determined, the means of study must be selected. A reasonable sample source must be identified, which is often a considerable problem. Sometimes high schools will provide lists of students, and some may make facilities available for interviews, if that is the chosen form of data collection; many do not permit access even to the names of students. Denominational colleges can often rely on lists from denominational sources, perhaps originating with the individual churches. Some testing agencies may permit the use of their lists for certain purposes by institutions or groups of institutions. (At present the College Board's Student Search Service files and the American College Testing Program files cannot be used for research purposes.) A variety of other sources may be available and appropriate for certain purposes—membership lists of fraternal, social, or educational organizations; subscription lists; scholarship or honor societies; driver's license registrations; companies that compile lists of names from various sources.

The sponsorship of the research is important, particularly when the research is presented to its subjects. An institution can hardly send out a questionnaire asking blatantly whether the student has even heard of the institution if the cover letter lists its name on the letterhead. Depending on the group and the issues being studied, certain types of sponsorship may enhance cooperation; in certain instances they may intrude upon the validity of the answers. In our project the sponsorship by the College Board of a survey of high salience to students is believed to have contributed substantially to the relatively high rate of return of a very long questionnaire. It was also believed to be a relatively neutral sponsorship and permitted asking questions about institutions by name, including Carleton. Because of the College Board sponsorship, however, asking income information was deemed especially undesirable in the middle of the college-selection process. There are often important trade-offs to be made in this area, and there are often important ethical questions to be resolved. In no way can intentional deception of research subjects be condoned (see Litten 1981a for a preliminary discussion of some of these issues).

Interviews or mail questionnaires? The former have a number of advantages: they can handle more complex issues; obtain certain specific information before obtaining subsequent information that might contaminate the earlier responses (e.g., unprompted recall or associations before asking for answers about named colleges or other phenomena); assure that the intended subject, and only the the intended subject, responds; and generally achieve a higher rate of cooperation. They are also considerably more expensive than mail questionnaires, although telephone interviews cost substantially less than those conducted in person.

Mail questionnaires have the advantage of being inexpensive and considerably less costly than interviews; they often achieve much lower rates of cooperation, however. In the pretest of the Carleton College–College Board project, both interviews and mail questionnaires were tested. The cooperation rate on the telephone interviews was about twice the rate a single mailing achieved (in the eventual mail survey, the second mailing doubled the rate of return achieved by the first), but the quality of the responses was judged to be very similar.

Assessing the Costs and Benefits of Market Research. Research is never a free good. It is critical, therefore, to take a hard look at both its costs and its potential benefits before embarking on a project. All costs should be assessed to the degree possible: finances, personnel, other resources, goodwill (from a job poorly done). These costs should include not only the execution of the project (design, data collection, analysis, reporting), but also the costs of legitimation and approval, effective dissemination of the results, and implementation of the suggested marketing activities. Some of these costs can only be grossly *estimated*, and some can only be recognized as existing at the time the research is conceived — but even their recognition is vital to a full understanding of the research potential and the requirements for realizing its full potential.

Benefits must also be assessed, and these are even more elusive than costs in many instances. Anticipated improvements in market share can be estimated (and stemming deterioration is an "improvement" that may require as much work as standing still in a swift adverse current). However, increases in goodwill (if the job is done well) and heightened sensibilities are much more difficult to estimate, particularly because some of them may have an extended payback period.

After deciding what the college seeks to learn about whom from such an undertaking, and assessing the likelihood of getting the answers via research, the investigators must decide whether the information obtained will be worth the costs incurred or, conversely, whether the lack of information bears potential costs that exceed those of the research. Models exist for calculating the costs and benefits of information and the potential costs of not having information (see Thompson 1979). These models deal effectively with research that is directed to specific program development; however, they do not relate well to research intended to produce a better general understanding of an institution's position in the market and the nature of the market in which it operates. Probably the best way of answering the questions of costs and benefits is to try some research on a limited, but sufficient, scale and then to monitor the effects of activities induced by the research in an experimental context (i.e., with control groups) with sufficient time allotted to permit results to occur. In almost all instances, however, it will be difficult to institute adequate controls, since there are many confounding factors in a given market. It is also difficult to judge whether lack of results, or cost-justifiable results, faults the research or the implementation of activities intended to exploit the research findings. (If the research fails to have any practical implications, its value may well be limited; one must bear in mind, however, that avoiding changes that are unnecessary or unlikely to produce benefits is as practical as successful changes.) Furthermore, the heightened sensibilities that come from even a limited study may well spill over into improvements in the marketing activities directed to nonresearched markets. On the other hand, *limited* experiments may well fail to have the critical mass required to achieve the desired objectives; thus our suggestion above that the research and marketing activities be undertaken on a limited, *but sufficient*, scale. There is no general formula that can specify this threshold. Qualitative evaluations ("Did we really learn something useful from this research, and what?" "Were we able to take some new actions, or persist more confidently in those we were taking as a result of this research?") will be as important as quantitative assessments of marketing research results.

Even with these limitations, the appropriate quantitative data should not be eschewed; what is *appropriate*, however, will depend on the nature of the marketing activities or policies that flow from the research. It will be necessary to set up an efficient system to identify individuals or groups that have received specific marketing treatments – and to have appropriate control groups that have not received such treatment – and then to track certain types of behavior associated with these targeted groups: inquiries (including returns to Student Search mailings), applications, yield from admitted applicants, and so forth. A critical consideration is to allow sufficient time to elapse for the various effects, intended and otherwise, to have a reasonable chance of occurring before the evaluation is terminated. Where no effects are observed, it may be necessary to determine whether the competition also engaged in offsetting marketing activities and (with as much honesty as possible) whether "no observable effect" was really a positive indication of a lack of the deterioration of market share that might have come without the research and the corresponding marketing activity.

THE EVALUATION OF MARKETING ACTIVITIES

In addition to understanding the nature of competition in the market and the values, perceptions, and behavior of consumers, it is important for an institution to evaluate its own marketing activities. General market-share data and assessments of student perceptions and behavior provide some basic information of this sort. An institution should also evaluate the effects of specific recruiting and promotional activities, changes in pricing practices or financing developments, program developments, and other activities (see above). To do this, a college must have an information system that permits monitoring of people from specific markets or the members of groups that have been exposed to a particular marketing practice (and, where possible, the monitoring of control groups of identical or similar people who have not been exposed to the marketing practice in question). The details of such a monitoring system are beyond the scope of this volume; we would emphasize, however, both the need to have effective mechanisms in place to track the inquiry, applications, and enrollment behavior of specific groups and the need to run the evaluation for a length of time sufficient for the effects of the marketing activity to be observable. We would also encourage strict quantitative accounting and other rigorous, but more impressionistic, observations.

It is also important to evaluate the costs and the staffing of recruitment and promotional activities. It is often difficult to assign a "bottom line" in the "net income" sense to academic activities. A more common measure of performance comes from comparative data from peer institutions. The principal problem with such data results from the important structural and procedural variations across institutions (e.g., admissions and financial aid may be combined or separate; volunteer workers perform different types or amounts of work; support services — publications, data processing, etc. — may be performed within or outside the office or the institution; and budgets and organization charts may variously capture operational realities). Nevertheless, periodic efforts to generate comparable data can contribute significantly to refining an institution's understanding of its own operations and assessing potential changes in practice or policy.

The periodic need for operations assessment data is readily apparent, given the rapid changes in costs induced by inflation and marketing developments. One model for generating such comparative data is the research study conducted by an independent agency. See the Lupton and Moses (1978) report on staffing, costs, and activities among colleges, produced by the Academy for Educational Development. The American Association of Collegiate Registrars and Admissions Officers and the College Board (1980) produced a survey of activities and policies in a large variety of institutions, although institutional data are not reported. Likewise, the National Association of College Admissions Counselors and Project Choice have reported general data on recruiting activities (Johnson, Chapman, Dominick, and Griffith, 1980). Another model is for a set of similar institutions to share cost, operations, and staffing data and to produce a comparative report. Smith (1981) has reported a survey of recruiting activities and admissions office staffing and costs among public institutions. The Consortium on Financing Higher Education has conducted a similar study among selective private institutions (the report is confidential, although the survey instrument is available as a model for use by other groups of institutions). For a final resource, see the reports that can be obtained from the basic data bank on small colleges' admissions costs, staffing, and operations, which is administered by the Council of Independent Colleges (formerly the Council for the Advancement of Small Colleges, under which their 1979 publication is listed in the References).

THE VALUES OF MARKET RESEARCH CONSORTIA

An institution's market share is directly related to its well-being and future security. Information that enhances an institution's position in the market and its prospects for increasing or maintaining its share is very valuable—both to the institution and to its competitors. A finite number of students, particularly in certain categories (e.g., the traditional, high-ability student), means that the competition for such students is often a zero-sum situation—one institution's gain is another's loss. Nevertheless, there are powerful arguments for the development of research consortia composed of similar institutions. If groups of similar institutions can join together to increase their *collective share* of the market, and to focus on their collective market share instead of their intra-group competition, each participating institution may well gain (admittedly to the detriment of some other set of institutions). If such collective competition is conducted with full and open commitment to sound educational principles and with a concern for effective social policy, then students will also gain from improvements in services, access, economies. The critical element is the adherence to sound educational and civic principles; consortia can force a number of these issues out into the open and increase the probability that appropriate basic principles will be observed.

Consortia also have a number of practical advantages in market research. Market research is expensive and risky (it is impossible to assure practical answers to complex questions). Consortia can help spread the costs and the risks across a number of institutions. Consortia can enhance the legitimacy of a research undertaking in two important ways. Research subjects may be reluctant to give of their time simply for the benefit of an individual institution (unless they have personal involvements with that institution). More broadly based efforts can appeal to a sense of altruism, since another individual or a particular institution is not expected to reap all the benefits. Second, it is difficult to obtain certain types of information (e.g., awareness or perceptions of a given institution) without some kind of sponsorship that does not broadcast the identity of the individual sponsor(s) but is a legitimate umbrella under which the research can be presented and executed. Consortia can provide such an umbrella.

Finally, as mentioned above, the absence of a hard cost-benefit criterion in higher education makes comparative data of particular value to academic institutions. Consortia can provide this kind of comparative perspective for institutional decisions. Although the provision of data on institutional operations and the sharing of data on the market run counter to nonacademic norms of proprietary information, the entire higher education system will benefit if colleges and universities carry out their commitments to rational inquiry and informed behavior through their own actions. What better testimonial to the principles for which we collectively stand than cooperative investigation of the circumstances that affect each academic institution and affect us all?

Although consortial efforts may reduce the direct costs to the participating institutions associated with a given project, consortial efforts can be dear. The political effort required to legitimate the undertaking and to develop sufficient consensus on a given project should not be underestimated. (See Litten, forthcoming, for further discussion of an existing consortial research enterprise, COFHE, and these several considerations.) The major key to the success of such consortia appears to be both a mutuality of respect among the institutions and a sense of commonality of interest. A major obstacle to achieving such conditions is the common discrepancy between those institutions a given college respects (and would like to be like) and those with which it has a true convergence of interest.

SOME SYSTEMIC CHANGES FOR THE IMPROVED MARKETING OF HIGHER EDUCATION

Our concern has been the value of market research for colleges and universities and the marketing developments associated with such activities. Our work has also impressed us, however, with the need to improve some aspects of the higher education system if the colleges' marketing activities are to serve the public interest effectively and if students and their families are to realize their college preferences.

As noted in Chapter 4, the pervasive effects of the gross price on the eventual college choices came as an unanticipated finding. To a substantial degree, stated preferences for types of colleges are not being met in the choices made during the college-selection process. More specifically focused research is needed to determine the precise nature of these phenomena:

- To what extent is it ignorance of net cost possibilities after financial aid?
- To what extent is it a lack of commitment or values that support the stated preferences in the face of alternative opportunities for spending?
- To what extent is it cash flow problems?

Our conversations with college admissions and financial personnel and with high school counselors following this research suggest that all of these phenomena may be operating and that each requires different educational efforts. A failure by students and parents to understand or appreciate financial aid and financing options requires much more effective information and counseling regarding these matters and effective planning for financing a college education. A failure to appreciate sufficiently the value of investments in higher education, especially high-cost education, suggests the need for a major public relations effort to present the benefits that have been associated with education in various types of institutions.

We also believe that there is insufficient appreciation of the value of selectivity in colleges and the contributions it can make to the creation of a student body that is itself an educationally rich resource. Although it will be difficult for many institutions to increase their selectivity in an era of demographic decline, the promotion of more extensive application activity by students could have benefits for institutions as they seek to assemble diverse student bodies, and for students as they are afforded greater exposure to different institutions.

This will be an exciting, although difficult, era for colleges and universities. We anticipate considerable enterprise in meeting the challenges that are before us. Our optimism leads us to believe that many positive developments will emerge over the next decade in student recruiting and in meeting the needs of individuals and society through the services of colleges and universities. We also expect to see less desirable developments as some institutions try too hard or exercise poor judgment. We strongly believe that the higher education process will have to engage in extensive and serious self-examination and monitoring of its marketing activities. The professional associations have major roles to play in these activities, as do the colleges themselves. We would like to see mechanisms develop through which we attend regularly to issues of the philosophy and the ethics of our intellectual life and the institutions in which it resides. We hope that all colleges that embrace the principles of marketing appropriate to higher education will also endeavor to nurture and sustain a discussion of what makes higher education worthwhile and how its benefits can best be achieved.

References

Internal Carleton College Market Research Reports

Dehne, George. Facts or Near Facts: Strategies. 1978.

Haselkorn, Deborah. An En-Littened Look at Carleton's 1980–81 Yield. November, 1980.

Lamson, George. How Does an Economist Look at College Marketing? [1978].

Litten, Larry H. A Brief Review of Attrition Research Relating to Carleton. February 1976.

Litten, Larry H. The Carleton Market Research and Marketing Program: Why and What. December 1978.

Litten, Larry H. Sharpened Reflections: A Reliability Report on Applicant/Matriculant Research at Carleton – 1976 and 1977. March 1978(a).

Litten, Larry H. Things Our Market Research Has Told Us. March 1978(b).

Litten, Larry H., Marcia Cohen, Donald Morrison, Karen Schilling, and Paul Trow. Mirror, Mirror: A Partial Reporting of Carleton College's 1976 Yield Research. September 1977.

Litten, Larry H., Jan Elder, David Welna, Michael Leahy, and Jennifer Harper. Student Attrition and Persistence at Carleton, or Tales from a SNARC* Hunt. (*Search for New Angle on Retention at Carleton.) October 1977.

Litten, Larry H., and Ellie Layton. An Analysis of High Schools' SAT Submission, Application, and Enrollment Rates at Carleton. November 1978(a).

Litten, Larry H., and Ellie Layton. Principal Competitors for Receipt of SAT Scores. November 1978(b).

Litten, Larry H., Ellie Layton, and Lori Ross. More Reflections from the Applicant Pool: Report on 1977–78 Applicant Research at Carleton College. November, 1978.

Metz, Linda, and Ian Evison. Interim Report on Admissions Research. Part 1, April 1973; Part 2, n.d.

Sullivan, Daniel. The Carleton Applicant Pool. August 1974.

Sullivan, Daniel, and Mona Sadow. Carleton's Image Relative to St. Olaf and the University of Minnesota as Seen by Minnesota High School Seniors. May 1980.

Young, V. Michael. Carleton Admissions: Who Are We Losing, Where Are They Going, and Why Are They Going There? August 1973.

Published Documents and Presentations to Professional Meetings

American Association of Collegiate Registrars and Admissions Officers and The College Board. *Undergraduate Admissions: The Realities of Institu-*

tional Policies, Practices, and Procedures. New York: College Entrance Examination Board, 1980.

Anderson, Richard E. Private/Public Higher Education and the Competition for High-Ability Students. *Journal of Human Resources* 10, 4 (February 1975): 500–511.

Anderson, Richard E. Determinants of Institutional Attractiveness to Bright Prospective College Students. *Research in Higher Education* 4 (1976): 361–371.

Ashby, Sir Eric. The Structure of Higher Education: A World View. *Higher Education* 2 (May 1973): 142–151.

Astin, Alexander W., Margo R. King, and Gerald T. Richardson. *The American Freshman: National Norms for 1980.* Los Angeles: Cooperative Institutional Research Program of the University of California at Los Angeles and the American Council on Education, [1980].

Barton, David W., Jr. Marketing: A Synthesis of Soul Searching and Aggressiveness. In David W. Barton, Jr., ed., *Marketing in Higher Education,* New Directions for Higher Education, no. 21. San Francisco: Jossey-Bass, 1978, 77–84.

Bassin, W. M. A Marketing Technique for Student Recruiting. *Research in Higher Education* 3 (1975): 51–65.

Bennet, Roger C., and Robert G. Cooper. Beyond the Marketing Concept. *Business Horizons,* June 1979, 76–83.

Berry, Leonard, and Bruce Allen. Marketing's Crucial Role for Institutions of Higher Education. *Atlanta Economic Review* 27, 4 (July–August 1977): 24–31.

Berry, Leonard, and William R. George. Marketing the University: Opportunity in an Era of Crisis. *Atlanta Economic Review,* July–August 1975, 4–8.

Berry, Leonard, G. Lynn Shostak, and Gregory Upah, eds. *Emerging Perspectives on Services Marketing.* Chicago: American Marketing Association, forthcoming.

Bowers, Thomas A., and Richard C. Pugh. A Comparison of Factors Underlying College Choice by Students and Parents. *Journal of College Student Personnel,* May 1973, 220–224.

Brodigan, David L. Notes on the Psychology of Price: An Exploratory Study. Paper presented at the Midwestern Regional Assembly of the College Board, Chicago, February 1982.

Brodigan, David L., Daniel Sullivan, and Larry Litten. The Effect of Concern about Price on Application Choices between Private and Public Higher Education Institutions. Paper presented at the Annual Forum of the Association for Institutional Research, Minneapolis, May 1981.

Brodigan, David L., Daniel Sullivan, Larry Litten, and Darrell Morris. The Effect of Concern about Price on College Choice. Paper presented to the Middle States Regional Assembly of the College Board, Philadelphia, February 1980.

Cass, James, and M. Birnbaum. *Comparative Guide to American Colleges.* New York: Harper & Row, 1977.

Chapman, David W. Improving Information for Student Choice: The

National Effort. *National Association of College Admissions Counselors Journal,* June 1979, 23.

Chapman, Randall. Pricing Policy and the College Selection Process. *Research in Higher Education* 10, 1 (1979): 37–57.

Chapman, Randall, and Richard Van Horn. Marketing Approaches to University Admissions. Planning and Administration Paper, Carnegie-Mellon University, Pittsburgh, August 1974.

Coffing, R., and T. Hutchinson. Needs Analysis Methodology: A Prescriptive Set of Rules and Procedures for Identifying, Defining and Measuring Needs. Paper presented at the annual convention of the American Educational Research Association, Chicago, April 1974.

The College Handbook, 1981–82, 19th ed. New York: College Entrance Examination Board, 1981.

Consortium on Financing Higher Education. Review of the Effects of Price on College Choice. Cambridge, Mass., July 1981.

Council for the Advancement of Small Colleges. *A Marketing Approach to Program Development.* Users Manual for CASC Planning and Data System. Washington, D.C.: CASC, 1979.

Cross, K. Patricia. The State of the Art in Needs Assessments. Paper presented at the Conference on Lifelong Learning: Assessing the Needs of Adult Learners, Akron, Ohio, April 27, 1979.

Crossland, Fred E. Learning to Cope with a Downward Slope. *Change* 12, 5 (July–August 1980): 18, 20–25.

Donnelly, James H., and William R. George, eds. *Marketing of Services.* Chicago: American Marketing Association, 1981.

Enis, Ben M., and Kenneth J. Roering. Services Marketing: Different Products, Similar Strategy. In James H. Donnelly and William R. George, eds., *Marketing of Services.* Chicago: American Marketing Association, 1981, 1–4.

Fram, Eugene. We Must *Market* Education – and Here Are Some Guidelines for Doing So, Effectively. *Chronicle of Higher Education,* April 17, 1972, 8.

Fram, Eugene. Marketing Higher Education. In D. W. Vermilye, ed., *The Future in the Making.* San Francisco: Jossey-Bass, 1973, 56–67.

Fram, Eugene. Marketing Revisited: Clarifying Concepts and Strategies. *College Board Review,* Winter 1974–1975, 6–8, 22.

Gaither, Gerald. Some Tools and Techniques of Market Research for Students. In John Lucas, ed., *Developing a Total Marketing Plan,* New Directions for Institutional Research, no. 21. San Francisco: Jossey-Bass, 1979, 31–68.

Garreau, Joel. *The Nine Nations of North America.* Boston: Houghton Mifflin, 1981.

Garvin, David A. Models of University Behavior. Working Paper 82-27. Graduate School of Business Administration, Harvard University, [1982].

Gelb, Betsy. The College of Business: An Industrial Marketer. *The* AASCB *Bulletin,* January 1976, 35–40.

Geltzer, Howard, and Al Ries. The Positioning Era: Marketing Strategy for College Admissions in the 1980s. In College Entrance Examination Board, ed., *A Role for Marketing in College Admissions.* New York: College Entrance Examination Board, 1976, 73–85.

Gilmour, Joseph E., Jr., Ira J. Dolich, and Lou M. Spiro. How College Students Select a College. Paper presented to the Annual Forum of the Association for Institutional Research, Houston, May 1978.

Glenny, Lyman A. Demographic and Related Issues for Higher Education in the 1980s. *Journal of Higher Education* 51, 4 (1980): 363–380.

Goodnow, Wilma E. Marketing Education through Benefit Segmentation. Paper presented at the 21st Annual Forum of the Association for Institutional Research, Minneapolis, May 1981.

Gorman, Walter P. Marketing Approaches for Promoting Student Enrollment in Higher Education Institutions. *College and University,* Spring 1974, 242–250.

Green, Kenneth C., Frank R. Kemerer, and J. Victor Baldridge. *Strategies for Effective Enrollment Management.* Washington, D.C.: American Association of State Colleges and Universities, in press.

Guseman, Dennis S. Risk Perception and Risk Reduction in Consumer Services. In James H. Donnelly and William R. George, eds., *Marketing of Services.* Chicago: American Marketing Association, 1981, 200–204.

Haley, Russell I. Benefit Segmentation: A Decision-Oriented Research Tool. In James F. Engel, Henry F. Fiorillo, and Murray A. Cayley, eds., *Market Segmentation: Concepts and Applications.* New York: Holt, Rinehart, and Winston, Inc., 1972, 196–205.

Hanson, Katharine H., and Larry H. Litten. Mapping the Road to Academe. In Pamela Perun, ed., *The Undergraduate Woman: Issues in Educational Equity.* Lexington, Mass.: Lexington Books, D. C. Heath & Co., 1982, 73–98.

Huddleston, Thomas Jr. Marketing: The Applicant Questionnaire. *College and University* 52 (1976): 214–219.

Hugstad, Paul S. The Marketing Concept in Higher Education: A Caveat. *Liberal Education,* December 1975, 504–512.

Hunt, Shelbey D. The Nature and Scope of Marketing, *Journal of Marketing,* 40 (July 1976): 17–28.

Ihlanfeldt, William. *Optimizing Enrollments and Tuition Revenues.* San Francisco: Jossey-Bass, 1980.

Jackson, Gregory. Public Efficiency and Private Choice in Higher Education. *Educational Evaluation and Policy Analysis,* in press.

Johnson, Dennis L. Market Approach Starts with Product Evaluation. *College and University Business,* February 1972, 48–51.

Johnson, Russell H., David W. Chapman, Charles A. Dominick, and John V. Griffith. Admissions Office Staffing and Policies: How Do You Compare? *National ACAC Journal* 24, 3 (May 1980): 10–13.

Kotler, Philip. A Generic Concept of Marketing. *Journal of Marketing* 36, 2 (April 1972): 46–54.

Kotler, Philip. Applying Marketing Theory to College Admissions. In College Entrance Examination Board, ed., *A Role for Marketing in College*

Admissions. New York: College Entrance Examination Board, 1976, 54–72.

Kotler, Philip. *Marketing for Nonprofit Organizations.* Englewood Cliffs, N.J.: Prentice-Hall, 1975; second edition, 1982.

Kotler, Philip. Strategies for Introducing Marketing into Non-Profit Organizations. *Journal of Marketing* 43 (Winter 1979): 37–44.

Kotler, Philip, and Sidney J. Levy. Broadening the Concept of Marketing. *Journal of Marketing* 33 (January 1969): 10–15.

Krachenberg, A. R. Bringing the Concept of Marketing to Higher Education. *Journal of Higher Education* 43, 5 (May 1972): 369–380.

Larkin, Paul G. Market Research Methods for Improving College Responsiveness. In John Lucas, ed., *Developing a Total Marketing Plan,* New Directions for Institutional Research, no. 21. San Francisco: Jossey-Bass, 1979, 11–30.

Lay, Robert, and David Bradley. Analyzing the Inquiry Pool to Develop Positioning Strategies: Research at Two Universities. Paper presented to the North East Association for Institutional Research, Princeton, N.J., October 1981.

Lay, Robert, and John Maguire. Identifying the Competition in Higher Education: Two Approaches. *College and University* 55, 3 (Fall 1980): 53–65.

Lay, Robert, John Maguire, and Larry Litten. Identifying Distinctive Groups in a College Applicant Pool. *Research in Higher Education* 16, 3 (1982): 195–208.

Lay, Robert, Charles Nolan, and John Maguire. Assessing Market Potential in the Inquiry Pool. Paper presented at the Annual Forum of the Association for Institutional Research, Denver, May 1982.

Lee, Wayne A., and Joseph E. Gilmour, Jr. A Procedure for the Development of New Programs in Postsecondary Education. *Journal of Higher Education* 48, 3 (May–June 1977): 304–320.

Leister, Douglas V. Identifying Institutional Clientele. *Journal of Higher Education* 46, 4 (July–August 1975): 381–398.

Leister, Douglas V., and Douglas L. MacLachlan. Assessing the Community College Transfer Market. *Journal of Higher Education* 47, 6 (November–December 1976): 661–680.

Leister, Douglas V., Robert K. Menzel, and Jane A. Shanaman. Assessing Potential New Student Markets: Meta-Marketing Applications. In Northwest Area Foundation, ed., *Choice or Chance.* St. Paul: Northwest Area Foundation, 1976, 23–45.

Levitt, Theodore. The Industrialization of Service. *Harvard Business Review,* September–October 1976, 63–74.

Lewis, Gordon, and Sue Morrison. A Longitudinal Study of College Selection. Technical Report no. 2, School of Urban and Public Affairs, Carnegie-Mellon University, Pittsburgh, February 1975.

Litten, Larry H. Market Structure and Institutional Position in Geographic Market Segments. *Research in Higher Education* 11, 1 (January–February 1979): 40–59.

Litten, Larry H. Marketing Higher Education: Benefits and Risks for the American Academic System. *Journal of Higher Education* 51, 1 (January–February 1980): 40–59. (1980a).

Litten, Larry H. Marketing Higher Education: A Reappraisal. In the College Board, ed., *Marketing in College Admissions: A Broadening of Perspectives*. New York: College Entrance Examination Board, 1980, 148–157. (1980b).

Litten, Larry H. Avoiding and Stemming Abuses in Academic Marketing. *College and University* 56, 2 (Winter 1981): 105–122. (1981a)

Litten, Larry H. Educational Essentials and the Marketing of Higher Education. In James H. Donnelly and William R. George, eds., *Marketing of Services*. Chicago: American Marketing Association, 1981, 134–137. (1981b)

Litten, Larry H. Different Strokes in the Applicant Pool: Some Refinements in a Model of Student College Choice. *Journal of Higher Education* 53, 4 (July–August 1982): 383–402.

Litten, Larry H. An Independent Perspective on Enrollment Management Issues and Initiatives in the Independent Sector. In J. Victor Baldridge and Kenneth C. Green, eds., *Enrollment Management and the Challenges of the Eighties* (tentative title). San Francisco: Jossey-Bass, forthcoming.

Litten, Larry H., and David L. Brodigan. On Being Heard in a Noisy World: Matching Media and Messages in College Marketing, *College and University* 57, 3 (Spring 1982): 242–263.

Litten, Larry H., Ellen Jahoda, and Darrell Morris. His Mother's Son and Her Father's Daughter: Parents, Children and the Marketing of Colleges. Paper presented at the Middle States Regional Assembly of the College Board, Philadelphia, February 1980.

Litten, Larry, Carol Finney, and Timothy Welsh. *A 3-D Perspective on COFHE Markets*. Cambridge, Mass.: Consortium on Financing Higher Education, September 1981.

Litten, Larry H., Daniel Sullivan, David L. Brodigan, and Darrell Morris. Twixt Cup and Lip: Evidence on the Effects of Price on College Choice. Paper presented at the Midwestern Regional Assembly of the College Board, Chicago, February 1980.

Lovelock, Christopher. *Services Marketing*. Englewood Cliffs, N.J.: Prentice-Hall, forthcoming.

Lovelock, Christopher. Why Marketing Management Needs to be Different for Services. In James H. Donnelly and William R. George, eds., *Marketing of Services*. Chicago: American Marketing Association, 1981, 5–9.

Lovelock, Christopher, and Michael Rothschild. Uses, Abuses and Misuses of Marketing in Higher Education. In the College Board, ed., *Marketing in College Admissions: A Broadening of Perspectives*. New York: College Entrance Examination Board, 1980, 31–69.

Lovelock, Christopher H., and Charles B. Weinberg. *Readings in Public and Nonprofit Marketing*. [Palo Alto]: The Scientific Press, 1978.

Lucas, John, ed. *Developing a Total Marketing Plan.* New Directions for Institutional Research, no. 21. San Francisco: Jossey-Bass, 1979.

Lupton, Andrew, and Kurt Moses. *Admissions/Recruitment: A Study of Costs and Practices in Independent Higher Education Institutions.* N.P.: Academy for Educational Development, Inc., 1978.

MacLachlan, Douglas, and Douglas Leister. Institutional Positioning: A Meta-Marketing Application. In Ronald Curham, ed., *New Marketing for Social and Economic Progress and Marketing's Contribution to the Firm and to Society,* 1974 Combined Proceedings. Chicago: American Marketing Association, 1975, 549–554.

McPherson, Michael S. The Demand for Higher Education. In David Breneman and Chester E. Finn, Jr., eds., *Public Policy and Private Higher Education.* Washington, D.C.: The Brookings Institution, 1978, 143–196.

McPherson, Michael. Quality and Competition in Public and Private Higher Education. *Change,* April 1981, 18–23.

Maguire, John, and Robert Lay. Modelling the College Choice Process: Image and Decision. *College and University* 56, 2 (Winter 1981): 123–139.

Marketing in College Admissions: A Broadening of Perspectives. New York: College Entrance Examination Board, 1980.

Monroe, Kent B., and Susan M. Petroshius. Buyers' Perceptions of Price: An Update of the Evidence. In Harold H. Kassarjian and Thomas S. Robertson, eds., *Perspectives in Consumer Behavior,* 3d ed. Glenview, Ill.: Scott, Foresman, 1981, 43–55.

Northwest Area Foundation, ed. *Choice or Chance: Planning for Independent College Marketing and Retention.* St. Paul: Northwest Area Foundation, 1976.

Peterson, Robin. *Marketing: A Contemporary Introduction.* Santa Barbara: John Wiley and Sons, 1977.

Rados, David L. *Marketing for Non-Profit Organizations.* Boston: Auburn House, 1981.

Richards, James M., Jr., and John L. Holland. A Factor Analysis of Student "Explanations" of Their Choice of a College. ACT *Research Reports,* no. 8, October 1965.

Ries, Al, and Jack Trout. *Positioning: The Battle for Your Mind.* New York: McGraw-Hill, Co., 1980.

Riesman, David. *On Higher Education: The Academic Enterprise in an Era of Rising Student Consumerism.* San Francisco: Jossey-Bass, 1980.

A Role for Marketing in College Admissions. New York: College Entrance Examination Board, 1976.

Rothschild, Michael L. *An Incomplete Bibliography of Works Relating to Marketing for Public Sector and Non-Profit Organizations,* 3d ed. Madison, Wis.: Graduate School of Business, University of Wisconsin, 1981.

Rowse, Glenwood, and Paul Wing. Assessing Competitive Structures in Higher Education. *Journal of Higher Education* 53, 6 (November–December 1982): 656–686.

Russick, Bert, and Paul Olsen. How High School Seniors Choose a College. In Northwest Area Foundation, ed., *Choice or Chance: Planning for*

Independent College Marketing and Retention. St. Paul: Northwest Area Foundation, 1976, 65–75.

Sacks, Herbert. "Bloody Monday": The Crisis of the High School Seniors. In Herbert Sacks and Associates, *Hurdles: The Admissions Dilemma in Higher Education.* New York: Atheneum, 1978.

Saunders, J. A., and G. A. Lancaster. The Student Selection Process: A Model. *Higher Education Review* 13, 1 (Fall 1980): 57–69.

Seymour, Warren R., and Morgan Richardson. Student and Parent Perceptions of a University: A Generation Gap? *Journal of College Student Personnel,* July 1972, 325–330.

Shaffer, Peter Brooks. The Identification of Market Positions of Wisconsin Private Colleges. Unpublished dissertation, University of Wisconsin-Madison, 1978.

Shils, Edward. Governments and Universities. In Sidney Hook, Paul Kurtz, and Milo Todorovich, eds., *The University and the State: What Role for Government in Higher Education.* Buffalo: Prometheus, 1978, 177–204.

Shostak, G. Lynn. Breaking Free from Product Marketing. *Journal of Marketing,* April 1977, 73–80.

Shostack, G. Lynn. How To Design a Service. In James H. Donnelly and William R. George, eds., *Marketing of Services.* Chicago, Ill.: American Marketing Association, 1981, 221–229.

Shostak, G. Lynn. The Service Marketing Frontier. *Review of Marketing 1978,* 1978, 373–388.

Small, H. G. Co-citation in the Scientific Literature: A New Measure of the Relationship between Two Documents. *Journal of the American Society for Information Sciences* 24 (July–August 1973): 265–269.

Smith, Judith L. *A Report on the Staffing, Budget, and Expenditures of Admissions Offices at Selected Institutions.* SAREO Report no. 223 (Peer Institution Studies, no. 3). Amherst, Mass.: University of Massachusetts, Student Affairs Research and Evaluation Office, 1981.

Solmon, Lewis C., and Alexander W. Astin. A New Study of Excellence in Undergraduate Education. Part One: Departments without Distinguished Graduate Programs. *Change,* September 1981, 23–28.

Spies, Richard R. *The Effect of Rising Costs on College Choice.* New York: College Entrance Examination Board, 1978.

Sternberg, Robert J., and Jeanne C. Davis. Student Perceptions of Yale and Its Competitors. *College and University* 53, 3 (Spring 1978): 262–279.

Stewart, Ian, and Donald Dickason. Higher Education Faces: Hard Times Ahead. *American Demographics* 1, 6 (June 1979): 13–17.

Sullivan, Daniel. The Carleton Applicant Pool: An Empirical Study. In Northwest Area Foundation, ed., *Choice or Chance: Planning for Independent College Marketing and Retention.* St. Paul: Northwest Area Foundation, 1976, 47–67.

Sullivan, Daniel, and Larry Litten. Using Research in Analyzing Student Markets: A Case Study. In College Entrance Examination Board, ed., *A Role for Marketing in College Admissions.* New York: College Entrance Examination Board, 1976, 86–106.

Sullivan, Daniel, D. Hywel White, and Edward J. Barboni. Co-citation Analysis of Science: An Evaluation. *Social Studies of Science* 7 (1977): 223–240.

Sullivan, Daniel, and Michael Zuckert. Demography and the Carleton Applicant Pool. *The Carleton Voice* 45 (Fall 1979): 5–9.

Surface, James R. Universities Aren't Corporations. *Business Horizons*, June 1971, 75–80.

Thompson, Fred. The Cost and Value of Marketing Analysis. *Research in Higher Education* 10, 1 (1979): 83–93.

Tierney, Michael L. *The Impact of Institutional Net Price on Student Demand for Public/Private Higher Education.* The Pennsylvania State University, Center for the Study of Higher Education, University Park, Pa., May 1980.

Turner, William H. Courting the Prospective Student. In David Barton, Jr., ed., *Marketing Higher Education,* New Directions for Higher Education, no. 21. San Francisco: Jossey-Bass, 1978, 23–35.

University of California. *Factors Affecting Student Choice.* Berkeley, Calif.: University of California, Systemwide Administration, June 1980.

Webster, Frederick E., Jr., *Social Aspects of Marketing.* Englewood Cliffs, N.J.: Prentice-Hall, 1974.

Windham, Douglas M. Student Marketing, the Public Interest and the Production of Social Benefits. In the College Board, ed., *Marketing in College Admissions: A Broadening of Perspectives.* New York: College Entrance Examination Board, 1980, 121–131.

Wright, Peter, and Maryanne O. Kriewall. State-of-Mind Effects on Predictions of College Choices from Derived and Reported Utility Functions. Unpublished paper, Graduate School of Business, Stanford University, August 1979.

Zeithaml, Valerie. How Consumer Evaluation Processes Differ between Goods and Services. In James H. Donnelly and William R. George, eds., *Marketing of Services.* Chicago: American Marketing Association, 1981, 186–190.

Zemsky, Robert. Toward a Discussion of Price. Unpublished paper, University of Pennsylvania, [1981].

Zemsky, Robert, and Penney Oedel. *The Structure of College Choice.* New York: College Entrance Examination Board, 1983.

Appendixes

APPENDIX A. GLOSSARY OF KEY MARKETING AND MARKET RESEARCH CONCEPTS

This is a glossary of some key marketing and market research terms, with particular emphasis on how they apply to higher education and how they are used in this book. Five other terms (marketing concept; marketing mix; segment, segmentation; position, positioning; market research) are discussed in Chapter 1.

Markets, Marketer, Marketing

A market is an aggregation of individuals or organizations that seek to obtain certain benefits or satisfy certain needs or desires through the *products*[1] provided by others. The demand side of the market consists of the people or organizations (see *consumers*) whose needs are met by the providers (see *suppliers*) on the supply side. Transactions in a market are exchanges between parties on both sides, such that there is some type of reciprocated demand and supply. Usually money flows from the demand to the supply side of a market and a product from the supply side to the demand side — except in markets such as financial markets, where money flows both ways, or political markets, where votes and influence are exchanged.

Marketing is the full set of activities that a supplier of products undertakes in order to manage its relationships with the demand side of the market. *Marketing consists of much more than advertising or promotion* (see *marketing mix* in Chapter 1), although even the "voice of business" — *The Wall Street Journal* — fails to comprehend this at times. Marketing activities that are related to colleges and universities we have labeled "academic marketing" for parsimony.

A profession of marketing has developed among persons who set marketing policies for suppliers and who carry out marketing activities. Marketing is also the term applied to the systematic study of the activities and effects of marketing and the formulation of

---

1. Terms defined elsewhere in this appendix or in Chapter 1 are italicized when first mentioned in relation to a specific concept.

principles to guide the effective conduct of such activities. A marketer is someone who practices or studies marketing. The practitioner is involved in studying the markets in which an enterprise operates and in managing, or advising on, the elements of the marketing mix that determine the enterprise's relationships with its environment.

The terms "marketing" and "markets" have had little currency in higher education, and they often grate on academic ears – particularly those that are attached to heads that fail to comprehend that marketing is not a synonym for advertising. (We have found it curious that English professors, with their professional commitment to precision in the use of language, can be among the most flagrant abusers of the term "marketing.") Nevertheless, colleges and universities do exist in, and operate in, markets; they provide services in exchange for resources controlled by students (or people who support students). A college must conduct marketing activities if the institution is to continue to exist. We have found no other terms to describe these phenomena.

It is unlikely that colleges and universities will develop vice-president for marketing positions, although it has been suggested (Kotler 1979). Marketing will always be diffused throughout a service organization that is populated by professionals who are also intellectuals. The closest that a college might come to a chief academic marketer's position would be an academic dean or a provost to whom admissions, and perhaps alumni relations, also reported (in addition to academic department heads, the librarian, etc.). Diffused marketing responsibilities are not only likely, given current academic structures; they are probably the most effective mode of organization in a service organization that depends on highly complex "technologies" (the academic disciplines). Lovelock and his colleagues suggest as much in their extensive writings on the particular marketing requirements of service organizations, the genre of which colleges are members (Lovelock and Rothschild 1980; Lovelock 1981). What is needed is to assure that these dispersed marketing functions are carried out by personnel with marketing sensibilities and market information, and that marketing policy and practice is informed by a coordinated discussion of such matters (see Chapter 9).

Education, Higher Education, Postsecondary Education

Education consists of activities planned and carried out for the purpose of increasing the knowledge, skills, and sensibilities of individuals. Higher education consists of a set of purposefully interrelated activities that build on the skills and knowledge obtained through secondary schooling. These activities must be marked by discipline and rigor and conducted and evaluated by highly educated or highly accomplished professionals. The purposes of higher education must be to increase intellectual skills and the understanding of oneself *and* the social and physical world in which one lives. Postsecondary education is simply educational activity that follows secondary schooling; it is a broader category, which includes higher education but does not require the latter's intellectual focus or the coherence of its component activities. We are concerned with higher education, although many of the market research techniques we describe can be useful in understanding the markets for postsecondary education.

Consumers

The consumers are the people or organizations on the demand side of the market. They are also called clients in professional markets, buyers in some markets, students in educational markets. Although the term "consumer" is generically used in marketing, it stretches the sense of demand in an educational market, where the passive connotations of the word detract from the active requirements placed on students for successful participation in educational activities. It also blurs the distinctive roles of students (who participate in, and benefit directly from, an educational activity) and parents (who pay a substantial portion of the costs of such participation). The term also slights the investment aspect of expenditures on education, whether made by individuals or by society. We use the terms "students" and "parents" to denote not only roles in the educational process but the principal sources of demand in educational markets.

Suppliers

The individuals or organizations that control or produce the *products* that satisfy *consumer needs* or *desires* are the suppliers. For market exchanges to occur, these suppliers must be willing to provide these products to *consumers* for some consideration (most often in our economy it is money). We use the term "college" to refer to institutions that supply *higher education* to students. (Our use of college generally subsumes universities, and their undergraduate operations, except when we are distinguishing between institutional types.)

Product

A product is any benefit-providing resource that an individual or organization creates expressly to offer to *consumers* in exchange for money or other instrumental resources (e.g., votes for a politician). Such a definition excludes interpersonal affective exchanges, kind deeds, noncommercial athletic activity, and so forth. Products may be physical goods, services (such as *education*), or a combination of the two (e.g., sales and subsequent servicing of physical goods). We are concerned here with the provision of higher education services to students and try to avoid the use of the term "product," since many people equate product with goods. (Colleges and universities produce other outputs that are more like goods when faculty conduct scholarly research that can be distributed via nonhuman vehicles such as books and reports.)

Consumer Needs, Desires, and Preferences

Consumers have needs and desires that can be satisfied by the *products* provided by *suppliers*. Needs and desires are not necessarily synonymous. Needs are the requisites for human existence and may include goods and services that contribute to a philosophically defensible "good life" (beyond mere existence). Specific needs must be compatible with other needs, either because they don't stand in conflict or by striking a balance between conflicting needs – for example, freedom and discipline, strength and compassion, comfort and challenge. Desires may reflect needs, but they can also reflect unresolved or incompatible wants and may lead to unanticipated negative consequences. Some philosophical criterion may define needs that often are not felt naturally by individuals as desires (without education); there is no reason to believe that instincts are sufficient for full individual growth or social existence.

Preferences are the tendencies or dispositions to favor one means (or set of means) for fulfilling needs or desires over alternative means. This may be one product over another or one brand of a given product over another. Since products are bundles of attributes and characteristics (each component of the *marketing mix* defines at least one attribute of a product), preferences for certain characteristics may be contingent upon the existence or nature of other characteristics (e.g., certain levels of quality are preferred only at certain prices).

We believe that educational *needs* have to be the driving principle in developing and delivering educational service; we recognize, however, that desires exist in the marketplace and that a major task of the academic marketer is to help orient desires toward educational needs. Thus a major task of market research is to determine the desires and preferences of consumers so that institutional marketing activities can be sensitive to these very real phenomena.

Consumer Behavior

Consumer behavior comprises the activities in which consumers engage in order to learn about *products* that will meet their needs or desires, to evaluate the options that are discovered, and to obtain the product(s) chosen. The academic marketer's challenge is to understand consumer behavior so that the institution can effectively engage students in interactions, either by accommodating institutional behavior to consumer behavior or by providing means and incentives to change the latter.

Attribute, Characteristic

Products have a variety of defining attributes (e.g., in goods: size, durability, cost, complexity; in services: duration, number of individuals involved, location(s), consumer effort required). Each product possesses a specific characteristic for each attribute—for example, a college's size (the attribute) may be small, medium, or large (the characteristic).

Price, Cost

Price is the stated value of a *consumer*'s resources that a *supplier* expects in exchange for the supplier's *product*. Discounts from the stated price often create a different net price. Discounts are initiated by suppliers to make it less costly for consumers to try an unfamiliar product or to induce particularly desired consumers to buy (e.g., consumers who may bring nonmonetary resources to the supplier—contacts with other consumers, skills, prestige, etc., that can be of benefit to other consumers of a service).

Cost is the amount of consumer resources actually required to obtain a given product. This is often measured in terms of money required, but it also involves time, comfort, effort, self-perceptions, or psychological well-being. The purchase of services generally involves a greater array of costs than does the acquisition of goods.

We use price to refer to published tuition, fees, and residential charges; our use of cost generally refers to net financial outlay (price minus discounts, or financial aid) by students and parents. We do not have relevant data regarding other types of costs, although they may be as important as financial costs—for example, the psychological costs that geographic removal from family may impose, apart from its educational benefits.

Prior conditions to be met by the consumers are also an important component of some costs (e.g., admissions requirements in education). In services marketing, the duration of the service can also be related to costs (as well as to benefits)—graduation requirements are major cost-setting elements in education marketing.

The general category of price in the marketing mix also includes financing arrangements and options.

Access, Availability, Distribution, Place

One of the four P's of the *marketing mix* is place—where and how *consumers* can obtain goods or services that they seek. This most often refers to physical locations, but it also includes when a *product* is available. For colleges this means not only campus (or course) locations, but also academic calendars, course scheduling, residency or fieldwork requirements.

Market Share

The amount of a particular activity or resource that a given *product* or *supplier* enjoys (compared with competitors) is the market share. This may be measured by incidence of recognition by consumers, units sold, dollar value of sales, proportion of *consumers* who buy, or other components of *consumer behavior*. Market share can be measured with respect to total markets or within specific segments. We employ several specific measures of market share.

Market Structure

The demand side of a market is divided into *segments* of various sizes, which are differentiated from other segments on the basis of *consumer behavior*, *needs*, interests, demographic characteristics, or other phenomena that relate to the nature of demand. The totality of these segments and their relationships to each other constitute the structure of the demand side of the market. Knowledge of this structure helps a marketer anticipate how the market will be affected by, and will react to, a particular *marketing mix*.

The supply side of the market is also structured with *products* and *suppliers* exhibiting various *market shares* and having particular characteristics on the various components of the marketing mix.

Some products are more similar to each other than to other products and therefore more readily substituted for each other. The relationships between these products and suppliers constitute the structure of the supply side. It is also known as the structure of competition.

The structures of the demand and supply sides of a market can often be graphically portrayed through various types of plottings or maps.

Elasticity, Responsiveness

Elasticity and responsiveness are terms for the degree to which people, or a particular group of people, are responsive to changes in components of the *marketing mix*. Higher levels of elasticity mean greater responsiveness. There is little point in altering components of the marketing mix unless sufficient elasticity for such changes exists to permit recovery of the costs of the change. We use responsiveness as a term instead of elasticity and often use the concepts of importance or strength of preference as indicators of "potential elasticity"—the more important an attribute is, or the more strongly a characteristic is preferred, the more likely students or parents are to respond to changes made therein.

APPENDIX B. THE RESEARCH-BASED CARLETON COLLEGE STUDENT SEARCH BROCHURE

Carleton College

For more information:

Carleton College
Director of Admissions
Northfield, Minnesota 55057
507/645-4431 • Toll Free 800/533-0466
(Oct. 1 to May 1 only)

"Carleton College stands among the best institutions of higher education in America... Several things account for the distinction of Carleton... A strong faculty which remains alive professionally, yet which is devoted to teaching and serving the student well ... A student body which by conventional criteria stands among the best in the country and which thus helps to create a vital learning center."
Accrediting Commission, North Central Association of Colleges and Secondary Schools

Carleton College
Northfield, Minnesota

Since no small publication can tell you everything about a college, this brochure starts with a basic assumption: you are the kind of student who knows something about Carleton College, or who perhaps should. Maybe a guidance counselor mentioned us as a possible choice for you. Perhaps you learned about us from your parents or friends. Maybe you read about Carleton in one of the college guides or in the national press. If so, you probably know we are one of the nation's highly selective, small, co-ed liberal arts colleges.

We assume you also have some questions about Carleton. We expect that you would like to know what majors we offer, the size of the library, the student/faculty ratio and so forth; but, at this point in your search for a college, you probably want some more general information. Many students who are just beginning to consider Carleton ask about the kind of students we seek, the climate in southern Minnesota, opportunities for students who do not want to go to graduate school, the College's reputation and other things. At this stage, we are counting on your being more interested in finding out about the faculty or the endowment than about how many swimming pools we have or exactly what courses are required. If we are right, you should find this publication helpful.

This brochure is obviously not designed to answer all your questions. In fact, we hope it prompts you to request more information.

Q CARLETON IS REPUTED TO BE ONE OF THE BEST SMALL COLLEGES IN THE NATION. HOW DO YOU EVALUATE SOMETHING LIKE THAT?

A college is judged in one way or another by everyone who has contact with it. Their judgments are based on both objective studies and subjective evaluations.

Many people judge Carleton by our faculty. These people point to the number of Ph.D's, publications, honors and awards, grants received, and similar objective criteria. (The fact sheet in the back of this publication lists many statistics like these.) Our reputation in academic circles is often based in part on this kind of evaluation.

Others argue that our reputation is derived from our success in placing students in professional and graduate schools. Approximately 45-50 percent of the students who graduate from Carleton continue their studies immediately. As many as eight out of ten have elected further study within five years of graduation. We don't do this alone, however; we start with very good students.

Some cite our alumni as the basis of our reputation. These people count the many physicians and lawyers we have in our ranks or discover we have more than our share of alumni who are top business executives. Some notice the large number of our alumni who teach at other fine colleges and universities. This does not imply that a Carleton education is a ticket to success. Prestigious alumni simply indicate that many intelligent people have benefited from a Carleton education.

The size and quality of the physical plant also enhance our reputation. For example, the 400-acre arboretum is a unique academic and recreational resource. We are proud of the physical facilities, but we

suspect it is how these facilities are used by the students, faculty and staff which sets us apart.

Subjective judgments also play a role. Some students argue that the involvement of faculty members in the life of the College contributes to our reputation. These students would cite, as evidence of Carleton's strength, the number of times they have visited professors' homes, challenged faculty to a tennis match or dined together with professors.

Other students claim the quality of teaching is the basis for our reputation. Faculty enthusiasm for their own disciplines and the ability to integrate each subject into the liberal arts curriculum are seen as further evidence of the College's strength.

Still others claim that the eagerness of fellow students to learn and to share really provides the foundation for the College's reputation.

All these factors help separate and define Carleton, but we know this is an incomplete list. A reputation takes years to build, and there is no way to be certain how it evolved.

Q CARLETON IS KNOWN FOR ITS SUCCESS IN PLACING STUDENTS IN GRADUATE AND PROFESSIONAL SCHOOLS, BUT WHAT ABOUT THE MEN AND WOMEN WHO WISH TO START A CAREER IMMEDIATELY FOLLOWING COLLEGE?

It is true that for many years most Carleton students went to graduate school immediately after Commencement. Many students today have other career plans, and the College has responded to meet their needs.

The Office of Student Futures was established some years ago to aid students in their search for a career. A broad range of information on occupations, internships, and job opportunities, as well as material on graduate schools and fellowships, is available to all students. Students can start their search for a career early in their freshman year.

In addition to the internships currently offered throughout higher education, the Office of Student Futures arranges Career Exploration opportunities, two or three days spent informally observing and working with a Carleton graduate.

The credentials, resumes and references for all seniors and alumni are assembled by the Carleton

Placement Service for distribution, upon request, to prospective employers and graduate schools. The Placement Service provides career counseling, maintains contacts with businesses, industries, government and research agencies, and schedules on-campus interviews with prospective employers.

What happended to those in the Class of 1976 who did not choose graduate study is typical. Members of that class secured jobs with a variety of major corporations, including: Inland Steel, First Bank Corporation, Hewlett-Packard, Hormel, Cargill, IBM, Southwestern Bell, Monsanto, Merrill Lynch, Owens-Corning, Control Data, Univac and General Electric. Other Carls are working at government jobs with the U. S. Geological Survey, Civil Service, the Minnesota Highway Department, a county medical center, the Urban Coalition and the Railroad Retirement Board; one is an aide to the City Council and the Mayor of St. Paul, another is a legislative aide to a U. S. Representative, and a third is working for the Clean Water Action Project in Washington, D. C. In the communications field, '76 graduates are employed by such as the Chilton Publishing Company, the Augsburg Publishing Company, the St. Paul *Pioneer Press*, Random House, KTCA-TV in Minneapolis, the Guthrie Theater, the *National Review* and Time-Life, Inc.

Q CARLETON HAS A LOW STUDENT TO FACULTY RATIO, YET THE FACULTY IS WELL KNOWN FOR ITS SCHOLARSHIP. DOES THIS MEAN CARLETON'S FACULTY STRESSES RESEARCH RATHER THAN TEACHING?

Carleton has a teaching faculty. Many professors choose Carleton because they are more interested in teaching than in research-oriented positions, others because they want complete responsibility for their teaching and do not want to delegate that responsibility to graduate assistants.

Fortunately, these same people who love teaching are also highly regarded for their contributions to the research or the literature in their disciplines. In any given year, more than one-third of the faculty will have written for one or more scholarly publications, performed professionally or exhibited their works. Several science faculty members are awarded research grants annually from private and public sources. Faculty are often asked to serve as guest lecturers at other colleges and universities.

Carleton students benefit directly from the achievements of the faculty. Students may work with faculty members on significant scientific research or aid a professor preparing an article. These students normally receive recognition for their efforts.

Interest in both teaching and research distinguishes Carleton's faculty from those of many other small colleges.

Q IS THE FACT THAT CARLETON ENROLLS MEN AND WOMEN FROM ALL PARTS OF THE COUNTRY IMPORTANT TO THE STUDENTS?

This is a question higher education has been asking itself for decades. Many colleges with larger regional student populations argue that a small-town student from Minnesota is just like a small-town student from New Hampshire, Texas or Washington. We disagree. Students from different regions bring with them different backgrounds, perspectives and experiences.

One Carleton student from Honolulu explained the advantage this way: "In Hawaii, 'busing' was just something you read about. It had no meaning to me. But my roommate from Boston gave me a feel for the tension and trauma a city goes through after busing is instituted."

A woman from North Dakota wrote about the students on her floor during freshman year: "I found myself rooming with a poet from Berkeley and bordered by a cross-section of the world — a Presidential Scholar from Connecticut, a blind girl from Minneapolis, a biology major from Juneau, Alaska, a junior from Iran, a black student from Pittsburgh, a girl from Turkey and a southern belle from Little Rock. From them I discovered what it was like to work in a ghetto store during the summer, to spend a year in Germany, to ride a horse when you can't see, to hear Joan Baez in concert and to watch the sun set behind the Golden Gate Bridge."

Most students live in College housing, thereby benefiting from Carleton's geographical, cultural and racial diversity. To encourage the exploration of different living situations, the College offers both single sex and co-ed living in on-campus residences ranging in style from 50 year old Severance Hall, where rooms have working fireplaces, to the more modern Watson Hall, designed by Minoru Yamasaki. In addition, Carleton provides several off-campus houses designed for students who share common interests. Each year, groups of students with a fascination for such diverse subjects as natural history, foreign languages, Eastern religions and Jewish Studies request the use of an off-campus house to further those interests.

Q ACADEMIC PRESSURE IS EXPECTED AT CARLETON, BUT HOW INTENSE IS IT AND WHAT DO STUDENTS DO TO RELAX?

There is no doubt that much is expected of Carleton students. Faculty members put in long hours to prepare for courses and they expect students to do the same. Yet, academic pressure is a matter of personal style and depends on the view of the individual. Some freshmen and sophomores, anxious to succeed, seem to sense pressure the most. Upperclassmen, who have decided on a major and have "learned the ropes" often find pressures miraculously become less intense.

Carleton students, fortunately, seem to refrain from competing against each other. Instead, academic pressure arises from students' desires to make the most of a Carleton education and to meet their own expectations.

Though academic motivation is strong and genuine, Carleton students find hundreds of ways to spend their leisure time. Many men and women choose to participate in intercollegiate or organized intramural athletics. Some relax by making furniture in the Boliou workshop or process photographs in the Co-op darkrooms. In the winter, cross-country skiing through the Arboretum and ice skating under the lights are popular pastimes. Nearly any evening, a Carleton student can go to a student production at the Arena Theater, attend a recital in the Concert Hall, see a movie or hear a guest lecturer in the Chapel.

Trips to the Twin Cities, racquetball in the stadium, dinner at a professor's home, a dip in the pool, a bridge game in a residence hall lounge, and Frisbee on the Bald Spot are some other ways Carleton students unwind. Some even find relaxation in pursuing their studies.

The list goes on, because there are probably as many different ways to relax as there are Carleton students.

Q THE TWIN CITIES OF MINNEAPOLIS AND ST. PAUL ARE KNOWN AS CULTURALLY VIBRANT PLACES. CAN CARLETON STUDENTS TAKE ADVANTAGE OF THEM?

The *Wall Street Journal* recently said of Minneapolis: "This Capital of the upper Midwest, together with neighboring St. Paul, supports a world-renowned symphony orchestra, a cluster of exciting art museums, an innovative opera company and the best repertory theater in the country." Professional athletics, unusual architecture, fine restaurants, interesting shops, a fascinating month-long Renaissance Festival and the St. Paul Winter Carnival are other Twin City attractions.

Carleton students are urged to take advantage of this valuable resource. A student can go to the cities for a weekend or just an afternoon. A charter bus makes the 50-minute trip to the cities twice each weekday — three times a day on weekends — for $3.50 round trip. Commercial buses also serve Northfield four times a day. Once in "The Cities," you can spend a full day enjoying the Walker Art Center, walking the Skyway (the bridges which link buildings in Minneapolis), or spending an evening at the Guthrie Theater.

As one faculty member said of Carleton: "Located near the center of our country in a pastoral setting, yet close to a major metropolitan area, we enjoy the best of both worlds: we can meditate in tranquility as we cross-country ski, and, when we get restless, we can leave the rural behind us and head for the entertainments of the big city."

Q WHAT ARE THE WINTERS LIKE IN NORTHFIELD?

Snowy and cold, if a student comes from New Orleans. Comfortable, if a student's hometown is Chicago or Buffalo.

It would certainly be untrue to say it doesn't get cold in Northfield. It does. Sometimes it dips well below zero. Yet, those students who have tried downhill or cross-country skiing, love to ice skate or just like to hear the crunch of snow under their boots wouldn't have it any other way. The right gear — a down parka, a stocking cap and good boots — makes even the coldest days bearable and most days comfortable. Less hardy students who live in certain residence halls can get to meals and many classes without going outside by using the underground tunnel system.

It is also worth noting that the sun shines an average of seven out of ten days during a Minnesota winter, a nice change for students from many other parts of the country.

Minnesota is a four-season state. The falls are crisp and colorful; the springs warm and green; the summers sunny and hot.

259

Q CARLETON HAS A SIGNIFICANT ENDOWMENT BUT HOW DOES IT BENEFIT THE STUDENTS?

Alumni, parents, corporations, foundations and many friends who believe in the College have been most generous. As a result, our endowment ranks among the largest of small liberal arts colleges, and it is one important reason why Carleton can continue to offer an outstanding education to students from a variety of backgrounds.

The endowment serves two major purposes. First is the continual improvement of the academic program. Carleton has several endowed visiting professorships which permit us to bring scholars from around the world to teach their specialties, help instruct in one of our colloquia and add new dimensions to the academic program. Carleton students also benefit from endowed lectures series designed to bring important speakers or artists to the campus for single lectures or short residencies. The endowment also provides the flexibility we need to introduce promising new programs without sacrificing our traditional quality.

Second, the endowment helps put a Carleton education within reach of those who could not attend without significant financial assistance. About 50 percent of our students receive some form of financial aid. To assure that financial concerns do not keep a student from attending Carleton, the College uses a considerable portion of its endowment income for financial aid; over $1 million is budgeted each year for scholarships alone.

More than 75 percent of Carleton students work on campus regardless of their financial circumstances. Some work to defray the cost of college, others to earn spending money, still others because they find that working is important to their personal development. Whatever the reason, the College's financial strength allows it to provide a job for any student who wishes to work. In summary, as student fees meet only about 60 percent of the College's educational expenses, income from the endowment helps to make up the $2,500 difference between the annual comprehensive fee and the actual cost of a Carleton education.

Q CARLETON'S TUITION IS LOWER THAN THAT OF MANY FINE EASTERN COLLEGES. HOW DOES THIS AFFECT EDUCATIONAL QUALITY?

Carleton's tuition is the highest in Minnesota and among the highest in the Midwest, yet our total costs are lower than those of a number of major colleges in the East.

There is no easy explanation for the phenomenon. Offering a program like Carleton's is expensive. To maintain the quality our students expect and deserve we must purchase the best equipment for laboratories, studios and classrooms. We must pay competitive salaries. Our low student/faculty ratio and a wide choice of course offerings are also very costly. We, therefore, don't believe we cut corners on our educational programs.

Educational costs tend to rise with certain programs. For example, it does help that Carleton has no graduate programs. We are committed solely to undergraduate education and leave graduate and professional programs to the nation's many outstanding universities. This helps to keep our costs relatively low.

Our traditional program also keeps our costs competitive. We have retained a liberal arts curriculum, including distribution requirements, even when it was called old-fashioned. We think we know how to do it well, and we make a concerted effort to keep our costs down.

Q WHAT ARE CARLETON STUDENTS LIKE?

Carleton students are as diverse as their backgrounds, but generally are intelligent and highly motivated. In addition, successful Carleton students seem to have at least one of three traits.

First, most of our students truly appreciate the value of a good liberal arts education as the beginning of a lifetime commitment to learning. These students seem to benefit from the curriculum and succeed academically while enjoying a wide variety of other interests.

Second, many Carleton students contributed significantly to their schools and communities and will probably continue to do so in college. The student who plays in the orchestra, joins an academic club, works in a campus office, writes for the student newspaper, competes in intercollegiate athletics, participates in the governance system or adds to the campus in some less tangible way seems to be most satisfied with the Carleton experience. For some, their primary contributions to the campus are their academic achievements.

Third, our studies suggest that Carleton students are more adventurous than other college students. This is particularly true of those who travel long distances to attend the College. These students not only chose Carleton for its academic strengths, but they also chose to experience another part of the country and have made conscious decisions to resist the magnetism of "home." Our Minnesota students also show this willingness to explore. The College has virtually no commuter students, although the main population centers of Minnesota are only a short drive from Northfield, nor do Carleton students head for home on the weekends. When vacations come, many Minnesota students explore other regions of the country with their Carleton friends.

Carleton College has adopted and implements a policy of non-discrimination with regard to race, color, religion, sex, age, national origin, and non-disqualifying handicap in relation to students, applicants for admission, employees and applicants for employment.

FACTS

THE COLLEGE

Founded in 1866. A private, coeducational, residential liberal arts college.

Degree conferred: Bachelor of Arts

Location: Northfield, Minnesota (40 miles south of Minneapolis-St. Paul), population of 12,000, including students from two colleges

Campus: Over 900 total acres: main section of campus - 90 acres; Arboretum - 400 acres; other open space - over 400 acres

Buildings: 48, including 10 academic buildings, 9 on-campus residence halls, 9 special interest houses, 3 athletic facilities, Chapel, library

Total assets: $74,283,095 (June, 1977)

Endowment: $45,000,000 (June, 1977)

Governance: College Council, composed of faculty, students, administrators, trustees and alumni

CARLETON STUDENTS

1977-78 on-campus enrollment: Men - 888; Women - 773; Total - 1,661

Students on off-campus programs: annual average - 165

Secondary School Class Rank of Freshmen:
57% in top ten percent
79% in top 25 percent

181 Carleton students are National Merit Scholars: ranks 13th in nation, only small undergraduate liberal arts college in top 15.

Geographic Distribution of Students:
21% from the East
9% from the West
10% from the South
57% from the 14 Midwestern states

Percentage of Students Attending Graduate or Professional School (immediately following graduation):
Professional School (Medicine, Law, Dentistry, Business) - 24%
Graduate School in Academic Fields - 25%

STUDENT LIFE

Nine residence halls ranging in capacity from 78 to 211

Nine Special Interest Houses (e.g. Arts, Eastern Religions, Environmental Studies, French Studies, German, Jewish and Spanish Studies, Natural History).

Sayles-Hill Campus Center - "Great Space," bookstore, post office, snack bar, game room, student offices and lounge (completion, Summer 1979).

Great Hall - large social and meeting hall.

Cave - pub and snack bar in Evans Hall.

Dining Facilities - Goodhue, Evans, Burton and Severance Halls.

Average Number of Concerts per Term - 24

Average Number of Special Guest Lectures per Term - 50

Average Number of Events Open at no cost to Students (including concerts, lectures, movies, intercollegiate athletics) per Term - 135

CARLETONIAN - student newspaper

KRLX - student-run AM-FM radio station

ALGOL - yearbook

VOICE OF THE STRUGGLE - Third-World publication

CSA - student government

Co-op - student social organization

ACADEMIC FACILITIES:

Library: four-story structure
360,000 volumes
subscriptions to 1,300 periodicals
Federal depository
18 full-time staff members

Concert Hall (seats 550) and Arena Theater (seats 460) joined by gallery: 4 large ensemble rooms, 8 rehearsal rooms

Music Hall - 2 classrooms, 16 practice rooms, 15 offices

Olin Hall - biology, psychology, physics - 2 classrooms, seminar room, auditorium, 15 teaching laboratories, 17 faculty offices

Mudd Hall of Science - chemistry, geology - 2 seminar rooms, 12 teaching laboratories, science library, 2 geology specimen processing rooms, geology specimen museum, chemistry instrument room, 9 faculty offices

Willis Hall - economics, education, political science, sociology-anthropology - 3 classrooms, seminar room, 17 faculty offices

Leighton Hall - classics, religion, history, modern languages, philosophy - 11 classrooms, 42 faculty offices

Laird Hall - English - 4 classrooms, seminar room, 17 faculty offices

Scoville Hall - media center

Boliou Hall - art - 1 classroom, seminar room, 5 studios, 6 faculty offices, gallery, student workshop

Goodsell Observatory - mathematics, astronomy - 2 classrooms, 22 faculty offices, 16-inch visual refractor, 8-inch photographic refractor

Academic Computer Facilites:
Main System: PDP-11/60 with 16 terminals throughout campus
Four PDP-8L's provide graphic capabilities
PDP-11/20 for statistical research
PDP-8L's for interfacing laboratory equipment in chemistry, physics and psychology
Staff of 10

ACADEMIC STATISTICS

Calendar: 3-3-3 (Three ten-week terms)

Student/Faculty Ratio: 11.5 to 1

Average Class Size: 21 (27% of classes have under ten students)

Number of Full-time Faculty: 147

85% of Faculty have Terminal Degrees (PhD., MFA, MMus., etc.)

Eighteen Academic Departments:
Art
Biology
Chemistry
Classical Languages
Latin
Greek
Economics
Education
English
Geology
History
Mathematics
Modern Languages
French
German
Hebrew
Japanese
Marathi
Russian
Spanish

Music
Philosophy
Physics and Astronomy
Political Science
Psychology
Religion
Sociology & Anthropology
Special Programs:
   Asian Studies
   American Studies
   Black Studies
   Interdisciplinary Studies
   Environmental Studies
   Film Arts Program
   International Off-Campus Programs
   Arts Program
   Studies in Arts and Sciences
   F. Bruce Morgan Fellowship Program
   Latin American Studies
   Theater Arts
   Special Majors
   3-2 Engineering Program
   3-2 Nursing Program
   3-3 Law Program
   Computer Studies
   Urban Studies
   Russian Studies
   Women's Studies
   Jewish Studies

REQUIREMENTS FOR GRADUATION:

1. 204 credits (equivalent of 34 six-credit courses) plus six terms of physical education
2. Proficiency requirement in writing (English)
3. Proficiency requirement in foreign language
4. Distribution requirements:
   a. 2 courses (12 credits) from art, music and/or literature (classics, English, modern languages)
   b. 3 courses (18 credits) from biology, chemistry, geology, physics, astronomy and/or mathematics)
   c. 3 courses (18 credits) from economics, education, political science and/or sociology-anthropology
   d. 2 courses (12 credits) from history, philosophy and/or religion
5. A minimum of 7 courses (42 credits) in a major field and completion of a senior integrative exercise approved by the major department
6. At least two academic years in residence, including the senior year, with a minimum of 102 credits completed while enrolled at Carleton

ACCREDITATION AND AFFILIATIONS:

Accredited by the North Central Association of Colleges and Secondary Schools and by the National Council for Accreditation of Teacher Education; on the approved list of the American Chemical Society; member of the Associated Colleges of the Midwest and other national and regional associations; Phi Beta Kappa and Sigma Xi.

ATHLETICS

Men's Gym - 25-yard, six-lane pool with one- and three-meter diving boards, two basketball courts, wrestling room, locker and shower facilities. Seats 1,850 for basketball, 350 for swimming.
Women's Recreation Center - 25-yard, five-lane pool, dance studio, field house, gymnastic and basketball court area, sauna, locker and shower facilities.
Laird Stadium - 220-yard Tartan-surface indoor track, long jump, pole vault, high jump and shot put areas, five handball, squash and racquetball courts, universal gym, weightlifting room, training room, sauna, locker and shower facilities; 440-yard outdoor track, 10,000-seat football stadium.
Sixteen outdoor and one indoor tennis courts.
Five athletic fields.
Varsity Sports for men: football, soccer, cross country, basketball, swimming, wrestling, indoor track, baseball, track and field, tennis, golf.
Varsity Sports for women: tennis, field hockey, volleyball, basketball, softball, cross country, track and field, swimming.
Co-ed sports: downhill and cross-country skiing.
Memberships: Midwest Collegiate Athletic Conference, NCAA; Minnesota Association of Intercollegiate Athletics for Women, Region VI AIAW, National AIAW.

TUITION AND FEES 1978-79

Tuition	$3,992
Activity	45
Room	824
Board	864
TOTAL	$5,725

APPENDIX C. CARLETON COLLEGE ADMITTED APPLICANT FORMS

Dates in upper right corner indicate entering class(es) with which the form was used.

CARLETON COLLEGE

CANDIDATE'S REPLY FORM

Used: 1974

_____ I accept admission to Carleton. My $100 deposit is enclosed.

_____ I decline admission to Carleton. I intend to enroll at _____

Name _____ Date _____

Please help us with an evaluation of our admission process by completing both sides.

1. Please list the colleges to which you applied, including Carleton, and indicate your order of preference at the time you applied and whether you were accepted at each college. For colleges at which you were accepted. Please enter amount of aid offered.

Name of College	Preference	Accepted?	Scholar-ship	Loan	Work
_____	_____	_____	$_____	$_____	$_____
_____	_____	_____	$_____	$_____	$_____
_____	_____	_____	$_____	$_____	$_____

2. Following is a list of sources of information about Carleton. Please read the list and then circle the code letter of all sources through which you received information about Carleton

A. High school counselor
B. A teacher
C. A parent
D. A friend who attended Carleton
E. Another friend
F. A relative who attended Carleton
G. A Carleton publication
H. An Admissions Representative
I. An Alumni Representative
J. A college guide or handbook
K. Other (Specify) _____

_____

2A. Through which source did you first hear about Carleton (One letter only) _____

2B. Which source of information was most important for your decision? (One letter only) _____

3. In the next column is a list of factors which sometimes affect decisions by students who attend a particular college.

3. (cont.)

Please circle code "1" for all the factors which influenced your decision about Carleton positively; circle "2" for all negative aspects.

	Positive	Negative
Size of the college	1	2
Location	1	2
Academic reputation	1	2
Coeducational	1	2
Coeducational housing	1	2
Presence of multiple living options	1	2
Friend(s) attending	1	2
A particular dept., major, set of courses, or off-campus program	1	2
Financial aid offered	1	2
Relatives or alumni who attended	1	2
Other (Specify) _____		
_____	1	2

3A. Place an X to the left of the factor which was most important in your decision.

4. Did you visit Carleton?

No . . . . 1 (Go to Q.5)

Yes . . . . . . 2 (Answer 4 a & 4B)

4a. When did you visit (Circle one
code)

During Carleton academic year. . .1

During Carleton vacation 2

Both 3

4B. Circle code "1" for each aspect
below which impressed you positively on your visit; circle "2"
for each negative aspect.

	Posi- tive	Nega- tive
Campus	1	2
Atmosphere	1	2
Students	1	2
Facilities	1	2
Faculty.	1	2
Location	1	2
Admissions interview	1	2
Admissions personnel.	1	2
Housing.	1	2

5. Did you visit with a Carleton Admissions Representative in your high
school or at a College Night or similar meeting?

No. 1   Yes. 2

6. Did you talk with a Carleton Alumni
Representative at any time during
the past year?

No. . . . . .1 (Go to Q.7)

Yes . . . . .2 (Please answer 6A and 6B)

6A. When did this contact take place?
(Circle codes for all that apply)

Before I applied 1

After I applied but before
I was accepted 2

After I was accepted 3

6B. What form did this contact take?
(Circle codes for all that apply)

Telephone call 1

Personal visit at your
high school. 2

Personal visit at your
home 3

Party or get-together at home
of alumni representative . . .4

Other (Please specify_____

_____5

7. What influence did the following have on your desire to attend Carleton? (Circle one
code for each influence)

	1. Greatly Increased	2. Slightly Increased	3. No Influence	4. Slightly Decreased	5. Greatly Decreased	6. Does not apply
Catalogue.	1	2	3	4	5	6
Other printed materials.	1	2	3	4	5	6
Campus visit	1	2	3	4	5	6
Talk with Admission Representative	1	2	3	4	5	6
Talk with Alumni Representative.	1	2	3	4	5	6
Your high school counselor	1	2	3	4	5	6
Present Carleton Student(s).	1	2	3	4	5	6
Friend(s).	1	2	3	4	5	6
Parent(s).	1	2	3	4	5	6

8. Please make any comments or suggestions you wish concerning our admissions process or
procedures. We are particularly interested in suggestions for improvements which
might be made.

Applying Market Research in College Admissions

Used: 1975

CARLETON COLLEGE
CANDIDATE'S REPLY FORM

Name _____   Date _____

_____ I accept admission to Carleton. My $100 deposit is enclosed.

_____ I decline admission to Carleton. I intend to enroll at _____.

Please help us evaluate our admissions process by completing both sides of this form.

1. List the colleges to which you applied, including Carleton, IN THE ORDER OF YOUR PREFERENCE
   AT THE TIME YOU APPLIED and whether you were accepted at each of the other colleges. For
   each college by which your application was approved, please enter the amount of aid offered.

Name of College	Accepted?	Scholarship	Loan	Work
(1)_____	_____	$_____	$_____	$_____
(2)_____	_____	$_____	$_____	$_____
(3)_____	_____	$_____	$_____	$_____
(4)_____	_____	$_____	$_____	$_____

2. Following is a list of sources of information about Carleton. Please read the list
   and then circle the code letter of all
   sources through which you received information about Carleton.

   A. High school counselor
   B. Teacher(s)
   C. Parent(s)
   D. Friend(s) who attend(ed) Carleton
   E. Relative(s) who attended Carleton
   F. Other friend(s) or relative(s)
   G. Carleton publication(s)
   H. Admissions representative(s)
   I. Alumni admissions representatives
   J. College guide(s) or handbook(s)
   K. Campus visit(s)
   L. Other source(s) (Specify)_____

   2A. Through which source did you first hear
       about Carleton? (One letter)_____
   2B. Which source (if any) was most impor-
       tant in your decision? (One letter)_____

3. Following is a list of factors which sometimes affect decisions by students to attend
   a particular college. Please circle "1" for
   all the factors which influenced your decision about Carleton positively; circle "2"
   for all negative factors.

	Positive	Negative
Size of the college	1	2
Distance from home	1	2
Location	1	2
Academic reputation	1	2
Academic rigor	1	2

3. (cont'd.)

	Positive	Negative
Friend(s) attending	1	2
Particular dept. or major	1	2
Which one? _____		
Financial aid	1	2
Carleton alumni	1	2
Cost	1	2
Other (Specify)		
_____	1	2

3A. Place an X to the left of the one
    factor most important in your decision.

4. Did you visit Carleton?

   No . . . . . 1 (Go to Q. 5)
   Yes . . . . 2 (Answer 4A & 4B)

4A. When did you visit? (Circle one code)

    During Carleton academic year . . . 1
    During Carleton vacation. 2
    Both. 3

4B. Circle code "1" for each aspect below
    which impressed you positively on your
    visit; circle "2" for each negative
    aspect.

	Positive	Negative
Campus	1	2
Academic atmosphere	1	2
Social atmosphere	1	2
Students	1	2
Facilities	1	2
Faculty	1	2

266

4B. (cont'd.)

Location. 1   2
Admissions
  interview 1   2
Admissions
  personnel 1   2
Housing 1   2

5. Did you visit with a Carleton Admissions
Representative in your high school or at a
College Night or similar meeting?

No . . . . . . .1 Yes 2

6. Did you talk with a Carleton Alumni
Representative at any time during the
past year?

No. . . . . .1 (Go to Q.7)
Yes . . . . .2 (Please answer 6A & 6B)

6A. When did this contact take place?
(Circle codes for <u>all</u> that apply)

Before I applied 1
After I applied but before
  I was accepted 2
After I was accepted 3

6B. What form did this contact take?
(Circle codes for <u>all</u> that apply)

Telephone call   1
Personal visit at your
  high School   2
Personal visit at your
  home   3
Party or get-together at home
  of alumni representative   4
Other (Please specify) _____

_____5

---

7. What influence did the following have on your desire to attend Carleton? (Circle one
code for each influence)

1. Greatly Increased
2. Slighly Increased
3. No Influence
4. Slightly Decreased
5. Greatly Decreased
6. Does not apply

	1	2	3	4	5	6
Catalog.	1	2	3	4	5	6
Other Carleton printed materials	1	2	3	4	5	6
Campus visit	1	2	3	4	5	6
Talk with Admission Representative	1	2	3	4	5	6
Talk with Alumni Representative.	1	2	3	4	5	6
Your high school counselor	1	2	3	4	5	6
Present Carleton Student(s).	1	2	3	4	5	6
Friend(s).	1	2	3	4	5	6
Parent(s).	1	2	3	4	5	6
College Guide(s) or Handbook(s).	1	2	3	4	5	6
Which one(s)?_____						

8. Please make any comments or suggestions you wish concerning our admissions process or
procedures. We are particularly interested in suggestions for improvements which
might be made.

CARLETON COLLEGE
CANDIDATE'S REPLY FORM

Used: 1976, 1977

Name _____   Date _____

____ I accept admission to Carleton. My $100 deposit is enclosed.

____ I decline admission to Carleton. I intend to enroll at _____.

Please help us evaluate our admissions process by completing both sides of this form.

1. List the colleges to which you applied, including Carleton, IN THE ORDER OF YOUR PREFERENCE
    AT THE TIME YOU APPLIED and whether you were accepted at each of the other colleges. For
    each college by which your application was approved, please enter the amount of aid, if any,
    offered.

Name of College	Accepted?	Scholarship	Loan	Work
(1)_____	_____	$_____	$_____	$_____
(2)_____	_____	$_____	$_____	$_____
(3)_____	_____	$_____	$_____	$_____
(4)_____	_____	$_____	$_____	$_____

2. Below are sources of information about college. For those which provided you with informa-
    tion about Carleton, please rate them according to how they influenced your desire to attend
    Carleton (circle a code in columns 1-5). Circle the code X for those sources from which you
    did not receive information.

```
                                    1.  Greatly Increased
                                      2.  Slightly Increased
                                        3.  No Influence
                                          4.  Slightly Decreased
                                            5.  Greatly Decreased
                                              6.  No Information
                                                  from this source
```

	1	2	3	4	5	X
Catalog	1	2	3	4	5	X
Other Carleton printed materials.	1	2	3	4	5	X
Campus visit.	1	2	3	4	5	X
Talk with Admissions Representative:						
At your high school . .	1	2	3	4	5	X
At a college fair . . .	1	2	3	4	5	X
On campus	1	2	3	4	5	X
Elsewhere	1	2	3	4	5	X
Talk with Alumni Representative	1	2	3	4	5	X
Other Alumni.	1	2	3	4	5	X
Your high school counselor.	1	2	3	4	5	X
A teacher at high school.	1	2	3	4	5	X
Present Carleton Student(s)	1	2	3	4	5	X
Friend(s)	1	2	3	4	5	X
Parent(s)	1	2	3	4	5	X
College Guide(s) or Handbook(s)	1	2	3	4	5	X

Which one(s)?_____

3. We are interested in learning more about the characteristics which differentiate the colleges to which our applicants apply and the characteristics on which colleges don't seem to differ much. In Column A, please rate Carleton on each of the following characteristics. If you are planning to attend Carleton, in Column B please rate the college at which you were accepted which you would most likely have attended had you not chosen Carleton. If you are planning to attend a college other than Carleton, please rate that college in Column B. Circle one code in each column for each characteristic; omit any item for which you have inadequate information.

	A. Carleton			B. 2nd Choice OR College Attending		
	Poor	Good	Very Good	Poor	Good	Very Good
A. The Admissions Process	1	2	3	7	8	9
B. Student/Faculty Ratio.	1	2	3	7	8	9
C. Quality of the Library	1	2	3	7	8	9
D. Racial/Ethnic Diversity.	1	2	3	7	8	9
E. Academic Quality	1	2	3	7	8	9
F. Distance from Home	1	2	3	7	8	9
G. Financial Aid Offer.	1	2	3	7	8	9
H. Graduate/Professional School Acceptance Rate	1	2	3	7	8	9
I. Off-campus Study Programs.	1	2	3	7	8	9
J. Music Opportunities.	1	2	3	7	8	9
K. Varsity Athletics.	1	2	3	7	8	9
L. Diversity of Residential Options	1	2	3	7	8	9
M. Policy on Student Cars	1	2	3	7	8	9
N. General Education Emphasis (e.g.,proficiency and distribution requirements)	1	2	3	7	8	9
O. Opportunity to Develop Special Major	1	2	3	7	8	9
P. Quality of Faculty	1	2	3	7	8	9
Q. Computer Facilities.	1	2	3	7	8	9
R. Particular Department(s) or Major(s) in which you are interested;(specify)_____	1	2	3	7	8	9
_____	1	2	3	7	8	9
S. Social Atmosphere.	1	2	3	7	8	9
T. Urban/rural Location	1	2	3	7	8	9
U. Geographical Location.	1	2	3	7	8	9
V. Size	1	2	3	7	8	9
W. Coeducation.	1	2	3	7	8	9
X. Cost	1	2	3	7	8	9
Y. Other (specify) _____	1	2	3	7	8	9
_____	1	2	3	7	8	9

Below please indicate, in the order of their importance, up to three characteristics which most differentiated Carleton and the other college which you rated and which influenced your choice. Use the letters from above.

First _____   Second _____   Third _____

4. Please make any comments or suggestions you wish concerning our admissions process or procedures. We are particularly interested in suggestions for improvements which you might have.

Used: 1978, 1979

Date_____

Dear Mr. Nicholson:

_____I am coming to Carleton in September. My $100 deposit is enclosed.

_____I decline admission to Carleton. I intend to enroll at_____

Name_____

With the financial assistance of a private foundation, Carleton is conducting research to help private colleges and universities find out more about their respective strengths and weaknesses. Please help in this endeavor by answering the following questions:

1. List up to four colleges to which you applied, INCLUDING CARLETON, in the order of your preference at the time you applied and indicate whether you were accepted at each of the other colleges. For each college by which you were accepted, please enter the amount of aid, if any, offered. If you did not request aid, draw a dash in the Scholarship column.

Name of College	Accepted?	Scholarship	Loan	Work
1st choice_____	_____	$_____	$_____	$_____
2nd choice_____	_____	$_____	$_____	$_____
3rd choice_____	_____	$_____	$_____	$_____
4th choice_____	_____	$_____	$_____	$_____

In questions 2 – 5, please tell us what you found most and least attractive or desirable about the school to which the question refers. Please be as specific as possible and indicate what gave you your impression about the things which you mention.

2. What did you like best about Carleton?

3. IF YOU ARE COMING TO CARLETON:*
in the following space, briefly describe what you liked best about the school which you would have attended had you not chosen Carleton.

IF YOU ARE NOT COMING TO CARLETON:*
what did you like best about the school which you will be attending? Name of school: _____

4. IF YOU ARE COMING TO CARLETON:*
why did you choose Carleton over the school which you named in question 3?

IF YOU ARE NOT COMING TO CARLETON:*
why did you choose the school which you will be attending over Carleton?

5. What aspects of Carleton might have made Carleton even more attractive if they had been different? (We are interested both in things which could be changed and those which are unchangeable.)

*the entire space can be used for your answer   1979 A

Since this is an exploratory effort, we need to be certain that we know about some key characteristics. For each of the following, please rate its importance to you in choosing the college which you are attending (scale A), and how **Carleton** rates in general on this characteristic (scale B).

Please describe briefly your impression of Carleton with respect to each of the named aspects of the colleges.

We are interested in why things are good or bad. For example, we want to know more than that Carleton is in a small town...we want to know why you might consider that positive or negative. Please also indicate how you formed your impression. Again, be specific. For example, instead of simply listing present Carleton students as a source of the impression, please state "Carleton students said this and that" or "Carleton students did this when I visited."

Rating Scales:
A. Importance to you   Not at all important   1 2 3 4 5 6 7   Extremely Important
B. Rating of Carleton   Terrible   1 2 3 4 5 6 7   Outstanding

THE FACULTY

A. Importance_____   B. Rating of Carleton_____
Your impression of Carleton's faculty: Source of impression:

THE STUDENTS

A. Importance_____   B. Rating of Carleton_____
Your impression of Carleton's students: Source of impression:

LOCATION (advantages / disadvantages)

A. Importance_____   B. Rating of Carleton_____
Your impression of Carleton's location: Source of impression:

SOCIAL ATMOSPHERE

A. Importance_____   B. Rating of Carleton_____
Your impression of Carleton's social   Source of impression:
atmosphere:

IMAGE OF THE COLLEGE HELD BY THE PUBLIC

A. Importance_____   B. Rating of Carleton_____
Your impression of Carleton's image: Source of impression:

Used: 1980

Carleton College
CANDIDATE'S REPLY FORM

Name _____ Date_____19____

____I accept admission to Carleton. My $100 deposit is enclosed. (Return form and deposit by May 1, 1980.)*

____I decline admission to Carleton. I intend to enroll at_____ .

Please help us evaluate our admissions process by completing both sides of this form.

1. List the colleges to which you applied, including Carleton, IN THE ORDER OF YOUR PREFERENCE AT THE TIME YOU APPLIED and whether you were accepted at each of the other colleges. For each college by which your application was approved, please enter the amount of aid, if any, offered.

Name of college	Accepted?	Scholarship	Loan	Work
(1)				
(2)				
(3)				
(4)				

2. Below are sources of information about college. For those which provided you with information about Carleton, please rate them according to how they influenced your desire to attend Carleton (circle a code in columns 1-5). **Circle the code X for those sources from which you did not receive information.**

	Greatly Increased	Slightly Increased	No Influence	Slighty Decreased	Greatly Decreased	No Information from This Source
Student Search letter and brochure	1	2	3	4	5	X
General Information Bulletin (Viewbook)	1	2	3	4	5	X
"See It Our Way"	1	2	3	4	5	X
Departmental descriptions	1	2	3	4	5	X
Catalog	1	2	3	4	5	X
Campus visit	1	2	3	4	5	X
Talk with admissions officer	1	2	3	4	5	X
At your high school	1	2	3	4	5	X
At a college fair	1	2	3	4	5	X
On campus	1	2	3	4	5	X
Elsewhere	1	2	3	4	5	X
Talk with alumni representative	1	2	3	4	5	X
Other alumni	1	2	3	4	5	X
Your high school counselor	1	2	3	4	5	X
A teacher at high school	1	2	3	4	5	X
Present Carleton student(s)	1	2	3	4	5	X
Friend(s)	1	2	3	4	5	X
Parent(s)	1	2	3	4	5	X
College Guide(s) or Handbook(s)	1	2	3	4	5	X
Which one(s)?						
Other (please specify)	1	2	3	4	5	X

*This is a non-refundable deposit, returned only upon graduation or withdrawal from the College with proper notice, upon withdrawal for illness, or if you are dropped from the College for academic reasons. Charges and unpaid obligations to the College will be applied against this deposit at the end of each academic year or at the time of withdrawal.

3. We are interested in learning more about the characteristics which differentiate the colleges to which our applicants apply and the characteristics on which colleges don't seem to differ much. In column A, please rate Carleton on each of the following characteristics. If you are planning to attend Carleton, in Column B, please rate the college **at which you were accepted** which you would most likely have attended had you not chosen Carleton. If you are planning to attend a college other than Carleton, please rate that college in Column B. Circle one code in each column for each characteristic; **omit any item for which you have inadequate information.**

	A. Carleton					B. 2nd Choice OR College Attending				
	Poor	Fair	Good	Very Good	Excel- lent	Poor	Fair	Good	Very Good	Excel- lent
A. The Admissions Process	1	2	3	4	5	1	2	3	4	5
B. Student/Faculty Ratio	1	2	3	4	5	1	2	3	4	5
C. Quality of the Library	1	2	3	4	5	1	2	3	4	5
D. Racial/Ethnic Diversity	1	2	3	4	5	1	2	3	4	5
E. Academic Quality	1	2	3	4	5	1	2	3	4	5
F. Distance from Home...............	1	2	3	4	5	1	2	3	4	5
G. Financial Aid Offer.................	1	2	3	4	5	1	2	3	4	5
H. Graduate/Professional School Acceptance Rate	1	2	3	4	5	1	2	3	4	5
I. Off-Campus Study Programs	1	2	3	4	5	1	2	3	4	5
J. Music Opportunities	1	2	3	4	5	1	2	3	4	5
K. Varsity Athletics	1	2	3	4	5	1	2	3	4	5
L. Diversity of Residential Options	1	2	3	4	5	1	2	3	4	5
M. Policy on Student Cars	1	2	3	4	5	1	2	3	4	5
N. General Education Emphasis (e.g., proficiency and distribution requirements)..........	1	2	3	4	5	1	2	3	4	5
O. Opportunity to Develop Special Major	1	2	3	4	5	1	2	3	4	5
P. Quality of Faculty	1	2	3	4	5	1	2	3	4	5
Q. Computer Facilities	1	2	3	4	5	1	2	3	4	5
R. Particular Departments or Major(s) in which you are interested; (specify)_____	1	2	3	4	5	1	2	3	4	5
S. Social Atmosphere..................	1	2	3	4	5	1	2	3	4	5
T. Urban/Rural Location	1	2	3	4	5	1	2	3	4	5
U. Geographical Location	1	2	3	4	5	1	2	3	4	5
V. Size	1	2	3	4	5	1	2	3	4	5
W. Coeducation	1	2	3	4	5	1	2	3	4	5
X. Cost	1	2	3	4	5	1	2	3	4	5
Y. Other (specify)_____	1	2	3	4	5	1	2	3	4	5
_____	1	2	3	4	5	1	2	3	4	5

Below please indicate, in the order of their importance, up to three characteristics which **most** differentiated Carleton from the other college which you have rated and which influenced your choice. Use the letters from above.

First_____   Second_____   Third_____

4. When did you first seriously consider the college you have selected?

Senior year_____   Junior year_____   Sophomore year_____   Freshman year_____   Earlier_____

5. Please make any comments or suggestions you wish concerning our admissions process or procedures. We are particularly interested in improvements which you might suggest.

_____

_____

_____

_____

APPENDIX D. SAMPLING DETAILS AND DESCRIPTION OF THE SAMPLE

Appendix D presents four types of information: (1) details on the drawing of the samples, (2) response rates among various groups of students and parents, (3) representativeness of the respondents in relation to the original sample, and (4) brief notes on the demographic distinctiveness of particular markets, where such exists.

The six metropolitan markets were defined to include the zip codes (first three digits) shown in Table D-1.

The intended majors included in the sample are listed in Table D-2.

Surveys were mailed on the dates and with the cumulative responses noted in Table D-3.

Table D-1. Zip Code Definitions of the Six Markets

San Francisco/Oakland 940–949
Denver/Boulder 800–806
Dallas/Ft. Worth 750–752, 760–762
Chicago 600–606
Minneapolis/St. Paul 550–554
Baltimore/District of Columbia 200, 202–212, 214, 217, 219,
220–221,* 223, 227

* Only two student respondents were from these northern Virginia zip codes.

Table D-2. Intended Majors

	% in Sample		% in Sample
Art (fine arts)	1.3	Music	3.6
Art (graphic design)	1.8	Philosophy	0.4
Biological sciences		Physical sciences	
(unspecified)	5.2	(unspecified)	0.8
Education (secondary)	0.6	Predentistry	1.0
English	2.6	Premedicine	12.7
History	2.1	Psychology	4.6
Languages (classical)	0.2	Theology, religious	
Languages (modern)	1.8	education	1.1
Liberal arts (unspecified)	3.8	Social sciences	
Literature (comparative)	0.1	(unspecified)	1.3
Mathematics (statistics)	4.7	Veterinary science	5.3
		Undecided	45.1

The response rate varied considerably across the six markets; Denver posted the highest rates of return among both students and

Table D-3. Mailing Details

Cumulative Response

Parents
October 20, 1978	Letter/survey	21%
November 14, 1978	Postcard reminder.	37
December 14, 1978	Letter/survey	47

Students
February 27, 1979	Letter/survey	23
March 20, 1979	Letter/revised survey**	42
March 30, 1979	Postcard reminder.	50

** A printing error, discovered after the first mailing of the student survey, was corrected; the second mailing included the revised questionnaire. Originally the same sequence was intended for students and parents.

parents, and Chicago the lowest. For the most part, the rates among students and parents were very similar in a given market. The return rates are shown in Table D-4.

Table D-4. Response Rates by Market*

	Students	Parents
San Francisco/Oakland.	49%	48%
Denver/Boulder	54	53
Dallas/Ft. Worth	45	42
Chicago	43	39
Minneapolis/St. Paul	49	48
Baltimore/D.C.	51	50

* Includes nondeliverables in denominator.

Table D-5 shows that in the total sample, women students were somewhat more likely to return the questionnaire than men were; among parents, the sex of the child did not influence response rates. Among students, there was a strong positive association between high school grades and return of the questionnaire; a much more modest association in the same direction occurred among parents. Among students, blacks and Hispanics were less likely to respond than other racial or ethnic groups; among parents, only blacks exhibited a distinctively low return rate.

As a result of these response rate differences among students, the characteristics of the respondents were somewhat different from those of the original sample; the distortions are not serious for our purposes, however. Table D-6 shows that the group available for analysis had about 5 percent more A students than did the

Table D-5. Response Rates by Demographic and Ability Characteristics*

Sex

	Men	Women
Students.	43% (1,457)†	53% (1,537)
Parents: sex of child . . .	46% (1,038)	47% (962)

(Men and women students in Denver and Baltimore/D.C. were almost equally likely to respond.)

High School Grade Average

	A	A−, B+	B or less
Students.	56% (1,019)	49% (1,259)	37% (709)
Parents: students' average grade	50% (644)	46% (835)	43% (515)

(A students in Denver had an especially high return rate of 61%; students with B or less in Dallas/Ft. Worth had an especially low return rate of 24%.)

Race/Ethnic Group

	White	Black	Hispanic	Asian	Missing Code
Students.	49% (2,430)	37% (54)	38% (21)	54% (85)	48% (373)
Parents: student's self-reported race	47% (1,615)	23% (30)	47% (17)	48% (50)	46% (267)

* Specific market deviations from general pattern are noted in parentheses below category.
† Number on which percentage is computed.

Table D-6. Discrepancies between Respondents and Original Sample (Students)

	Respondents	Original Sample
Grade point average		
A	39%	34%
A−, B+	43	42
B or less	18	24
	100%	100%
Sex		
Men	44%	49%
Women.	56	51
	100%	100%
Race		
Black	1%	2%
Hispanic.	0.5%	0.7%

original sample, and about 5 percent more women. The group used for analysis slightly underrepresented blacks and Hispanics, but they constituted a miniscule percentage of the original sample because of the sampling criteria.

Table D-7 presents descriptive statistics on each market for the student survey respondents. There are fairly marked intermarket differences on items such as average high school grades, race, parental education, and religion. The following notes highlight distinctive attributes of each market.

San Francisco/Oakland

Students in this market do not stand out for the most part as distinctive. They are the most likely to report "no religious preference" and to live with only their mothers (but the latter condition shows little intermarket variation). Three-fifths of the respondents are women. These students are the most likely to have withheld racial information and the least likely to be white; this market has the largest minority percentage – and they are all Asians.

Denver/Boulder

This market has the most extreme imbalance between men and women (in favor of the latter) and has a high level of respondents who reported "no religious preference." These students are the least likely among the six markets to be long-term residents of their present state. Parents are especially likely to have high levels of education; half of the mothers are college-educated.

Chicago

Almost equal proportions of men and women are found among Chicago respondents. There is a greater variety of minority students than in any other market, and a relatively large proportion of students who declined to provide this information. These students are the most likely among the six markets to report long residence in the state in which they were surveyed. Mothers are the least likely to have a college education (but barely behind mothers in the Twin Cities). This market is by far the most Catholic; over half the students report being Catholic.

Twin Cities

This is a relatively indistinctive group except for very low levels of parental education, especially among fathers. They are the most

Table D-7. Descriptive Statistics on Student Respondents by Market

	San Francisco/ Oakland	Denver/ Boulder	Chicago	Twin Cities	Dallas/ Ft. Worth	Baltimore/ D.C.
Verbal PSAT/NMSQT Mean	55.3	54.0	54.7	52.5	55.9	56.2
Math PSAT/NMSQT Mean	58.0	57.2	57.3	58.2	57.9	57.9
High School Grades						
A	35%	46%	39%	30%	62%	25%
A−, B+	46	40	41	53	29	47
B or less	19	14	20	17	9	28
Sex						
Male	41%	39%	49%	41%	46%	46%
Female	59	61	51	59	54	54
Race						
White	68%	86%	74%	88%	90%	83%
Black	–	–	3	–	–	4
Asian	10	2	3	1	2	–
Hispanic	–	–	2	–	–	–
Missing Codes	22	12	18	11	8	13
Mother's Education						
Bachelor's or more	44%	50%	32%	33%	45%	47%
Graduate work or degree	12	13	8	6	13	23
Father's Education						
Bachelor's or more	70%	71%	58%	47%	70%	73%
Graduate work or degree	37	43	28	26	35	44
Years Lived in State						
13 plus	77%	61%	86%	82%	72%	75%
Family Status						
Both parents in residence	83%	90%	87%	91%	81%	88%
Mother only in residence	12	6	9	4	11	10
Student's Religion						
Protestant	36%	46%	24%	57%	71%	35%
Catholic	27	20	55	25	16	32
Jewish	5	3	6	2	2	12
None	27	24	9	14	8	16

likely to be residing with both parents (just ahead of Denver by 1 percentage point) and among the most likely to be white. These students are also relatively likely to be long-term residents of their present state.

Dallas/Ft. Worth

This market has the highest percentages of whites and Protestants of the six markets. It also has the highest percentage of students who report A grades in high school, by a substantial margin; at the same time these students do *not* score exceptionally well on the PSAT/NMSQT. Grading practices appear to be distinctively soft in Dallas/Ft. Worth. Students are the least likely to report that they are living with both parents.

Baltimore/D.C.

These students exhibit a pattern of grades and test scores that is diametrically opposed to the pattern found in Dallas/Ft. Worth; they have the lowest grades among the six markets and among the highest test scores. Parents have high levels of education; almost a quarter of the mothers have been in graduate school. Students are almost equally likely to be Protestants or Catholics; the highest proportion of Jewish students is found in this market.

APPENDIX E. THE DEVELOPMENT OF THE SIX-MARKET STUDY QUESTIONNAIRES; QUESTIONNAIRE SAMPLES

The questionnaires for the Six-Market Study resulted from an extensive and valuable developmental process. Drawing on extensive readings in the marketing literature and on Carleton's market research tradition, the project director developed a detailed marketing and research plan that addressed the following issues:

- Objectives of the marketing strategy
- Tactics in a marketing strategy
- Market research objectives (listed by priority)
- Models, hypotheses, and specific questions to be addressed in the research
- Formulations of hypotheses, models, and modes of analysis
- Listing of tables and other analyses to be produced from the research

The first draft of the parents' questionnaire followed this specification of a marketing and research plan (we intended from the start to make the parent and student forms closely parallel). This form was criticized by student interns in the Carleton Office of Institutional Research and by members of the on-campus advisory groups, who also sought criticism from their spouses; these critics all performed their function by putting themselves into the role of a parent with a college-bound child and filling out the questionnaire. (Several of the parent-critics had sent children to college, or were about to.) The forms were also given to our alumni advisory group for their review.

At this point we anticipated conducting the survey via telephone interviews, which would be conducted by Carleton alumni volunteers to be trained and supervised by a professional survey research firm. (Legal complications surrounding use of the PSAT/NMSQT files prevented us from ultimately using interviewers for this project.) An early draft of the questionnaire was tested by the firm we proposed to engage for the interviewer training and supervision; they used a sample that was obtained through an administrator in a suburban Chicago high school. Nine interviews were conducted by two Carleton alumni who had previous interviewing experience; 25 were conducted by the firm's regular interviewing staff; and 218 surveys were distributed by mail (108 long forms, with one reminder letter, and 110 short forms, without a reminder). One of the principals of the survey research firm then submitted a written criticism of the questionnaire and the data collection methods. Two mailings of the long form produced a 38 percent return;

the single mailing of the short form produced a 45 percent return; the telephone interviews produced higher returns — at higher cost — with the two types of interviewers producing comparable quality; the mail surveys were judged to yield data that were equal in quality to the interview data.

A revised draft of the survey was tested with a sample of parents obtained through the high school counselor at Northfield High School (the town in which Carleton is located). They simply filled out the form, which was distributed and collected by mail, and we examined their responses and comments.

The student questionnaire was tested first with a dozen students from Northfield High School; they filled out the form in small groups and then discussed it with the Carleton project director. This test was followed by similar efforts at two high schools in the Twin Cities, and additional surveys were filled out by students at two other schools (the selection of students was made by teachers who were Carleton alumni). Following all these tests, the editorial staff of the College Board criticized the survey, and a final form was developed in which we sought to maintain maximum similarity to the parents' form but to take account of terminology and phrasing that might present problems for students.

High School Students and the College Selection Process

The College Board in cooperation with one of its member colleges is conducting a study of factors that relate to the college selection process experienced by high school seniors, and we are requesting that you assist us in this study by answering the following questions. These questions can be answered by short written statements or by checking the appropriate box or boxes where provided. Please be as specific as you can in your written answers.

We are in the early stages of extended research and are exploring the best way to ask specific types of questions. Some of the questions may seem slightly repetitious, but the differences are important and we need to have answers to each in order to determine the most effective means of conducting this type of inquiry.

This is not a test, and there are no right or wrong answers. Please do not look things up or consult other people. (A separate study is being conducted with parents of high school students.)

The answers you provide are confidential. The College Board does not engage in college recruiting, and your answers will not be seen by college admissions personnel.

Thank you for your assistance in a project that we hope will improve the recruiting and counseling efforts of colleges and the college selection process for parents and students.

Darrell Morris and Larry Litten
Study Directors

1. First we would like you to give us your emotional reaction to a variety of words or phrases that are associated with colleges or universities.

   For each word or phrase below, please check the box in the column that comes closest to your own reaction.

	Very negative	Somewhat negative	Indifferent	Somewhat positive	Very positive
	1	2	3	4	5
Private college	☐	☐	☐	☐	☐
Character building	☐	☐	☐	☐	☐
Upper Midwest	☐	☐	☐	☐	☐
Concern for the whole person	☐	☐	☐	☐	☐
International programs	☐	☐	☐	☐	☐
Traditional	☐	☐	☐	☐	☐
Liberal arts	☐	☐	☐	☐	☐
Minnesota	☐	☐	☐	☐	☐
Racial diversity	☐	☐	☐	☐	☐
Public university	☐	☐	☐	☐	☐
New England	☐	☐	☐	☐	☐
Ecumenical religious atmosphere	☐	☐	☐	☐	☐
Independent study	☐	☐	☐	☐	☐
California	☐	☐	☐	☐	☐
Private university	☐	☐	☐	☐	☐
The pursuit of excellence	☐	☐	☐	☐	☐
Small college	☐	☐	☐	☐	☐
Ohio	☐	☐	☐	☐	☐
Computer-assisted instruction	☐	☐	☐	☐	☐
Texas	☐	☐	☐	☐	☐

2. Here are some of the same words or phrases to which you already gave us your emotional reaction. Please briefly describe the positive and negative images you think of when you see these words. You can list both positive and negative images for each phrase if they occur to you, or just one kind.

   Small colleges
   Positive images _____
   Negative images _____

   Upper Midwest
   Positive images _____
   Negative images _____

   Public university
   Positive images _____
   Negative images _____

   Liberal arts
   Positive images _____
   Negative images _____

   New England
   Positive images _____
   Negative images _____

   Private college
   Positive images _____
   Negative images _____

   Minnesota
   Positive images _____
   Negative images _____

3. How would you define the following terms:

Small college . . . . . fewer than _____ students	
Medium-sized college . . . . . . _____ to _____ students	*(size of student body)*
Large college . . . . . more than _____ students	
Close to home . . . . . less than _____ miles	
Moderate distance from home . . . . . . _____ to _____ miles	
Far from home . . . . . more than _____ miles	
Low-priced college . . . . . . less than $_____	
Moderate-priced college . . . . . . $_____ to $_____	*(annual tuition, room and board, and other expenses)*
High-priced college . . . . . . more than $_____	

4. We are interested in the aspects and characteristics of postsecondary education that are important to you. From the list of institutional characteristics listed below, please rate them according to their importance to you in deciding which colleges or universities you have applied to or will apply to.

   For each aspect listed, rate its degree of importance to you by checking the box in the appropriate column.

	Not important	Slightly important	Moderately important	Very important
Student body	1	2	3	4
Proportion of applicants admitted	☐	☐	☐	☐
Average entrance test scores (SAT, ACT)	☐	☐	☐	☐
Social backgrounds of students	☐	☐	☐	☐
Extracurricular activities	1	2	3	4
Social atmosphere	☐	☐	☐	☐
Residential life and options	☐	☐	☐	☐
Size of student body	☐	☐	☐	☐
Religious atmosphere	☐	☐	☐	☐
Varsity athletics	☐	☐	☐	☐
Campus activities (sports, clubs, etc.)	☐	☐	☐	☐
Rules and regulations for students	☐	☐	☐	☐

	Not important 1	Slightly important 2	Moderately important 3	Very important 4
Outdoor recreation opportunities	☐	☐	☐	☐
Appearance of campus . .	☐	☐	☐	☐
Setting (neighborhood, character of town, etc.) . .	☐	☐	☐	☐
Physical facilities and buildings	☐	☐	☐	☐

Cost

Price (tuition, fees, room and board)	☐	☐	☐	☐
Financial aid	☐	☐	☐	☐
Net cost (price minus aid)	☐	☐	☐	☐

Curriculum

Teaching reputation of faculty	☐	☐	☐	☐
Scholarly reputation of faculty	☐	☐	☐	☐
Proportion of faculty with doctorates	☐	☐	☐	☐
Fields of study offered . .	☐	☐	☐	☐
Careers to which the college might lead . .	☐	☐	☐	☐
Library collection	☐	☐	☐	☐
Acceptance rate to graduate/professional schools	☐	☐	☐	☐
Computer facilities . . .	☐	☐	☐	☐

Other considerations not mentioned

(Please write in below and then rate.)

_____	☐	☐	☐	☐
_____	☐	☐	☐	☐
_____	☐	☐	☐	☐

You have indicated a variety of things that are important to you in the selection of a college or university. In the next two questions we wish to find out the **three most important** things, and how information about them could best be provided to you.

5. What are the three most important things you wish to know about the college(s) or university(ies) to which you apply.

1. Most important thing

_____

_____

2. Next most important thing

_____

_____

3. Third in importance

_____

_____

6. From which source of information would you prefer to learn about the things you listed in Question 5 as important. Write code letters from the following list of sources in spaces below.

A. High school counselor

B. High school teacher (non-counselor)

C. An admissions officer from the college

D. Faculty of the college

E. Alumnus (graduate) of the college

F. Student currently enrolled in the college

G. Parent of a current student in the college

H. Rabbi / priest / minister

I. Publications of the college (catalogs, brochures, etc.)

J. College guide books, such as *The College Handbook*

K. Other _____

L. Other _____

	Preferred source of information	Second preference
1. Most important thing listed in Question 5 . . .	_____	_____
2. Next most important thing in Question 5 . . .	_____	_____
3. Third in importance in Question 5	_____	_____

7. Considering campus atmosphere and academic quality, what colleges or universities do you think present the best opportunities for students with high academic potential?

Please name up to four colleges or universities on the lines below:

1. _____

2. _____

3. _____

4. _____

If you cannot think of as many as four, list as many names as come to mind and go on immediately to Question 8. Do not return later to add names. We are interested in knowing the name or names of those institutions with which you are most familiar.

8. A. From approximately how many colleges or universities have you received materials or contacts by mail or telephone through the Student Search Service of the College Board?

_____

(Number of colleges)

B. If you were contacted or received materials, which of the institutions particularly impressed you? (List names below.)

_____

_____

_____

Appendix E

9. Will you attend college full time in the fall of 1979?

Yes, definitely . . . . . . ☐ 1 ⎤
Yes, probably . . . . . . ☐ 2 ⎦ Continue with Question 10

Probably not . . . . . . ☐ 3 ⎤ Answer A at right and then
No . . . . ☐ 4 ⎦ go to Question 21.

A. If your answer is "probably not" or "no," please indicate briefly why you won't go to college full time and what you will be doing next fall.

_____

_____

_____

10. Listed below and grouped in pairs are contrasting types and characteristics of education institutions. Please check one box in each row to indicate your preference in each pair. The preferences you indicate should reflect the *ideal* freshman-year institution for you.

> **Example:** If you had a slight preference for an out of state college you would check box 2 in the following pair; you would check box 5 if you greatly preferred a college in your home state.
>
> Out of state college   1 ☐   2 ☐   3 ☐   4 ☐   5 ☐   In state college

	Greatly prefer 1	Slightly prefer 2	Unimportant or no preference 3	Slightly prefer 4	Greatly prefer 5	
Public	☐	☐	☐	☐	☐	Private
College	☐	☐	☐	☐	☐	University
Coeducational	☐	☐	☐	☐	☐	Single sex
Rural	☐	☐	☐	☐	☐	Urban
Students from varied social backgrounds	☐	☐	☐	☐	☐	Students from select social backgrounds
Junior (2-year) college	☐	☐	☐	☐	☐	4-year college
Church-related	☐	☐	☐	☐	☐	Inter-denominational or nonde-nominational religious atmosphere
Liberal arts	☐	☐	☐	☐	☐	Technical/Vocational
Commuter campus	☐	☐	☐	☐	☐	Residential campus
Academically select students	☐	☐	☐	☐	☐	Students of varied academic ability
Fraternities and sororities	☐	☐	☐	☐	☐	No fraternities or sororities
	1	2	3	4	5	
Mostly Caucasian	☐	☐	☐	☐	☐	Sizable minority representation
Studious atmosphere	☐	☐	☐	☐	☐	Social atmosphere
High priced	☐	☐	☐	☐	☐	Moderate priced
Moderate priced	☐	☐	☐	☐	☐	Low priced
Large size	☐	☐	☐	☐	☐	Medium size
Medium size	☐	☐	☐	☐	☐	Small size
Close to home	☐	☐	☐	☐	☐	Moderate distance from home
Moderate distance from home	☐	☐	☐	☐	☐	Far from home

285

11. You have indicated your preferences for the type of college you would prefer to attend. Please list up to four of these characteristics that are most important to you in your college selection, and briefly state why.

Characteristic   Why is this important to you?

1. _____

2. _____

3. _____

4. _____

12. Can you remember the institution(s) to which you thought you would apply at the end of last summer? Please list it (or them) below.

_____

_____

_____

_____

13. Now list all the institutions to which you have applied or to which you think you probably will apply. Please rank them according to your preference, beginning with the one that you would most like to attend. If you applied to an institution for "early decision," enter it as first choice, even if you were not accepted. Please indicate the month you applied or intended to apply, and for those to which you have already applied, check the status of your application.

	Applications made to	Month or probable month of application	Status of application		
			Accepted	Not accepted	No decision yet
First choice	_____	_____	1	2	3
Second choice	_____	_____	1	2	3
Third choice	_____	_____	1	2	3
Others	_____	_____	1	2	3

14. You have just ranked your preferences for certain institutions. Please briefly tell us why you prefer your first choice over your second choice.

_____

_____

_____

15. Please indicate whether your first or second choices (as listed in Question 13) include each of the following types of institutions, and *if they do not,* why that type of institution is not included. Please give both major and minor reasons.

	Yes	No	If NO: why not?
Is your first or second choice a:	1	2	
Public college or university	☐	☐	_____
Private college	☐	☐	_____
Private university	☐	☐	_____
College or university in the East	☐	☐	_____
College or university in the Midwest	☐	☐	_____
College or university in the West	☐	☐	_____

16. Whether or not you have mentioned them before, are there some institutions you would like to consider but probably will not apply to because the tuition and living costs are too high? Please check the appropriate box.

Yes ☐ 1
No ☐ 2

If your answer is "yes," please respond to A below. If "no," go to Question 17.

A. Which institutions are these? Please write in the name(s) of the institutions(s).

_____

_____

_____

_____

_____

_____

17. We would like to know how you learned about the colleges or universities you named as your first and second choices in Question 13.

Below is a list of information sources. Please check in Column A all the sources from which you have learned about your first choice, and in Column B check all the sources from which you have learned about your second choice. Check as many as apply

Information sources	A. First-choice college	B. Second-choice college
General reputation of college	☐ 1	☐ 1
High school counselor	☐ 2	☐ 2
Other high school teacher	☐ 3	☐ 3
Mother	☐ 4	☐ 4
Father	☐ 5	☐ 5
Admissions officer from the college	☐ 6	☐ 6
Faculty member from the college	☐ 7	☐ 7
A graduate or former student of the college who is a member of your family	☐ 8	☐ 8
Any other graduate or former student of the college	☐ 9	☐ 9
A student currently enrolled in the college	☐ 10	☐ 10
A parent of a student currently enrolled in the college	☐ 11	☐ 11
Minister / Priest / Rabbi	☐ 12	☐ 12
Unrequested mailings such as those of the Student Search Service	☐ 13	☐ 13
Requested publications of the college (catalogs, brochures, etc.)	☐ 14	☐ 14
Guidebooks, such as *The College Handbook*	☐ 15	☐ 15
Visit	☐ 16	☐ 16
Any other source(s) (Please specify)		
_____	☐ 17	☐ 17
_____	☐ 18	☐ 18

18. From which of the sources of information that you checked in Question 17 did you first learn about your first and second choice of colleges? Use the code number given in Question 17 to identify how you first heard about each college. *Code number of first information source*

First learned about first choice college from . . . . _____

First learned about second choice college from . . _____

19. Which of the information sources listed in Question 17 were most influential in helping you select the institutions to which you applied? Consider all your applications, not just your first and second choices. Write the code numbers listed in Question 17 in the spaces below and, as best as you can, list them in order of influence, starting with the most important influencing factor.

Code number of people who influenced your decision

Most influential. . . . . _____

Second in influence. . . . . _____

Third in influence. . . . . _____

■ Thank you for your assistance on this project. We are extremely grateful for your cooperation.

Please return questionnaire to:
The College Board
Cooperative Research Project
P.O. Box 2849
Princeton, New Jersey 08541

20. There are two parts to this question. In Part A we list 11 institutions and provide lines for you to write in a short phrase that comes to your mind when you see that name. If you have never heard of the institution, check (✔) the appropriate column and go on to the next name.

In Part B we would like you to rate the school, on a scale of 1-8 (poor to excellent), *considering its overall desirability for you*, on the basis of what you presently know about it. Circle one number for each institution you have heard of.

For each institution, please fill in Part A and circle your rating in Part B. Then go on to the next. Rate each on a scale of 1-8.

Name of school	Part A — Phrase that comes to your mind	I have never heard of it	Part B — My rating of the school — Poor ... Excellent
Harvard / Radcliffe	_____	____	1 2 3 4 5 6 7 8
Swarthmore	_____	____	1 2 3 4 5 6 7 8
Northwestern	_____	____	1 2 3 4 5 6 7 8
Carleton	_____	____	1 2 3 4 5 6 7 8
Stanford	_____	____	1 2 3 4 5 6 7 8
University of California Berkeley	_____	____	1 2 3 4 5 6 7 8
Oberlin	_____	____	1 2 3 4 5 6 7 8
Duke	_____	____	1 2 3 4 5 6 7 8
University of Wisconsin	_____	____	1 2 3 4 5 6 7 8
Pomona	_____	____	1 2 3 4 5 6 7 8
St. Olaf	_____	____	1 2 3 4 5 6 7 8

Now we have just a few background questions:

21. How many of your brothers or sisters, if any, have gone to college? _____

When did the brother or sister who most recently entered college first enroll; and where?

_____ _____
(Entering date)   *(Name of college or university)*

22. How many years have you lived in the state you now live in?

_____

23. With whom do you principally reside? Check all that apply.

Mother ☐ 1
Father ☐ 2
Other adult ☐

24. What is your religious affiliation and that of each person checked in Question 23 with whom you have regular contact? Check one box per column.

	Mother	Father	Other adult in residence	Your own religious affiliation
Protestant	☐ 1	☐ 1	☐ 1	☐ 1
Catholic	☐ 2	☐ 2	☐ 2	☐ 2
Jewish	☐ 3	☐ 3	☐ 3	☐ 3
None	☐ 4	☐ 4	☐ 4	☐ 4

Other (Please specify) _____

25. What is the occupation of each person checked in Question 23?

Mother _____

Father _____

Other adult in residence _____

26. What is the highest level of education completed by each person checked in Question 23? Check one box per column.

	Mother	Father	Other adult in residence
Elementary school (8th grade)	☐ 1	☐ 1	☐ 1
Some high school (9th – 11th grade)	☐ 2	☐ 2	☐ 2
High school (12th grade)	☐ 3	☐ 3	☐ 3
Associate degree	☐ 4	☐ 4	☐ 4
Some college	☐ 5	☐ 5	☐ 5
Bachelor's degree	☐ 6	☐ 6	☐ 6
Master's degree	☐ 7	☐ 7	☐ 7
Doctorate	☐ 8	☐ 8	☐ 8

27. If you told us that your mother, father, or other adult in residence earned a bachelor's degree or higher, please answer A – C below about the institution from which the bachelor's degree was earned.

If none of these persons received a bachelor's degree or higher, check this box. ☐

	Mother	Father	Other adult in residence
A. Was the institution:			
Private, church-related	☐ 1	☐ 1	☐ 1
Private, not church-related	☐ 2	☐ 2	☐ 2
B. Was it:			
A liberal arts colllege	☐ 1	☐ 1	☐ 1
University	☐ 2	☐ 2	☐ 2
Technical Institute	☐ 3	☐ 3	☐ 3
Comprehensive college (liberal arts plus vocational courses)	☐ 4	☐ 4	☐ 4
C. Was it:			
Coeducational	☐ 1	☐ 1	☐ 1
Single sex	☐ 2	☐ 2	☐ 2

The College Board

Parents and the College Selection Process

Darrell Morris and Larry Litten
Study Directors

This is a study of factors which relate to the college selection process as experienced by parents of high school juniors and seniors. Questions can be answered by short written statements or by checking the appropriate box or boxes where the latter are provided. Please be specific in your written answers (for example, when referring to geographic location, instead of simply responding "location" indicate whether it is distance from home, climate or social and cultural aspects which concern you).

We are in the early stages of some extended research and are exploring the best way to ask specific types of questions. Some of the questions may seem slightly repetitious, but the differences are important and we need to have answers to each in order to determine the most effective means of conducting this type of inquiry.

The answers which you provide are confidential. The College Board does not engage in college recruiting and your answers will not be seen by any college admissions personnel.

Thank you for your assistance in a project which we hope will improve the recruiting and counselling efforts of colleges and the college selection process for parents and students.

1. First we would like you to give us your emotional reaction to a variety of words or phrases that are associated with colleges or universities.

   For each word or phrase below, please check the box in the column that comes closest to your own reaction.

	Very negative	Somewhat negative	Indifferent	Somewhat positive	Very positive
	1	2	3	4	5
Private college	☐	☐	☐	☐	☐
Character building	☐	☐	☐	☐	☐
Upper midwest	☐	☐	☐	☐	☐
Concern for the whole person	☐	☐	☐	☐	☐
International programs	☐	☐	☐	☐	☐
Traditional	☐	☐	☐	☐	☐
Liberal arts	☐	☐	☐	☐	☐
Minnesota	☐	☐	☐	☐	☐
Racial diversity	☐	☐	☐	☐	☐
Public university	☐	☐	☐	☐	☐
New England	☐	☐	☐	☐	☐
Ecumenical religious atmosphere	☐	☐	☐	☐	☐
Independent study	☐	☐	☐	☐	☐
California	☐	☐	☐	☐	☐
Private university	☐	☐	☐	☐	☐
The pursuit of excellence	☐	☐	☐	☐	☐
Small college	☐	☐	☐	☐	☐
Ohio	☐	☐	☐	☐	☐
Computer—assisted instruction	☐	☐	☐	☐	☐

2. Here are some of the same words or phrases to which you already gave us your emotional reaction. Please describe the positive and negative images which these phrases bring to your mind. You can list both positive and negative images for each phrase if they occur to you, or just one kind.

POSITIVE IMAGES	NEGATIVE IMAGES
Small college:	
Upper midwest:	
Public university:	
Liberal arts:	
New England:	
Private college:	
Minnesota:	

3. How would YOU define the following terms:

Small college: fewer than _____ students
Medium-sized college: _____ to _____ students } (size of student body)
Large college: more than _____ students

Close to home: less than _____ miles
Moderate distance: _____ to _____ miles
Far from home: more than _____ miles

Low priced college: less than $ _____
Moderate priced: $ _____ to $ _____ } (annual tuition, room and board and other expenses.)
High priced: more than $ _____

4. Column A lists 6 types of schools. In column B, please write the name of the best quality college that you know of which fits the description in Column A. Do not repeat names. If you don't know of any schools of a particular type, or run out of different names, leave the space in Column B blank and go on to the next school type. Then in the columns under C, rate each named school on the characteristics listed. Use the following scale and write a rating number in each box.

Poor 1 2 3 4 5 6 7 8 Outstanding

| | | C. Ratings | | | | |
A. Type of school	B. Name of college of this type	Student Body	Faculty	Social atmosphere	Location	Overall desirability for your child*
Private university						
Small private college						
Public university						
Ivy League school						
Church-related school						
Single-sex college						

*The child named in the address on the envelope (your high school senior).

5. We are interested in the aspects of a college or university that are important to YOU AS A PARENT — not the particular characteristic you would desire, but which aspects are important to consider in the colleges or universities to which your child applies.

For EACH school aspect, rate its degree of importance to you by checking the box in the appropriate column.

	Not important	Slightly important	Moderately important	Very important
Student Characteristics:	1	2	3	4
Proportion of applicants admitted	☐	☐	☐	☐
Average entrance test scores (SAT, ACT)	☐	☐	☐	☐
Social backgrounds of students	☐	☐	☐	☐
Extra-curricular Characteristics:	1	2	3	4
Social atmosphere	☐	☐	☐	☐
Residential life and options	☐	☐	☐	☐
Size of student body	☐	☐	☐	☐
Religious atmosphere	☐	☐	☐	☐
Campus activities (sports, clubs, etc.)	☐	☐	☐	☐
Rules and regulations for students	☐	☐	☐	☐
Outdoor recreation opportunities	☐	☐	☐	☐
Appearance of campus	☐	☐	☐	☐
Setting (neighborhood, character of town, etc.)	☐	☐	☐	☐
Physical facilities and buildings	☐	☐	☐	☐
Financial:	1	2	3	4
Price (tuition, fees, room & board)	☐	☐	☐	☐
Financial aid	☐	☐	☐	☐
Net cost (price minus aid)	☐	☐	☐	☐
Curricular Aspects:	1	2	3	4
Teaching reputation of faculty	☐	☐	☐	☐
Scholarly reputation of faculty	☐	☐	☐	☐
Proportion of faculty with doctorates	☐	☐	☐	☐
Fields of study offered	☐	☐	☐	☐
Careers to which the college might lead	☐	☐	☐	☐
Library collection	☐	☐	☐	☐
Acceptance rate to graduate/professional schools	☐	☐	☐	☐
Computer facilities	☐	☐	☐	☐
Other aspects not mentioned:	1	2	3	4
PLEASE WRITE IN BELOW AND THEN RATE:				
_____	☐	☐	☐	☐

You just indicated how important to you a variety of aspects of a college are. In the next two questions we wish to find out which are the three MOST IMPORTANT aspects and who or what could best provide you with information about these aspects.

6. What are the three most important things which you, as a parent, wish to know about the college(s) or university(ies) to which your child applies.

   A. Most important thing   **B. Next most important thing**   **C. Third in importance**

7. From which source of information would you prefer to learn about the things which you listed in Question 6 as important. Write code letters from the following list of sources in spaces below.

   A. High school counselor
   B. High school teacher (non-counselor)
   C. An admissions officer from the college
   D. Faculty of the college
   E. Alumnus (graduate) of the college
   F. Student currently enrolled in the college
   G. Parent of a current student in the college

   H. Rabbi / priest / minister
   I. Publications of the college (catalogs, brochures, etc.)
   J. Commercial college guide books

   K. Other_____
   L. Other_____

	A. Most important thing listed in Question 6.	**B. Next most important thing in Question 6.**	**C. Third in importance in Question 6.**
Preferred source of information	____	____	____
Second preference	____	____	____

8. Considering academic quality and school atmosphere, what colleges or universities do you think present the best opportunities for students with high academic potential?

   Please name up to four schools on the lines below:

   _____   _____

   _____   _____

   > Please do not return to Question 8 and fill in any blanks after you have continued to the remainder of the questionnaire. We are interested in schools which come to mind WITHOUT PROMPTING, which may well be fewer than four.

9. Will the child named on the envelope attend college full time in the Fall of 1979?

Yes, definitely ☐ 1
Yes, probably ☐ 2   >Continue with Question 10
Probably not ☐ 3   Answer Part A and then go
No ☐ 4   to Question 20

A. If "probably not" or "no", please indicate briefly why this child won't go to college full-time and what he or she will be doing next Fall.

10. We would like to know how far you and your child have proceeded in the search for a college or university. Please place a check in Column A by the statement which best describes the stage where your child is in the search, and in Column B where you are.

Stage of search process	A Your child	B You
Not started search	☐ 1	☐ 1
Casually considered 1 or 2 colleges	☐ 2	☐ 2
Casually considered several colleges	☐ 3	☐ 3
Seriously investigated 1 or 2 colleges	☐ 4	☐ 4
Seriously investigated several colleges	☐ 5	☐ 5
Visited 1 or 2 colleges	☐ 6	☐ 6
Visited several colleges	☐ 7	☐ 7
Applied to 1 or 2 colleges	☐ 8	
Applied to several colleges	☐ 9	
Other (PLEASE SPECIFY)		
_____	☐ 10	☐ 10

11. A. From approximately how many colleges have you or your child received materials or contacts by mail or phone through the Student Search Service of The College Board?

_____
(Number of Colleges)

B. If you received any such contacts or materials, which of them, if any, particularly impressed you? (List the schools below.)

_____ _____

_____ _____

12. Listed below are several characteristics of colleges and universities. They are listed in pairs which represent contrasting types of colleges. Please indicate your preference for one of the types in each characteristic. Your preference should refer specifically to a school for the child named on the envelope.

EXAMPLE: If you had a slight preference for a junior college you would check box 2 in the following pair; you would check box 5 if you greatly preferred a 4-year college.

	1	2	3	4	5	
Junior College	☐	☐	☐	☐	☐	4-year college

	Greatly Prefer 1	Slightly Prefer 2	Unimportant or No preference 3	Slightly Prefer 4	Greatly Prefer 5	
Public	☐	☐	☐	☐	☐	Private
College	☐	☐	☐	☐	☐	University
...Co-ed	☐	☐	☐	☐	☐	Single-sex
Rural	☐	☐	☐	☐	☐	Urban
Students from varied social backgrounds	☐	☐	☐	☐	☐	Students from select social backgrounds

	1	2	3	4	5	
Church-related	☐	☐	☐	☐	☐	Ecumenical or non-denominational religious atmosphere
Liberal arts	☐	☐	☐	☐	☐	Technical / Vocational
Commuter campus	☐	☐	☐	☐	☐	Residential campus
Academically select students	☐	☐	☐	☐	☐	Students of varied academic ability
Fraternities and sororities	☐	☐	☐	☐	☐	No Greek letter societies

	1	2	3	4	5	
Mostly Caucasian	☐	☐	☐	☐	☐	Sizable minority representation
Studious atmosphere	☐	☐	☐	☐	☐	Social atmosphere
High priced	☐	☐	☐	☐	☐	Moderate priced
Moderate priced	☐	☐	☐	☐	☐	Low priced

	1	2	3	4	5	
Large size	☐	☐	☐	☐	☐	Medium size
Medium size	☐	☐	☐	☐	☐	Small size
Close to home	☐	☐	☐	☐	☐	Moderate distance from home
Moderate distance from home	☐	☐	☐	☐	☐	Far from home

13. You just indicated YOUR preferences for the type of college that your child will select. Which of these characteristics will you strongly suggest (or insist) that your child's college have. List UP TO 4 characteristics and briefly state why each is important.

Characteristic	Why is this important to you?

14. In this question we would like you to tell us about schools which have been suggested to your child by you, a spouse, another person or any other source (for example, materials from the college, guide books, etc.).

First, in Column A, please write the names of colleges or universities which have been suggested to your child. Start the list with the school that YOU would most like your child to attend.

Next, in Column B, please check, next to the schools you have listed, who FIRST suggested this school to your child. Check only one source for each school.

A. Name of school	B. First suggested to child by:			
	You or your spouse	Other person	Materials from college	Other
	1	2	3	4
Your first choice:_____	☐	☐	☐	☐
Your second choice:_____	☐	☐	☐	☐
Others suggested: _____	☐	☐	☐	☐
_____	☐	☐	☐	☐
_____	☐	☐	☐	☐
_____	☐	☐	☐	☐

15. You just indicated your first and second choices of schools for your child. Please briefly tell us why you prefer your number one choice over number two.

16. Whether or not you have mentioned them before, are there some schools which you would like your child to consider, but to which he or she probably won't apply because the tuition and living costs are too high?

Yes . . (Answer A) . . ☐ 1
No . . (Go to Q. 17). . ☐ 2

A. Which schools are these? Please write in the name(s) of the school(s).

17. Please indicate whether one of your first or second choices (as listed in Question 14) includes each of the following types of schools, and IF IT DOES NOT, why that type of school is not included. Please give both major and minor reasons.

Is your first or second choice a:	Yes 1	No 2	IF NO: Why not?
Public college or university	☐	☐	_____
Private college	☐	☐	_____
Private university	☐	☐	_____
School in the East	☐	☐	_____
School in the Midwest	☐	☐	_____
School in the West	☐	☐	_____

18. We would like to know how you learned about the colleges or universities you named as your first and second choice in Question 14.

Below is a list of information sources. Look down the list and check in Column A the ones from which you learned about your first choice, and in Column B the ones from which you learned about your second choice school. Check as many as apply.

Information Sources	A. First Choice School	B. Second Choice School
General reputation of school	☐ 1	☐ 1
High school counselor	☐ 2	☐ 2
Other high school teacher	☐ 3	☐ 3
Admissions officer from the college	☐ 4	☐ 4
Faculty member from the college	☐ 5	☐ 5
A graduate or former student of the college who is a member of your family	☐ 6	☐ 6
Any other graduate or former student of the college	☐ 7	☐ 7
A student currently enrolled in the college	☐ 8	☐ 8
A parent of a student currently enrolled in the college	☐ 9	☐ 9
Minister / Priest / Rabbi	☐ 10	☐ 10
Unrequested publications of the college (catalogs, brochures, etc.)	☐ 11	☐ 11
Commercial college guide books	☐ 12	☐ 12
Any other source(s) (PLEASE SPECIFY)		
_____	☐ 13	☐ 13
_____	☐ 14	☐ 14

19. There are two parts to this question. In PART A we list 11 institutions and provide a line next to each one for you to write in a short phrase that comes to your mind when you see that school name.

If you have never heard of the school, check (✓) the "Never heard of it" column, and go on to the next school.

In PART B we would like you to rate the school, on a scale of 1 – 8 (poor to excellent), CONSIDERING ITS OVERALL DESIRABILITY FOR THE CHILD NAMED ON THE ENVELOPE. (We have printed the numbers; all you have to do is circle one for each school you have heard of.)

For each school, please fill in PART A and circle your rating in PART B. Then go on to the next school. Rate each school on a scale of 1 – 8.

	PART A		PART B
Name of school	Phrase that comes to your mind	Never heard of it	My rating of the school
Harvard / Radcliffe			Poor 1 2 3 4 5 6 7 8 Excellent
Swarthmore			1 2 3 4 5 6 7 8
Northwestern			1 2 3 4 5 6 7 8
Carleton			1 2 3 4 5 6 7 8
Stanford			1 2 3 4 5 6 7 8
U. of Calif. Berkeley			1 2 3 4 5 6 7 8
Oberlin			1 2 3 4 5 6 7 8
Duke			1 2 3 4 5 6 7 8
U. of Wisconsin			1 2 3 4 5 6 7 8
Pomona			1 2 3 4 5 6 7 8
St. Olaf			1 2 3 4 5 6 7 8

20. Now we have just a few background questions:

How many of your children are of college age or older? _____

How many of your children have gone to college? _____

When did the child who most recently entered college first enroll and where?

_____ _____
(Entering Date)   (Name of college or university)

21. What is your relationship to the child named on the envelope?

Mother ☐ 1
Father ☐ 2
Other (SPECIFY)
_____ ☐ 3

22. With whom does the child principally reside? Check all that apply.

Mother ☐ 1
Father ☐ 2
Non-parental adult ☐ 3

23. What is the religious affiliation of each person checked in Question 22 with whom your high school junior has regular contact? Check one box per column.

	Mother	Father	Non-parental adult in residence
Protestant	☐ 1	☐ 1	☐ 1
Catholic	☐ 2	☐ 2	☐ 2
Jewish	☐ 3	☐ 3	☐ 3
None	☐ 4	☐ 4	☐ 4
Other (PLEASE SPECIFY)	_____	_____	_____

24. What is the occupation of each person checked in Question 22?

Mother _____

Father _____

Non-parental adult in residence_____

25. What is THE HIGHEST LEVEL of education completed by each person checked in Question 22? Check one box per column.

	Mother	Father	Non-parental adult in residence
Elementary school (8th grade)	☐ 1	☐ 1	☐ 1
Some high school (9th – 11th grade)	☐ 2	☐ 2	☐ 2
High school (12th grade)	☐ 3	☐ 3	☐ 3
Associate degree	☐ 4	☐ 4	☐ 4
Some college	☐ 5	☐ 5	☐ 5
Bachelor's degree	☐ 6	☐ 6	☐ 6
Master's degree	☐ 7	☐ 7	☐ 7
Doctorate	☐ 8	☐ 8	☐ 8

26. If you told us that Mother, Father, or Non-parental adult in residence have earned a Bachelor's degree or higher, please answer A — D below about the institution from which the Bachelor's degree was earned.

    If none of these persons received a Bachelor's degree or higher, check this box. ☐

		Mother	Father	Non-parental adult in residence
A.	What was the size of the school at the time of attendance?			
	1,000 or fewer	☐ 1	☐ 1	☐ 1
	1,001 to 2,000	☐ 2	☐ 2	☐ 2
	2,001 to 4,000	☐ 3	☐ 3	☐ 3
	4,001 to 10,000	☐ 4	☐ 4	☐ 4
	10,001 to 20,000	☐ 5	☐ 5	☐ 5
	More than 20,000	☐ 6	☐ 6	☐ 6
B.	Was it:			
	Private, denominational,	☐ 1	☐ 1	☐ 1
	Private, non-sectarian,	☐ 2	☐ 2	☐ 2
	or Public?	☐ 3	☐ 3	☐ 3
C.	Was it:			
	A liberal arts college,	☐ 1	☐ 1	☐ 1
	University,	☐ 2	☐ 2	☐ 2
	Technical Institute,	☐ 3	☐ 3	☐ 3
	or a Comprehensive college (liberal arts plus vocational courses)?	☐ 4	☐ 4	☐ 4
D.	Was it a co-ed school or single sex?			
	Co-ed	☐ 1	☐ 1	☐ 1
	Single sex	☐ 2	☐ 2	☐ 2

THANK YOU FOR YOUR ASSISTANCE ON THIS PROJECT.

Please return questionaire to: Educational Testing Service
Cooperative Research Project
P.O. Box 2849
Princeton, New Jersey
08541

APPENDIX F. MARKET SHARE AND FIRST-CHOICE APPLICANT CHARACTERISTICS FOR CARLETON, ST. OLAF, AND THE UNIVERSITY OF MINNESOTA AMONG TWIN CITIES STUDENTS

In Appendix F, both market-share and applicant-pool-characteristics data are shown for Carleton and two of its principal competitors in the Twin Cities. Market share data are of most use to a marketer when seeking to understand an institution's position in a market and when designing a marketing strategy. These data were not included in Chapter 6, however, because the numbers on which they are based are extremely small and the interinstitutional differences are generally quite small. They are presented in the Appendix to illustrate the type of data that a market researcher would seek through larger samples in a given market.

Table F-1. Institutional Shares of Twin Cities Ability/Educational Segments (*A*) and Ability/Educational Characteristics of Institutional Applicant Pools (*B*) (Includes Only Students Listing College as First Choice)

	Carleton		St. Olaf		University of Minnesota		
	A	B	A	B	A	B	N*
Verbal PSAT/NMSQT							
60 or greater	11%	45%	11%	29%	16%	16%	44
55–59	5	18	10	23	12	12	42
50–54	6	36	4	18	23	37	69
Less than 50	0	0	5	29	16	35	92
		99%		99%		100%	
Family educational level							
Both parents with high school or less	2%	9%	5%	18%	23%	35%	64
One with college work/degree	2	9	4	12	18	21	51
Both with college work/degree	3	18	8	29	20	30	66
One with graduate work/degree	7	36	9	29	11	14	56
Both with graduate work/degree	30	27	20	12	–	–	10
		99%		100%		100%	
N =	11		17		43		

Note: Column A percentages show market share and are calculated across the page; the shares of institutions not listed constitute the remaining share needed to add to 100 percent. Column B percentages show the characteristics of each institution's pool of applicants and are calculated down the columns.
* Number on which Column A percentages are based.

Table F-2. Institutional Shares of Twin Cities Preference Segments (*A*) and Preference Orientations of Institutional Applicant Pools (*B*) (First Choice Only)

Preferences	Carleton A	Carleton B	St. Olaf A	St. Olaf B	University of Minnesota A	University of Minnesota B	N
Private	10%	100%	11%	71%	6%	14%	113
Indifferent	0	0	5	12	26	23	39
Public	0	0	5	18	30	63	89
		100%		101%		100%	
College	10%	73%	15%	71%	3%	8%	78
Indifferent	0	0	6	29	11	21	80
University	4	27	0	0	37	70	82
		100%		100%		99%	
Rural	6%	36%	16%	59%	8%	12%	62
Indifferent	7	36	9	29	13	16	56
Urban	3	27	2	12	26	72	120
		99%		100%		100%	
Academically selective	8*	91%	11%	82%	13%	40%	124
Indifferent	0	0	0	0	17	20	46
Academically diverse	2	9	5	18	26	41	76
		100%		100%		101%	
Studious atmosphere	7%	73%	8%	59%	14%	40%	121
Indifferent	0	0	4	12	25	28	48
Social atmosphere	4	27	7	29	19	33	72
		100%		100%		101%	
Mostly Caucasian	4%	18%	9%	29%	16%	21%	55
Indifferent	3	27	7	41	21	47	97
Racial diversity	7	55	6	29	16	33	89
		100%		99%		101%	
Church-related	2%	9%	14%	50%	7%	9%	58
Indifferent	0	0	9	31	23	28	53
Nondenominational	8	91	2	19	21	63	129
		100%		100%		100%	
N =	11		17		43		

* Carleton has 15% of the "strongly prefer" selective market (*N* = 41) versus 7% for St. Olaf and 12% for Minnesota.

Table F-3. Institutional Shares of Attribute-Importance Market Segments (A) and Attribute-Importance Orientations of Institutional Applicant Pools (B) (First Choice Only)

Attribute importance	Carleton		St. Olaf		University of Minnesota		
	A	B	A	B	A	B	N
Scholarly reputation							
Slightly/not important	0	0	7%	12%	18%	12%	28
Moderately important	2%	18%	6	35	15	33	96
Very important.	7	82	7	53	20	56	123
		100%		100%		101%	
Faculty doctorates							
Slightly/not important	3%	27%	9%	47%	19%	37%	86
Moderately important	3	27	5	35	20	56	118
Very important.	12	45	7	18	7	7	43
		99%		100%		100%	
Career outcomes							
Slightly/not important	29%	18%	4%	6%	4%	0	7
Moderately important	14	18	6	19	6	14%	54
Very important.	4	64	11	75	20	86	185
		100%		100%		100%	
Graduate school acceptance							
Slightly/not important	5%	18%	5%	12%	19%	19%	42
Moderately important	3	27	6	29	17	36	88
Very important.	5	55	9	59	16	45	116
		100%		100%		100%	
Campus activities							
Slightly/not important	3%	18%	6%	24%	22%	33%	65
Moderately important	7	64	6	35	18	44	106
Very important.	3	18	9	41	13	23	76
		100%		100%		100%	
N =	11		17		43		

Table F-4. Institutional Shares of Market Segments Giving Very Positive Ratings to Selected Phrases (A) and Percentages of Institutional Applicant Pools Giving Such Ratings (B) (First Choice Only)

Phrases	Carleton		St. Olaf		University of Minnesota		
	A	B	A	B	A	B	N
Character building	6%	36%	13%	47%	13%	20%	63
Concern for the whole person	3	27	8	53	14	36	
International programs.	5	36	7	35	13	26	86
Independent study	7	36	10	35	18	27	60
N =	11		17		43		

DATE DUE
